Nightmare Japan

Contemporary Cinema

Contemporary Cinema is a series of edited volumes and
single-authored texts focusing on the latest in film culture, theory,
reception and interpretation. There is a concentration on films
released in the past fifteen years, and the aim is to reflect important
current issues while pointing to others that to date have not been
given sufficient attention.

Nightmare Japan

Contemporary
Japanese Horror Cinema

Jay McRoy

Rodopi

Amsterdam - New York, NY 2008

Institutional support:
The Centre for Cinema Studies, Department of Theatre and Film,
University of British Columbia

Illustration cover:
Fukasaku Kinji's *Battle Royale* (© Tartan Video).

Cover design:
Pier Post

The paper on which this book is printed meets the requirements
of "ISO 9706:1994, Information and documentation - Paper for
documents - Requirements for permanence".

ISBN: 978-90-420-2331-4
ISSN: 1572-3070
©Editions Rodopi B.V., Amsterdam - New York, NY 2008
Printed in the Netherlands

To Amy, as Always...

CONTENTS

List of Illustrations

Acknowledgments

As any author knows, books are rarely assembled without the assistance of dedicated colleagues, friends, and family. Consequently, I express my warmest gratitude to Ernest Mathijs and Steven Jay Schneider for their confidence and generosity throughout this book's conceptualisation and production. For their careful reading and valuable comments on this work throughout its various stages, my deepest appreciation likewise extends to Christa Stevens, Guy Crucianelli, Steffen Hantke, Richard J. Hand, Ruth Goldberg, Tony Williams, Christopher Sharrett, Harmony Wu, Bryan Wehr, Emily Wood, Joshua Diefenbach and Nathaniel Carlson. Thanks are likewise due to my colleagues around the globe, and to my students, with whom I am honoured to share ideas about film and literature. Lastly, my sincerest thanks and deepest affections go out to my family, for their unwavering support; to my friends, for their honest insights and excellent company; and to my wife, Amy, for saving my life and giving me a reason.

The images in this book remain the property of the production or distribution companies concerned. They are reproduced throughout this book in the spirit of publicity and the promotion of the films under discussion.

Kenosha, Wisconsin
July 2007

Introduction: 'New Waves', Old Terrors and Emerging Fears

Japan's Screaming

In his compact primer, 'An Exquisite Nightmare: New Asian Horror Sprays the Screen', Todd Wardrope notes that contemporary Asian horror cinema is 'well on its way to becoming a staid film studies expression like "French New Wave"' (2004: para 1). Concentrating almost exclusively upon the genre's most popular cinematic offerings, from the stylish gut-wrenching *Audition* (*Ôdishon*, 1999), helmed by Japan's hyper-prolific Miike Takashi, to Hong Kong director Herman Yau's brutal thriller, *Ebola Syndrome* (*Yi bo la beng duk,* 1996), Wardrope remarks briefly upon 'New Asian Horror''s similarities to and differences from Western horror film traditions and motifs. In the process, he reiterates casual observations about the films' cross-cultural appeal, commenting perfunctorily upon the filmmakers' seemingly paradoxical reliance upon atmosphere and restraint over gore on the one hand, and 'juicy violence and sexual perversion' (para 23) on the other. Of course, the often thought-provoking content and arresting visual styles that comprise works of 'New Asian Horror' come as no surprise to veteran horror film aficionados, many of whom would undoubtedly argue that the narratological and visual tropology on display in these works has long been a primary component of cinematic traditions that are only now getting the critical attention (and international distribution) they have so long deserved. However, as an increasing number of university syllabi

and on-line fan sites illustrate, 'New Asian Horror' has, within the last
two decades, become both a genre deemed worthy of intellectual inquiry,
as well as one of international cinema's most compelling and marketable
commodities. Japanese director Nakata Hideo's wildly successful *Ringu*
(1998), for example, is not only one of the most discussed, re-made, and
imitated horror films in recent memory, but, as Mark Cousins points out,
it is also 'the most commercially successful [motion picture] ever
released in [Japan]' (2004: 475).

Ringu's sensational reception and influence evinces Japanese
horror cinema's position as one of the most vital and expansive filmic
traditions constituting 'New Asian Horror', a moniker that, like 'French
New Wave' or even 'Japanese horror cinema', serves a classificatory
function that inevitably risks privileging generic similarity over culturally
and historically specific conceptions of monstrosity, terror, and
apocalypse. This is not to suggest that each nation's contributions to what
has come to be known as 'New Asian Horror' exist in a vacuum,
emerging uninflected from the imaginations of specific filmmakers; such
a claim would ignore the varying extent to which works of 'New Asian
Horror' borrow from, or emerge as reactions against, the aesthetic and
thematic content informing works of filmic horror from around the globe.
Nakata Hideo, for instance, admits that *Ringu*'s mounting dread and
terrifying visual economy owes as much to William Friedkin's *The
Exorcist* (1973) as it does Mizoguchi Kenji's haunting 1953 masterpiece,
Ugetsu monogatari, and the Suzuki Koji novel, *Ring* (Japan, 1991), from
which *Ringu* borrows its fundamental premise (475). South Korean
filmmaker Kim Dong-bin likewise adapts Suzuki's novel with *Ring*
(1999). One may even go so far as to posit that by retaining the novel's
focus on transgendered identity, Kim's *Ring* is the more faithful film
adaptation of Suzuki's novel, though one must also consider the multiple
narrative and thematic occlusions that necessarily accompany any cross-
cultural translation. Of course, such cultural cross-fertilisation in the form
of film adaptation is nothing new. Like many nations' cinemas, Japanese
film has a lengthy history of international cultural exchange. As Richard
J. Hand notes, 'Kurosawa Akira...takes Shakespeare's *Macbeth* (1600)
and creates *Throne of Blood* (*Kumonosu jô,* 1957)' (2005: 18), a film

encoded with visual motifs from both Noh and Kabuki theatrical traditions and set in medieval Japan. Meanwhile, US directors like John Sturgis, George Lucas, and Gore Verbinski take Kurosawa Akira's *The Seven Samurai* (*Shichinin no samurai*, 1951) and *The Hidden Fortress* (*Kakushi-toride no san-akunin*, 1958), and Nakata Hideo's *Ringu*, and fashion, respectively, *The Magnificent Seven* (USA, 1960), *Star Wars* (USA, 1977) and *The Ring* (USA, 2002), works that erase 'Japanese cultural specificity' in favour of 'American modes of social and political organization' (Blake 2006: 1-2).

While a lengthy consideration of the politics of cross-cultural adaptation in 'New Asian Horror' cinema in general and Japanese horror film in particular would make for a compelling book-length study in its own right, such an exploration ultimately exceeds this volume's focus. Nevertheless, *Nightmare Japan: Contemporary Japanese Horror Cinema* by no means elides relevant cultural excavations; in the pages to follow, this book offers a sustained interrogation of contemporary Japanese horror cinema that carefully considers the 'intricate matrix' of social, cultural, and historical 'relations' (Cohen 1996: 2-3) that give rise to this influential tradition in world cinema. It is also a book whose time has come. Scholars, surprisingly, have allotted remarkably little extensive critical attention to the contemporary profusion of Japanese horror films. Individual, and frequently groundbreaking, articles by noted scholars like Jaspar Sharp and Tom Mes, as well as successful mass-market writers from Chris Desjardins to Patrick Macias, provide valuable insights into the social dynamics that render certain aspects of Japanese horror cinema impenetrable to some viewers. In the process, their writings establish valuable critical and historical groundwork, paving inroads for future academic sojourns. In addition, several vital anthologies on international horror cinema provide interested readers with crucial opportunities for gaining an increased understanding of both familiar and lesser-known works of Japanese cinematic horror, as well as some of the cultural, political, and economic factors that shape these unique and disquieting visions. These collections include, among others, *Fear Without Frontiers: Horror Cinema from around the Globe* (Schneider, 2003), *Horror Film: Creating and Marketing Fear* (Hantke, 2004), and *Horror International*

(Schneider and Williams, 2005). To date, however, only one volume of criticism dedicated exclusively to the current deluge of horror films from Japan has been published: *Japanese Horror Cinema* (McRoy, 2005). Comprised of individual essays investigating the genre's dominant aesthetic, cultural, political, and technological underpinnings, *Japanese Horror Cinema* addresses, among other key topics, the debt Japanese horror films owe to various Japanese theatrical and literary traditions, recent permutations of the "avenging spirit" motif, the impact of atomic warfare upon the popular imaginary, the influence of recent shifts in audience demographics upon horror movie fandom, and the developing relations and contestations between Japanese and Western (Anglo-American and European) horror film tropes and traditions.

Given the absence of a sustained single-authored academic engagement with the latest offerings of filmic horror from Japan, *Nightmare Japan: Contemporary Japanese Horror Cinema* offers a much-needed aesthetic and critical introduction to some of the genre's most significant works. As a substantial component of Japanese popular culture, horror films allow artists an avenue through which they may apply visual and narrative metaphors in order to engage aesthetically with a rapidly transforming social and cultural landscape. Furthermore, given Japan's complex and often contradictory responses to the impact of Western – as well as neighboring Asian – cultures, the liminal physiognomies that frequently populate Japanese horror films (be these corporeal formations traditionally monstrous, phantasmagoric, or representations of the human form dismantled) offer useful models for interrogating what H.D. Harootunian describes as Japan's 'cultural particularity', its malleable 'relationalism (*aidagamshugi*)' that 'reflects the diversity of Japanese society at a given moment', as well as its ability to 'accommodate change throughout time' (73). Thus, *Nightmare Japan* advances current studies in Japanese horror film through close readings of politically-charged motion pictures emerging within an historical moment when the artificiality of social, national, and physiological boundaries has never been more apparent, and during which the desire to re-inscribe these borders has never been, in the eyes of some cultural theorists, more pressing. This book, in other words, positions Japanese horror cinema's major thematic and aesthetic trends within a specifically Japanese cultural context that takes into account both the radical economic and political fluctuations of the last half century, and an ever-emerging politics of identity informed by shifting gender roles, reconsiderations of the importance of the extended family as a social institution, and re-conceptualisations of the very notion of cultural and national boundaries. In the process, *Nightmare Japan* maps not only how both prominent and obscure horror film directors bring their individual and, at times, collaborative, talents to the construction of compelling narratives, but also how these texts function as a mode of critical discourse engaging a transforming culture at a vital crossroads, a society at once increasingly nationalistic and global.

Written to offer readers an expansive socio-cultural analysis of this vital film genre, *Nightmare Japan* at once contributes to existing critical dialogues on the current state of the horror genre in Japanese cinema, and provides a platform from which future academic and popular inquiries into this exciting tradition in world cinema may commence. Additionally, as spatial restrictions inevitably limit the number of films and directors a single volume can address, undoubtedly some readers may be disappointed if a favourite film is not explored in as much detail as others. It is, after all, virtually impossible to address *every* Japanese horror film produced over the last two decades. As such, it is important for readers to note that this book is by no means intended to be 'exhaustive' or 'the last word' on this compelling topic. Such a claim would be an act of indefensible hubris, not to mention foolish. One of the primary goals of this book, then, is to stimulate further writing and discussion on the plethora of exciting and important new visions that constitute so much of contemporary Japanese horror cinema.

Before commencing upon a discussion of the chapters that comprise *Nightmare Japan*, a brief survey of the horror genre in the latter half of twentieth century Japanese cinema is in order. Given that this book constitutes an aesthetic and cultural analysis of Japanese horror cinema in its most contemporary manifestations – with an extensive concentration on the last two decades – such a review of the genre's rich history may provide some crucial contextualisation. By no means, of course, should readers construe this succinct review as anything even remotely approaching comprehensive. Indeed, no scholars have yet authored a thorough book-length study of the history of the horror genre in the one-hundred plus years of Japanese film. This is an unfortunate omission; such a tome would prove an invaluable contribution to cinema studies. Certainly, the specific historical and cultural moments I explore in the impending chapters disallow for such an extensive generic archaeology. However, as one can trace back many of the motifs and themes comprising contemporary Japanese horror films to prominent works within this abundant cinematic tradition, sketching out some of the most prominent contributions over the last fifty years seems an appropriate, if not vital, rhetorical gesture.

Post-War Japanese Horror Cinema

Although horror cinema existed in Japan previous to the end of World War II, Japanese film culture of the 1950s and 1960s was the site for a virtual explosion of tales of terror and apocalypse. These films generally conformed to two dominant genres: the *kaidan*, or ghost story, dominated by the *onryou* (avenging spirit) motif, and the disaster narrative, perhaps best – and certainly most famously – exemplified by the *daikaiju eiga*, or giant monster film. Drawing on a multiplicity of religious traditions, from Shintoism to Christianity, as well as the plot devices from traditional folklore, literature and theatre (including *Noh* theatre's *shunen-* [revenge-] and *shura-mono* [ghost-plays], and *Kabuki* theatre's tales of the supernatural), *kaidan* films depicted the incursion of supernatural forces into the realm of the ordinary, largely for the purposes of exacting revenge. In the majority of cases, visual representations of the 'avenging spirit' assumed the form of a 'wronged', primarily female entity returning to avenge herself upon those who harmed her. A continuation of a cinematic tradition in place long before the second world war began, prominent features associated with the *onryou* include long black hair and wide staring eyes (or, in some instances, just a single eye). These physiological details carried a substantial cultural and aesthetic weight, as long black hair is often aligned in the Japanese popular imaginary with conceptualisations of feminine beauty and sensuality, and the image of the gazing female eye (or eyes) is frequently associated with vaginal imagery.[1]

Though restrictions imposed by US colonialist forces following the war's end initially prohibited the production of *kaidan* that were set during historical periods that might, in the eyes of the occupation forces, inspire an ideologically inconvenient form of nationalism, the progressive loosening of limitations facilitated the genre's re-emergence in the form of thematically rich and visually stunning productions by some of Japan's most celebrated auteurs. Directors responsible for some of the best known *kaidan* of the 1950s and 1960s decades include Mizoguchi Kenji (*Ugetsu monogatari*, 1953), Kobayashi Masaki (*Kaidan*, 1964), and the noted Japanese new wave filmmaker, Kaneto Shindô (*Onibaba*, 1964).

Works of *daikaiju eiga*, with their over-the-top representations of Japanese urban centres under assault by giant dinosaurs and insects (among other fantastically and gargantuan creatures), are among the most immediately recognisable films in Japanese cinema. Prolific director Honda Ishirô led the way with *Godzilla* (*Gojira*, 1954) and its twenty-plus sequels, as well as his *Rodan* (*Sora no daikaijû Radon*, 1956), *Mothra* (*Mosura*, 1961), and *Dogora the Space Monster* (*Uchu daikaijû Dogora*, 1965). Yuasa Noriaki also contributed substantially to this deluge of giant monster films with his *Gamera* (*Daikaijû Gamera*, 1965) series, as did Yasuda Kimiyoshi, with his 1966 feature, *Majin: Monster of Terror* (*Daimajin*) and its sequels. These *daikaiju eiga* provided the perfect arena for the expression of numerous social anxieties, not the least of which constellate about the dread of mass destruction, mutation and the environmental impact of pollution resulting from rapid industrialisation. As Japan remains the only nation to have suffered a direct attack by atomic weapons, a devastating incident followed by decades of exposure to US military exercises and atomic tests in the

---

[1] See Barrett, G. (1989) *Archetypes in Japanese Film: The Sociopolitical and Religious Significance of the Principle Heroes and Heroines*, Selinsgrove, PA: Susquehanna University Press. For a detailed study of hair in Japanese culture, see Batchelor, John (2000), *Ainu of Japan: The Religion, Superstitions and General History of the Hair*, Mansfield Centre: Martino Publishing.

Pacific, these mutated monstrosities' aquatic and aerial assaults seem only appropriate, as do their intentional, and sometimes unintentional, annihilations of major cities. Tokyo in particular endures repeated destruction, a narrative device that has received notable critical attention in texts ranging from Darrell William Davis's *Picturing Japaneseness: Monumental Style, National Identity, Japanese Films* (1995) to Mick Broderick's anthology, *Hibakusha Cinema: Hiroshima, Nagasaki and the Nuclear Image in Japanese Film* (1996).

Such apocalyptic visions also found articulation in films that correlated the Japanese social body with 'apocalypse' and 'transcendence' (La Bare 2000, 43). The cataclysmic events that bring about the 'end of the world as we know it' can be technological, religious, or both; similarly, bodies undergoing radical disassembly can be individual, national, or global. In their fusion of the technological and the biological as a locus for terror, films like Honda Ishirô's body horror masterpiece, *Attack of the Mushroom People* (*Matango*, 1963), and Matsubayashi Shuei's World War III fantasy, *Last War* (*Sekai daisenso*, 1961), are particularly noteworthy. Not only do these texts function as exemplary models of this cinematic tradition, but they anticipate the fusion of cyberpunk and splatterpunk conceits that permeate Tsukamoto Shinya's techno-fetishist nightmare, *Tetsuo: The Iron Man* (1988), one of the most influential Japanese horror films ever produced and a picture that, along with Ishii Sogo's *Burst City* (*Bakuretsu toshi*, 1982), Fukui Shozin's *964 Pinocchio* (1991), and Ikeda Toshiharu's *Evil Dead Trap* (*Shiryo no wana*, 1988), spurred the emergence of an increasingly visceral and graphically violent wave of Japanese horror films in the mid 1980s. The success of these latter films was instrumental in refocusing international attention upon the works of numerous Japanese directors inclined towards frightening audiences with their visions of liminal entities and human bodies undergoing radical transformations or extreme physical trauma.

Finally, this introduction would be incomplete if it failed to acknowledge the influence of Tsuruta Norio, whose *kaidan*-inspired video productions *Scary True Stories* (*Honto ni atta kowai hanashi*, 1991; *Honto ni atta kowai hanashi: Dai-ni-ya*, 1992) were a direct influence on the reinvigoration of the *kaidan* as one of Japanese cinema's most durable and economically viable film genres. As Alex Zahlten and Kimihiko Kimata likewise recognise, fans of contemporary Japanese horror cinema should not underestimate Tsuruta's role in the emergence of the so-called 'J-horror' boom.

In the 1980s, Japanese Horror was painted in bright streaks of red, spurting from gashing wounds and blood-spouting intestinal spillings, a far cry from the late 1990s films filled with young women simply standing there with hair hanging over their face. The shift from bloody spectacle to intense atmospheric tension based on showing less was initiated by a barely-known director originating from Japan's straight-to-video world, usually called V-Cinema. Norio Tsuruta not only turned the horror methodology around by 180 degrees, but also established extremely successful and resilient storylines and iconography, influencing all the big names in Japanese horror film today (yes, all!), and ultimately leading to the worldwide J-horror boom and spate of American remakes. (2004-2005: para 2)

Of course, 'booms' and international 'remakes' in any film genre fall prey to perhaps the most pernicious of economic stressors, namely the desire on the part of producers and studio executives to produce more 'product' for ready mass consumption and, consequently, to dilute the latest cinematic trends through the rapid creation of multiple shallow, ultimately interchangeable regurgitations of fashionable plotlines and clichéd images. Contemporary Japanese horror cinema is by no means immune to such pressures, and if this tradition is to not only survive, but thrive, directors must be willing to innovate rather than simply immitate. In this sense, Tsuruta's recent *Premonition* (*Yogen*, 2004), the second instalment in a series of stand-alone feature-length films in the 'J-Horror Theater' series, may very well provide the kind of visual and intellectual energies necessary to cement Japanese horror's reputation as a consistently evolving genre. Hence, despite the emergence of numerous films designed to mimic the structure and style of works by directors like Shimizu Takashi, Tsukamoto Shinya, Miike Takashi, and other filmmakers instrumental to establishing the genre's current global status, it may well be these very same groundbreaking visionaries that push

Japanese horror cinema in important, visually-inventive, and intellectually-engaging new directions.

Nightmare Japan

Nightmare Japan is divided into six chapters. Chapter One consists of an extensive study of four short but brutal films, each an example of one of world cinema's most notorious genres: the 'torture film'. Long popular in Japan, this thorny branch of the horror genre has become increasingly attractive to an ever-wider array of Western audiences searching for films that push the portrayal of violence and gore to new extremes. Mobilising brutal and, occasionally, darkly comical images of dismemberment and biological violation, these films offer gruesome yet crucial insights into shifting conceptions of corporeal, social, and national cohesion, exposing a larger socio-political body in a state of cultural crisis. Shot primarily on video, Satoru Ogura's *Devil's Experiment* (*Za ginipiggu: Akuma no jikken*, 1985), Hino Hideshi's *Flowers of Flesh and Blood* (*Za ginipiggu 2: Chiniku no hana*, 1985), Tabe Hajime's *Devil Woman Doctor* (*Za ginipiggu 6: Peter no akuma no joi-san*, 1990) and Kuzumi Masayuki's *He Never Dies* (*Za ginipiggu 3: Senritsu! Shinanai otoko*, 1986) mobilise documentary aesthetics even as they deconstruct traditional verist filmmaking practices. Infused with gruesome special effects and shot with an amateur, guerrilla filmmaking aesthetic, these disturbing films offer visceral visions interlaced with a degree of stinging social satire rarely seen in works of Western horror directors. *Flowers of Flesh and Blood*, for instance, differs so radically from virtually any Western horror film that US actor Charlie Sheen famously mistook Hino's text for an actual snuff film.

Chapter Two likewise explores horror films that take corporeal disassembly as their primary conceit. Specifically, it consists of close readings of two works of postmodern body horror films by Sato Hisayasu: *Naked Blood* (*Naked Blood: Megyaku*, 1995) and *Muscle* (*Kurutta Butokai*, 1988). Positing the human body as an indiscrete, transformative, and immanent space that reveals the potential for imagining new economies of identity, Sato explores the abject dread and infinite promise of the human body in a state of perpetual becoming. Fusing splatterpunk, cyberpunk, and erotic cinema (or *pinku eiga*) motifs, *Naked Blood* and *Muscle* locate the human body as a liminal construction, a flexible and ever-encodable space that is 'at once a target for new biological and communicational technologies, a site of political conflict, and a limit point at which ideological oppositions collapse' (Shaviro 1993: 133-4).

Chapter Three focuses upon one of the most popular motifs in Japanese literary, dramatic, and visual arts: the *kaidan*, or 'ghost story'. An exceedingly flexible and persistently revisited trope in contemporary Japanese horror cinema, particularly those dependent upon representations of the *onryou*, or 'avenging spirit' motif, these uncanny narratives draw upon a plurality of religious traditions, including Shintoism and Christianity, as well as plot devices from *Noh* and *Kabuki* theatre, to relate tales of incursion upon the natural world by spectral entities eager to exact revenge on, or in some way intervene with, the living. Specifically, this chapter analyses three acclaimed works by two of Japanese horror cinema's best known directors: Nakata Hideo (*Ringu* [1998] and *Dark Water* [*Honogurai mizu no soko kara*, 2002]) and Shimizu Takashi (*Ju-on: The Grudge* [2002]). Inspired by films like Shindô Kaneto's *Onibaba* (1964) and Kobayashi Masaki's *Kwaidan* (1965), Nakata and Shimizu re-envision the 'avenging spirit' motif in these tales of 'wronged', primarily female entities who return to curse the living. Careful considerations of the focus of, and motivations behind, these spirits' wrath offer valuable insights into the historical, political, and economic logics informing contemporary social and cultural tensions between nostalgic imaginings of a 'traditional Japanese' past and the steady emergence of women as both single parents and active members of Japan's work force.

Chapter Four investigates the bleak, nihilistic, and criminally under-explored motif of 'dove style violence', a term that finds its genesis in Thomas Weisser's and Yuko Mihara Weisser's description of the detached cruelty exemplified by 'certain species of bird' that, when it discovers that 'a flock member is *different* or weaker', will peck 'dispassionately' at the meeker animal 'until it's dead" (1997: 21). This theme, best illustrated by the works that comprise Matsumura Katsuya's dark and 'controversial' (21) *All Night Long* series (*All Night Long* [*Ooru naito rongu*, 1992], *All Night Long 2: Atrocity* [*Ooru naito rongu 2: Sanji*, 1994], and *All Night Long 3: Atrocities* [*Ooru naito rongu 3: Saishuu-shô*, 1996]), as well as films as seemingly diverse as Iwai Shunji's quietly brutal meditation on *ijime* (or bullying), *All About Lily Chou-Chou* (*Riri Shushu no subete*, 2001), and Miike Takashi's sadomasochistic splatterfest, *Ichi the Killer* (*Koroshiya 1*, 2001). These works present viewers with protagonists that seemingly embody the most destructive and extreme consequences of scholastic competition, economic recession, shifting gender and sex roles, and cycles of sadism and masochism informing constructions of group and individual identity.

Chapter Five analyses three prominent apocalyptic horror films. In their representation of contemporary civilisation under assault or in ruins, the ominous yet captivating images that comprise Sono Shion's *Suicide Circle* (*Jisatsu saakuru*, 2002), Higuchinsky's *Uzumaki* (2001), and Kurosawa Kiyoshi's *Pulse* (*Kaïro*, 2001) recall a history of annihilation and reconstruction that has resulted, both nationally and internationally, in the correlation of the Japanese social body with cycles of cataclysm and rebirth. Similarly, Chapter Six, the book's final chapter, engages notions of demolition and renovation as social and generic transformations. Consequently, *Nightmare Japan*'s sixth and final chapter interprets some of the emerging visual, narratological and philosophical trends in contemporary Japanese horror cinema. In the process, I speculate upon some of the potential new directions in which this important cinematic tradition is progressing, as well as how it may continue to develop in the future. In the process, I consider multiple short and feature films that, despite occasionally contributing to a creative climate that encourages derivative plots and clichéd images, nevertheless provide avenues for forward-looking artists to innovate in important new ways. Ochiai Masayuki's *Infection* (*Kensen*, 2004) and Tsuruta Norio's *Premonition* (*Yogen*, 2002), for example, advance sophisticated meta-filmic considerations of the cultural fears and anxieties informing the social functions of not only horror movies, but also the visual representation of fear itself. Lastly, in the chapter's final pages, it is to Shimizu Takashi and Tsukamoto Shinya, two of contemporary Japanese horror cinema's premier and most consistently influential filmmakers, that I once again direct my attention. In particular, I examine how Shimizu Takashi's *Marebito* (2004) and Tsukamoto Shinya's *Vital* (2004) offer not only indispensable new visions, but construct fertile points of departure for Japan's next wave of horror directors.

Chapter One:
Guinea Pigs and Entrails:
Cultural Transformations and Body
Horror in Japanese Torture Film

Will You Be My Guinea Pig?

In 1990, Charlie Sheen, the Hollywood actor and star of such spectacles of cinematic violence as *Red Dawn* (USA, 1984), *Platoon* (USA, 1986), and *The Wraith* (USA, 1986), viewed a video tape containing *Flowers of Flesh and Blood* (*Chiniku no hana*, 1985), an episode from the Japanese *Guinea Pig* series. '[B]elieving it to be a real snuff film', Sheen 'contacted the Motion Picture Association [of America]' (Weisser and Weisser 1997: 123), and then immediately initiated a crusade dedicated to ensure that the roots of this cinematic flora would never find *terra firma* on the shelves of US video stores. Although this incident has been recounted so frequently among 'hard core' aficionados of world horror cinema that, with each re-telling, it comes closer and closer to assuming 'urban legend' status, Charlie Sheen and the authorities he alerted are far from the only people who have found themselves compelled to investigate the origin of these controversial texts. In Sweden, police called upon a physician to determine whether an episode of the *Guinea Pig* series was a recording of an actual or simulated murder, and in 1992, a 26-year old British man named Christopher Berthoud was fined £600 for importing the very same *Guinea Pig* film that spawned Charlie Sheen's misguided campaign. According to the prosecution in the Berthoud case, although the film did not consist of footage from a homicide, it nevertheless fell 'into the category of a snuff video' ('The Christopher Berthoud Case' 2003: para 1). In a rhetorical gesture that raises a myriad of compelling questions about the dynamics of film spectatorship and the power of cinema as a medium for *representing* 'reality', the prosecution elaborated by stating that: 'This [the central protagonist/victim] is not an Asian girl alive being murdered, but something that is so well simulated that that is the impression it creates' (para 1). Mr. Berthoud, perhaps wary of the film's potential dramatic and emotional impact, elected to accept whatever judgment the court deemed appropriate rather than subject the jury to 'the anxiety of having to watch the shocking footage' (para 3).

The *Guinea Pig* films have also inspired some legal and ethical debate in Japan, where, according to one of the series' primary distributors, the films were wildly successful upon their release, outselling 'most mainstream Hollywood releases two months in a row' (Biro 2003: para 5). Perhaps the most pronounced example of the *Guinea Pig* series achieving an extensive degree of notoriety in Japan occurred following the so-called '*otaku* murders' of four young girls. During these killings, Miyazaki Tsutomo, a recluse with a vast collection of violent videos, allegedly re-enacted some of the more graphic scenes from *Flowers of Flesh and Blood*. Despite attempts by the Tokyo Metropolitan Government to cite the *Guinea Pig* series as an example of an entertainment industry in need of restraint, much of the blame was targeted towards Japanese culture itself for 'creating a society that bred such a [violent] mentality' (para 6).

This socially self-reflective stance is particularly interesting, especially if one understands the *Guinea Pig* films as not only innovative works of horror cinema that challenge and redefine many of the genre's narrative and visual conventions, but also as texts in which the depiction of splattered and splattering physiognomies both provides a critical commentary upon, and aesthetically intervenes with, a transforming Japanese body politic. Through a critical survey of these controversial texts, this chapter understands the infamous series as a collection of texts that mobilise images of corporeal disintegration, and the (on-screen) forces responsible for their methodical yet gory disassembly, as metaphors for shifting conceptions of corporeal, social, and national cohesion. They are films, in short, about bodies in crisis. Narratives in perhaps the loosest sense of the term, the films under examination in the pages to follow nevertheless chart the trajectory of a culture in transition. By turns sadistic and contemplative, gruesome and elegiac, each film is its own 'flower of flesh and blood', sprouting forth and blooming its bloodiest shade of red where traditional conceptions and emerging notions of gender, class, and nation intersect.

'A Japanese Thing': Social Bodies, Cinematic Horror

Western horror films have long been obsessed with bodies – both corporeal and social – and the rhetoric (including visual and philosophical) of embodiment. Frequently marked by a thematic preoccupation with monstrosity in all its polymorphic, anthropomorphic and 'all-too-human' manifestations, horror films provide insight into not only a culture's dominant ideologies, but also those multiple subject positions that question or contest the status quo. This has particularly been the case in much of western culture, where analytical approaches from the 'psychoanalytic' critiques advanced by scholars like Robin Wood, Barbara Creed, and Steven Jay Schneider, to the 'Marxist' inquiries set forth by theorists like Christopher Sharrett and Tanya Modleski, have offered valuable insights into the extents to which horror literature and film facilitate or challenge the circulation of capitalist disciplinary power. In short, western horror films, whether progressive or ideologically recuperative, function metaphorically, participating in a larger discourse of embodiment by mobilising notions of containment, flexibility and identity (individual, national, etc.). In the process, these texts reveal volumes about the socio-political geometries from which, and against which, they arise.

How, then, might Japanese horror cinema differ from and/or resemble its western counterparts? To what extent can we understand images of corporeal cohesion and radical or 'monstrous' alterity in Japanese horror films as allegories for larger socio-political concerns? To answer these questions, we must first acknowledge the importance of the body as a metaphorical construct in Japanese society. However, before embarking upon such a discussion, it is important to note that the following paragraphs are by no means intended to serve as an exhaustive analysis of this complex discursive phenomenon. Such an exploration would certainly constitute a valuable contribution to Japanese cultural studies, but it is also an avenue of inquiry far beyond this chapter's scope. Rather, my object in the following paragraphs is to illustrate the presence, within Japanese cultural and political discourse, of the consolidated and fragmented body as an operative allegorical motif. By extension, the subsequent paragraphs aim to provide a historical basis from which one may understand contemporary Japanese horror cinema and the models of embodiment that so frequently accompany conceptions of the horrific and 'monstrous'.

In discussions of modern and contemporary Japanese society, western sociologists and historians frequently articulate the island nation's often turbulent past via a discursive paradigm that foregrounds a propensity for adaptability[1] and change in the face of socio-political crises and transformation. However, since at least the mid-nineteenth century and the Meiji restoration, numerous Japanese scholars have imagined the construction and maintenance of a consolidated – and distinctly Japanese – cultural and national identity in both implicitly and explicitly physiological terms. Thus, the application of the body as metaphor for larger socio-political formations is by no means the exclusive domain of western culture. As scholars as varied in their critical methodologies as Marilyn Ivy, Ramie Tateishi, Darrell William Davis

---

[1] Such discussions of cultural adaptability as a particularly Japanese trait are, of course, reductive in that similar claims can be made about most cultures, especially when studied over many years or during periods of significant cultural, national or even ecological transition.

and H. D. Harootunian demonstrate,[2] Japanese artists and intellectuals often employ the image of the body, and the integrity of its 'boundaries', within a larger allegorical framework; as such, it frequently provides a vital component for imagining modern and contemporary notions of 'Japanese-ness'.

For instance, one can clearly discern a discourse of 'monstrosity' and dangerous transmutations underlying contesting interpretations of Japan's so-called 'modernisation' in the years following the Meiji restoration of 1868, a tumultuous period during which Japan emerged from a relatively isolationist paradigm as a response to not only the impact of Western cultural and military imperialism, but also the rapid process of industrialisation it engendered.[3]

As Tateishi notes, Inoue Tetsujiro, in his writings on 'monsterology' during the 1890s, merges metaphors of monstrosity with a pathologisation of pre-'modern' Japanese theological (or 'super-stitious') precepts in an attempt to reify convictions that 'the conflict between the past and the modern' represented 'a battle against monstrous forces', and that the 'eradication of superstition…was instrumental to the constitution of a healthy, modern Japanese state' (Tateishi 2003: 296). Marilyn Ivy advances a similar thesis in her description of the construction of an increasingly discrete Japanese social body during the mid- to late-nineteenth century. In particular, Ivy links Japan's self-identification as a 'nation-state' with 'the threat of domination by European and American powers' (Ivy 1995: 4). In this sense, one can understand the very idea of a 'Japanese culture' as 'entirely *modern*' (4). A response to colonialist overtures, the creation and maintenance of a definitive Japanese social body evolved within the cultural imaginary

---

[2] As Elizabeth Ann Hull and Mark Siegel note in 'Science Fiction,' '[t]he industrial revolution was not simply imported by the Orient; it was forced upon it, either through imperialistic exploitation or, in the case of Japan, as a defense against exploitation.' See Powers, R. G. and Kato, H. (1989) *Handbook of Japanese Popular Culture*. New York: Greenwood Press, p. 245.

[3] One manifestation of this 'disintegrating' effect was the apparent rise in individualised, 'autonomous disciplines', a system of social compartmentalisation in which an emerging concentration on specialised fields of 'knowledge' led to the establishment of 'barriers between different areas of culture, causing mutual isolation and preventing genuine self-understanding.' Harootunian 1989: 74.

even as the trappings (both material and ideological) of western culture became progressively familiar.

In contrast to writers like Inoue, twentieth-century Japanese scholars and cultural theorists like Kamei Katsuichirō and Hayashi Fasao perceived the introduction/incursion of western (largely US) culture as contributing to a dissolution of a 'sense of "wholeness" in life among the Japanese' (Harootunian 1989: 70). From this perspective, Westernising forces are a deforming and disintegrating influence; the impact of western culture disrupts a spiritually and socially coded 'Japanese-ness' that, as Darrell William Davis asserts, had been shaped and reshaped 'for a very long time, even before Japan's mid-nineteenth-century encounter with American gunboats and the Meiji restoration of 1868' (Davis 2001: 60-1). Even to this day, over a half century after the Allied occupation further facilitated the proliferation of western cultural hegemony, this impulse to recover a perceived sense of social cohesion can still be observed.

In contemporary Japan there has been a relentlessly obsessive 'return' to 'origins': an orchestrated attempt by the state to compensate for the dissolution of the social by resurrecting 'lost' traditions against modernism itself, and by imposing a master code declaring 'homogeneity' in a 'heterogenous' present. (Harootunian 2003: 66) Like Inoue's 'monsterology', which depicts enduring religious models (or 'superstitions') as a 'monstrous' pre-'modern' past threatening the emergence of a newly modernist, industrial and internationally engaged Japan, discourses that call for a resistance of western cultural and military imperialism through the restoration of a conspicuously unified and 'Japanese' past promote a narrative in which a return of a 'repressed' and/or 'oppressed' identity figures prominently.[4] Both ideologies,

---

[4] D. P. Martinez recognises the logic behind this narrative as a rhetorical (and frequently aesthetic) construct that presents an almost panicked reification of a illusory 'wholeness' through a depiction of the Japanese national identity as discrete and homogenous: 'Japan is similar to many modern nation-states in that it has had to construct a model of a unitary identity shared by all citizens. Identity no longer depends on religious models or on loyalty to one particular ruler, leader, but on the wider construct of the imagined national community. This nationalism depends on the mass production of mass culture and, while the logic of capitalism (late or otherwise) demands diversification, the underlying logic of one identity (the Japanese) as different from that of their neighbors (let us say, Korea or China) remains crucial

informed by metaphors of imperiled ocial bodies, co-exist in the larger cultural imaginary. Likewise, as Davis shows, both positions depend upon an understanding of nationalism as an invention made possible only through the acknowledgement of a 'relative' as (as opposed to binary) difference that re-affirms the inescapability and permanence of cross-cultural 'syncretism', or contamination (Davis 2001: 65). Furthermore, the contesting ideologies that were discussed above can be understood as

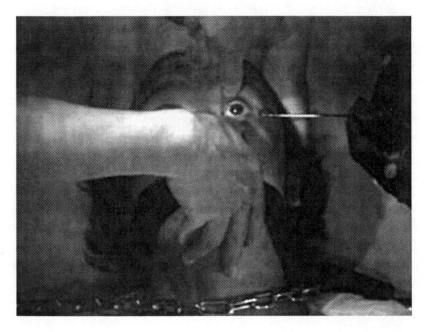

Image 1: Buñuel revisited – Satoru Ogura's *Devil's Experiment* (© Ecclectic DVD Distributors)

having achieved varying degrees of metaphorical translation through the iconography and dominant scenarios of Japanese horror cinema,

---

to the nation state.' See Martinez, D. P. (1998) 'Gender, Shifting Boundaries, and Global Cultures', in Martinez, D. P. *The Worlds of Japanese Popular Culture: Gender, Shifting Boundaries and Global Cultures*. Cambridge: Cambridge University Press, p. 10.

particularly those texts created in the tumultuous decades following World War II. Metaphors of the body, like bodies themselves, are surprisingly flexible and porous; as Matsui Midori notes, '(a)ccording to each historical application, the return of the repressed Japanese "body" can be made either regressive or liberating, reactionary or revolutionary' (2002: 144).

Of course, to contextualise not only the recent 'explosion' of Japanese horror cinema, but also the general popularity of horror films in Japan over the last fifty years, one cannot underestimate the impact of such crucial events as Japan's catastrophic defeat in World War II (and the subsequent years of foreign occupation), the decades of dramatic economic recovery and the similarly spectacular financial recession of the 1990s upon both the national psyche and, consequently, the artistic creations that inevitably emerged. In addition, it is equally essential to recognise how these larger social transformations inform the shape and significance of those institutions and behavioural codes central to the development and preservation of a sense of national and cultural identity. As Tim Craig notes, large-scale political and economic shifts invariably produce 'new social conditions', including 'urbanization, consumer cultures, changing family structures and gender roles, and lifestyles and values that are less purely traditional and more influenced by outside information and trends' (2000: 16). Correspondingly, given the influence of such novel 'social conditions' and transformations upon the cultural imaginary, it seems only fitting that they would find reflection within the 'popular culture' (16) as well.

As a substantial product of Japanese popular culture, horror films provide one of the more valuable and flexible avenues through which artists can apply visual and narrative metaphors to engage a changing cultural terrain. Furthermore, given Japan's aforementioned complex, and often contradictory, responses to the 'permanence of imprints left by the contact with the West' (Ivy 1995: 241), the liminal physiognomies that frequently populate Japanese horror films (be these corporeal formations traditionally monstrous, phantasmagoric or representations of the human form dismantled) are ideal models for interrogating Japan's 'cultural particularity', a malleable 'relationalism (*aidagamshugi*)' (Harootunian

1989: 80-1) that 'reflects the diversity of Japanese society at a given moment', as well as its ability to 'accommodate change throughout time' (Martinez 1998: 3). Therefore, it is to the *Guinea Pig* series, arguably Japanese cinema's most extreme works of cinematic terror and body horror that I now turn, endeavoring, over the next several pages, to note the extent to which their themes and motifs may reveal a culture at once increasingly nationalistic and global.

Bloody Fragments and the Body in Pain:
Devil's Experiment and *Flowers of Flesh and Blood*

In her essay, 'Horror and the Carnivalesque', Barbara Creed notes that '(t)he image of the transforming body is central to the horror genre' in that '(t)he possibility of bodily metamorphosis attacks the foundations of the symbolic order which signifies law, rationality, logic, truth' (137). In other words, cinematic representations of radical biological malleability or violent corporeal disintegration disrupt notions of identity (national, cultural, gendered) as 'fixed' or 'natural', even as some artists and cultural critics with variably conservative, reactionary, or intransigent subject positions mobilise such imagery to reify their political agendas.

Often cited as among world cinema's most notorious motion pictures, Satoru Ogura's *Devil's Experiment* (*Akuma no jikken*, 1985) and Hino Hideshi's *Flowers of Flesh and Blood* are works of 'body horror cinema' in that they are 'obsessed with limits – with the skin as a boundary, with the tolerance of audience expectation and desire, and with the connection between the two, as on-screen the visceral violation provokes visceral response' (Williams 2000: 34). Similar to Japanese films like Ishii Teruo's *Joys of Torture* series (*Tokugawa onna keibatsu-shi*, 1965-9), Suzuki Norifumi's *Beautiful Girl Hunter* (*Dabide no hoshi: bishoujo-gari*, 1979), Sato Toshio's *Guts of a Beauty* (*Bijo no harawata*, 1986), and Hashimoto Izo's *Bloody Fragments on a White Wall* (*Shiroi kabe no kekkon*, 1989), especially in their vivid depiction of the human body tortured and dismembered, *Devil's Experiment* and *Flowers of Flesh and Blood* have become increasingly attractive texts to an ever-wider array of horror fans and paracinemaphiles[5] hungry for films that push the portrayal of violence and gore to new extremes. Merging the aesthetics of *cinéma vérité* and *cinema vomitif*, they are 'total theater' (Brottman 1997: 3) impacting viewers on the most visceral level through a consistent barrage of graphic scenes of physical and psychological abuse framed by little more than scrolling title cards. Such a cinematic presentation at once gestures towards alienating the viewer (in an almost Brechtian sense) from the graphic content to follow, and threatens to collapse the psychic distance between spectator and spectacle. Presented in a visual style that mimics the 'look' and 'feel' of 'nonfiction films' that purport to document what André Bazin calls the 'raw reality' of everyday life, these 'topographical narratives of the human body split open, infested, rendered asunder, penetrated, truncated, cleft, sliced, suspended, and devoured' (14) arise from a myriad of diverse Japanese cinematic traditions, ranging from *pinku eiga* (the "pink" or soft-core film) to *chanbara eiga* (the samurai film).   In addition, the scenes of ritualised brutality that define these texts provide a barometer of sorts for a plethora of social concerns.   The evisceration of the female body in *Flowers of Flesh and Blood*, for instance, is reminiscent of rituals like *hara kira*, 'an ancient act in which female votives would offer up the "flower" of their entrails and blood by a self-inflicted knife wound' (Hunter 1998: 159-60), while the apportioning of gender roles within both films address concerns about the stability of traditional sex and, by extension, gender-based divisions of labor at the height of Japan's late capitalist 'bubble economy'.

Given their substantial focus on the body as a site of trauma and radical reconfiguration, the *Guinea Pig* films' position within Japanese cinema seems appropriate for the period of economic prosperity, rapid technologisation, and extreme cultural transformation that began with the

---

[5] 'Paracinema' is Jeffrey Sconce's term for a set of reading practices clustered around a variety of film texts that lend themselves to ironic and/or counter-hegemonic reading protocols in the hands of viewers who focus their sophisticated reading skills on texts ignored by 'legitimate' taste cultures. In other words, paracinema is 'less a distinct group of films than a particular reading protocol, a counter-aesthetic turned subcultural sensibility devoted to all manner of cultural detritus...[T]he explicit manifesto of paracinema culture is to valorise all forms of cinematic "trash", whether such films have been either explicitly rejected or simply ignored by legitimate film culture' (Sconce 372).

end of US military occupation, and which would eventually – and perhaps inevitably – culminate with the devastating recession of the 1990s. To this day, metaphors of both corporeal integrity and imperiled social bodies permeate the Japanese cultural imaginary, a discursive phenomenon best evidenced when one considers how the demands of an increasingly global economy at once conditions and perpetually threatens to collapse the always already illusory notion of a discrete and homogenous national identity. In this sense, then, Japan resembles 'many modern nation-states in that it [Japan] has to construct a model of a unitary identity shared by all citizens' (Martinez 1998: 10). Such a paradigm depends on 'the wider construct of the imagined national community' (10), a form of nationalism linked with the content and circulation of filmic and other popular culture texts. Hence, 'while the logic of capitalism (late or otherwise) demands diversification, the underlying logic of one identity (the Japanese) as different from that of their neighbors…remains crucial to the nation state' (14). In the turbulent, yet economically productive decades following the end of World War II, this seemingly paradoxical drive to establish an imagined homogeneity in an increasingly global arena is marked by concurrent drives to repress or forget a pre-modern past in favor of a postmodern global community and to rescue vanishing or abandoned traditions in what H.D. Harootunian describes as 'a relentlessly obsessive "return" to "origins": an orchestrated attempt by the state to compensate for the dissolution of the social by resurrecting "lost" traditions against modernism itself' (Harootunian 1989: 66).[6] Indeed, if we understand the 'discursively constructed' corporeal and social body in late capitalist Japan as a 'central site for the reconfiguration of Japan's national image' (Igarashi 2000: 13), it is then possible to read the violated and violating

---

[6] In light of Japan's political and cultural climate since the Meiji restoration, Rey Chow's brief essay, 'Film and Cultural Identity', offers a compelling introduction to the complex, and explicitly modern, relationship between the photographic image (including, but not limited to, film) and "cultural identity". Chow argues that the complex "multiple significance of filmic visuality" in numerous non-Western cultures must be understood within a postcolonial framework "in which to become 'modern' signifies an ongoing revisioning of indigenous cultural traditions alongside the obligatory turns towards the West or 'the world at large'. In this light, it is worth remembering that film has always been, since its inception, a *transcultural* phenomenon, having as it does the capacity to transcend 'culture'" (172).

physiognomies in the *Devil's Experiment* and *Flowers of Flesh and Blood* as emblematic of wider socio-cultural tensions resulting from a post-colonial climate of economic development?

Composed of progressively brutal vignettes with brief, albeit accurate titles ('Hit', 'Kick', 'Claw', 'Unconscious', 'A Sound', 'Skin', 'Burn', 'Worm', 'Guts', and 'Needle'), Satoru Ogura's *Devil's Experiment*, the most visually fragmented of the *Guinea Pig* films, is explicitly concerned with testing the very notion of boundaries, be these limit points corporeal, narratological, or political. This thematic agenda is clear from the opening sequence, in which the anonymously penned text that precedes the film's action scrolls upwards against a black background, spelling out, in the process, the film's main premise:

Image 2: Pseudo-snuff or nostalgic nationalism? Hino Hideshi's *Flower of Flesh and Blood* (© Ecclectic DVD Distributors)

> Several years ago, I obtained a private video under the title GUINEA PIG. Its commentary said that 'this is a report of an experiment on the breaking point of bearable pain and the corrosion of people's senses'…but it was, in fact, an exhibition of devilish cruelty as three perpetrators severely abused a woman. Note: 'Guinea Pig' is defined as any experimental material.

The use of the ambiguously plural 'people' is particularly instructive, as the 'breaking point' that this filmed/filmic 'experiment' purports to test extends beyond that of the victim, whose suffering the director presents as 'real' torture captured on tape, to include the audience as well. Indeed, as is the case with many films and film genres, audience perceptions of the 'reality' of the action transpiring before them is perhaps the most vital component of all when considering the text from an aesthetic and socio-political perspective.

Episodic in its portrayal of the torture and mutilation of an unidentified female by three male figures clad in black pants, black T-shirts, and dark sunglasses, *Devil's Experiment* is a gut-wrenching forty minutes of 'video' designed to confound viewers expecting the narrative and visual trappings of traditional horror film. It is, instead, a text that increases the viewer's dis-ease via a process of continuous visual and narrative dislocation; through a layering of anonymity within the film's diegesis, as well as a series of meticulously orchestrated compositions, Saturo's lens evokes simultaneously sadistic and sympathetic viewing positions. The scrolling, written text that opens the film, for instance, constitutes a carefully articulated rhetorical gesture deliberately poised to blur audience distinctions between fact and fiction, thus heightening the visceral impact generated by the 'experiment's' verisimilitude. Whether the images that form the body of the text are a re-creation of the original 'experiment' or the 'real' 'experiment' is likewise left ambiguous, and the absence of a traditional credit sequence further confounds spectator assumptions of what is 'real' or 'simulated', investing the images with an aura of 'authenticity'.

However, once a prudent viewer closely examines the film's deeper structures, dedicating special attention to Satoru's practiced manipulation of not only *what* is shown, but also of *how* (and in *what order*) images are represented, it becomes obvious that not only is *Devil's Experiment* not a 'snuff movie', but that its categorization within the documentary – or, for that matter, the 'mockumentary' – genre is problematic at best. The film appeals to documentary conceits by mobilising the notion that its content constitutes 'found footage' (the images we watch were, after all, ambiguously 'obtained', and its aesthetic is, at times, consistent with the conventions of 'direct cinema', particularly in the implication that the images represent a directly and intimately observed 'reality'. At the same time, however, the director creates a text that by turns establishes and frustrates audience expectations regarding the text's documentary authenticity. Any initial anxiety or dread conjured by the potentiality of seeing something illicit, culturally aberrant, or taboo is soon countered by meticulously staged and edited sequences that, as we shall soon discover, variously destabilise the viewing process. Indeed, Satoru's editing, as Jack Hunter observes in *Eros in Hell: Sex, Blood and Madness in Japanese Cinema*, reveals a remarkable level of technical sophistication and artistry that designates the film as 'professional', if not downright 'well crafted' (Hunter 1998: 145):

> [U]tilizing such techniques as slow-motion, freeze-frame, fades, intercuts, overhead shots, point-of-view shots, close ups, anamorphs, rapid-fire editing, captioning and sound tracking in its composition...*Devil's Experiment* is, in fact, an effective and surprisingly low-key meditation on the cumulative dehumanization that violence causes in both aggressor and victim alike. (145)

Hunter's assessment of the film as meditative in tone is particularly astute, as the film's episodic structure allows for periodic moments of reflection upon (if not recuperation from) the preceding events, as well as "setting up," via the inter-title, the next session of torture.

Furthermore, by repeatedly varying the audience's perspective during the torture sequences, Satoru complicates the distribution of the object, trajectory, and implication of the audience's gaze. Throughout the majority of the film, the abuse is lensed in slightly high-angle close ups and medium shots, heightening the victim's helplessness at the hands of her captors and positioning the spectator as an intimate witness to, if not somewhat complicit in, the horrific events that transpire. At other moments, we adopt the victim's POV, staring helplessly through her eyes as we are spun around and beaten. In still other instances, we are seemingly removed from the visceral proximity of the film's action, viewing the victim in an extreme long shot as she rotates slowly within a mesh sack dangling from a tree in the woods; this detached perspective becomes the film's visual refrain, providing a 'break' that extends the respite afforded by the text's inter-titles and, thus, allows audiences to more thoroughly divest themselves from the visceral immediacy of the brutally graphic images.

How, then, does this variable allocation of the viewer's gaze impact the experience of viewing *Devil's Experiment*? In additions, how might we understand the film's content in relation to social transformations in late capitalist Japanese culture?

Satoru's careful manipulation of the film's variable and fragmented/fragmenting *mise-en-scène*, coupled with the aforementioned recurring visual and aural motifs, ruptures conventional cinematic processes of identification, as well as typical expectations of how a documentary should function. In doing so, Satoru draws attention to the film as artifice, as a deliberately arranged aesthetic 'experiment' comprised of a series of spliced and sutured images selected for both their urgent visual impact, as well as their contribution to a larger, socio-cultural meta-narrative informed by anxieties over the apportioning of sex and gender roles in late capitalist Japan. One can comprehend *Devil's Experiment*, for instance, as contributing to a popular tradition of sadomasochistic imagery within Japanese cinema, a pervasive visual rhetoric that, as Maureen Turim reminds us, arises both as a result of restrictions on the representation of male and female genitalia in Japanese *pinku eiga*, and as a misogynist 'appeal to desires', within a transforming social landscape, 'to contain women socially, economically, and sexually' (1994: 83). There is little escaping the film's femicidal and misogynist overtones;[7] the recipient of the sadistic attacks is, after all, a woman. In

---

[7] For and extensive (primarily Western) historical and cultural analysis of the practice and consequences of this most heinous form of misogyny, see Radford, J. and Russell, D. E. H. (1992) *Femicide: The Politics of Killing Women*. New York: Twayne Publishers.

scenes that merge what Jane Caputi identifies as 'pornographic and gorenographic images' (1992: 213), the female victim's body is continually reduced to an object, a 'thing' to be abused and butchered. As a result, *Devil's Experiment* depicts 'an extreme expression of patriarchal "force"' (206). A demonstration 'of sexual politics' and 'male domination', the film is a visual 'form of terror that functions to maintain the power of the patriarchal order' (206).

This is not to suggest that Satoru's film is explicitly pornographic (or porno-graphically explicit), though its visual rhetoric repeatedly adopts the fragmentation of human body as its central metaphor. Nor am I claiming that *Devil's Experiment* is irrevocably misogynistic. Given Satoru's aesthetics of disruption, in which everything from the text's deconstruction of its initial claims of documentary authenticity to the director's manipulation of the audience's gaze is designed to undermine conventional viewing practices, we can also understand this text as providing a politically charged meditation on cultural dynamics akin to the practices of world cinema's more accomplished experimental, and politically-progressive, filmmakers. Through its vacillating POV, *Devil's Experiment* collapses subjective and objective vision in a manner that resembles the 'dissolution of the boundary between inside and outside…private and public' that Elaine Scarry locates in the practice of torture. As such, the film can be understood as a complex study of power, specifically the 'regime' of violent male authority wielded against the feminine form.

Thus, the 'experiment' that Satoru's film offers viewers is a distinctly cinematic one, approaching, at times, a level of socio-cultural critique most frequently attributed to experimental or avant-garde filmmaking. In the film's climactic moment, for example, the three torturers push a needle into the woman's temple, angling it until it emerges through her eye. Immediately reminiscent of the famous eyeball slicing scene from the Luis Buñuel – Salvador Dali collaboration, *Un Chien Andalou* (France, 1929), the retinal puncturing in *Devil's Experiment* is a seemingly inevitable yet powerful moment of ocular horror, its immediacy providing an ultimate corporeal violation of the female victim, as well as a final, visceral intrusion upon the spectator's wavering distance from the film's explicit content. As blood pools from the corner of the victim's eye, the point of the needle perforating her cornea, viewers witness the ultimate articulation of patriarchal authority as a dominating social (and socializing) force. Through the violent destruction of the very organ most frequently associated with 'vision' and 'enlightenment', Satoru presents viewers, through the metaphor of torture, with an unforgettable representation of an aggressive regime's total infusion of the corporeal and social body; the female form is reduced to an object of abusive inquiry (and inquiry through abuse), its physical and psychic parameters pushed to – and past – the 'breaking point' by an impassive masculine collective that is quite literally never out of control. Thus, unlike Buñuel and Dali's *Un Chien Andalou*, which approached the political by way of a personalised surrealism and the creation of 'meaning' through imagistic conflation, *Devil's Experiment* confronts viewers with an externalised hyperreality informed by a logic of disruption via a *mis-en-scène* that fluctuates between immersion and alienation. In the process, it maps an ever-emerging discursive legacy of brutality, offering audiences a gruesome exposition of a transforming postwar Japanese body waging a ferocious war with itself.

Flowers of Flesh and Blood, the controversial cinematic creation of renowned *manga* artist Hino Hideshi, resembles Saturo's film in that Hino, too, uses a written text scrolling against a black background to frame the film's primary 'narrative'. Unlike Saturo, however, Hino does not set out to create even the faintest illusion that the material the viewer sees on the screen is 'real' (although, given the aforementioned account of the film's infamous reception history, the gory content has nevertheless been understood as such). Rather than transmit the notion that what we are about to see is actual – i.e. not simulated – violence captured on camera, Hino posits the film's content as a *re-creation* of a snuff film delivered to a 'bizarre cartoonist' with the curiously familiar sounding moniker, Hideshi Hibino:

> It was in April 1985...[that]...Bizarre cartoonist Hideshi Hibino eceived one horrible parcel from an unidentified person who calls himself an enthusiastic fan of the cartoonist Hideshi Hibino. The parcel contained one 8mm film, 54 still pictures and a 19 page letter: The letter to the cartoonist that [sic] a

horrible and bizarre crime seems to have been performed by the [sic] person of aesthetic paranoia in some secret place. The 8mm film was considered to be a vivid and authentic film showing an unidentified man chop [sic] the body of a woman into pieces and put [sic] them into his collection. Therefore, this film should not be shown to other people. Hideshi Hibino newly created this video as a restructured semi-documentary based on the 8mm film, pictures and letter.

Similar to *Devil's Experiment*, *Flowers of Flesh and Blood* at once conforms to and confounds standard documentary practice. Defined as a 'restructured semi-documentary', a genre classification that, in its very syntax, conflates the expectations of fiction and so-called 'non-fiction' filmmaking, *Flowers of Flesh and Blood* is nothing less than a cleverly articulated work of cinematic metafiction. A 'fake documentary', it derives the majority of its effectiveness through the skillful application of familiar documentary techniques, most notably the dramatic 're-enactment' of events which, for one reason or another, either could not be captured on film or can not be rebroadcast in their original form. Thus, from its opening sequence, Hino's film, informed by documentary techniques, advocates an understanding of its gruesome content as a 'restructured' and, consequently, fictionalised narrative based upon an already imaginary 8mm film. In the process of crafting this complex and inventive layering of realistic unreality, Hino creates a text that explores profound cultural anxieties surrounding gender- and class-based transformations in Japan's socio-cultural climate.

Likewise akin to *Devil's Experiment*, *Flowers of Flesh and Blood's* primary action consists of increasingly violent attacks upon a female body punctuated by mainly low angle close ups of the killer staring directly into the camera's lens and discussing his next assault ('And now her bowels start dancing wildly on her body and bloom many blossoms.'). These intimate moments of direct address portion the film into tiny sanguine chapters and, together with numerous lengthy panning shots, slow fades, and non-diegetic moans and wails, provide periods of almost poetic reflection. Indeed, the film's lyricism is perhaps never more pronounced than during the film's penultimate sequence, during which a mournful lamentation of 'man's' descent into hell – a veritable 'lullaby of hell' – plays over the camera's slow pan through the killer's 'collection', a combination of exquisitely detailed scrolls depicting warriors and demons from Japanese folklore, and a gruesome, yet artfully arranged tableaux of eviscerated bodies, skinned faces and jars of eyeballs, vaginas, and chicken heads.

Unlike *Devil's Experiment*, however, Hino's film depicts the victim's abduction from an urban street through a grainy sequence that, shot at night on location, is immediately reminiscent of a 'direct cinema' approach to filmmaking in both the camera's mobility (the shots seem hand-held) and the director's use of available light within the *mise-en-scène*.[8] As a result, the film's action is rendered less ambiguous and fragmentary. Viewers learn how the woman has come to be at the mercy of her captor. Additionally, as the camera's angle and motion suggests that the images on the screen may in fact represent the stalker's point-of view, the viewer's gaze aligns with that of the killer in a manner familiar to audiences of mass-market horror films. Further, by coding the lone, well-dressed woman (the object of the camera's gaze and soon-to-be-victim) as an office worker most likely on her way home at the end of the day, Hino engages cultural apprehensions over not only the threat of women entering the work force in larger numbers, but also, by extension, the alteration in the woman's role within the domestic realm (Napier 2000: 145). Walking both with purpose and without escort, the women in the film's opening scenes, including the film's protagonist/victim, can be read as figures representative of a wider, more discursive threat to conventional notions of masculine authority, a fear 'commonly expressed' within Japanese popular culture through images, both literal and figurative, 'of the socially respected white collar man becoming impotent' (145). This femicidal tone permeates the entire film, at once revealing masculinist anxieties over changing gender roles, and perpetuating misogynist representations of violence against women that, like those in Satoru's *Devil's Experiment*, contribute to a larger 'gorenographic' imaginary (Caputi 1992: 213).

---

[8] Indeed, the only moment when available light is not used during this sequence is in the killer's pursuit of his eventual victim. During this event, a small spotlight (most likely attached to the hand-held camera) illuminates the scene.

As if in recognition of the imagined 'dangers' that may accompany this potential reversal of social power, the killer in *Flowers of Flesh and Blood* wears samurai armor, a black leather butcher's apron, and latex gloves throughout the lengthy dismemberment sequences; in a similar fusion of the traditional and the modern, he wields a battle axe, an assortment of rusty tools, and a variety of contemporary surgical utensils against his victim's prone and securely tied body. While clearly reminiscent of the previously discussed inclination within Japanese popular culture to envision a homogenous past, a 'relentlessly obsessive "return" to "origins"' (Harootunian 1989: 66), *Flowers of Flesh and Blood*'s conflation of historical (and cinematic) signifiers likewise calls to mind what Christopher Sharrett calls postmodernism's 'catastrophe', a condition defined as 'the simultaneous affirmation and denial of historical views of reality, the nostalgia for the past simultaneous with its derision, and the constant attempt to prop up mythic readings of history even as they are seen as risible' (1999: 421).

This catastrophic 'will-to-myth' about which Sharrett writes – the impulse to 'legitimate false consciousness and to reassert primitive views of human interchange' (422), including torture and murder – underlies Hino's vision of corporeal apocalypse in which the bound physiognomy of the female victim is methodically annihilated. In its depiction of historically-coded Japanese iconography (the figure of the samurai), as well as in its visual, verbal, and poetic allusions to traditional Japanese ritual (*hara kiri* is, as Hunter notes, the most obvious), the film evokes nostalgia for an idealised, if illusory, past at once longed for and yet impossible to recover. While attired in samurai armor made ridiculously anachronistic given the dilapidated urban environment in which he 'operates', the killer seems to be literally rotting away from the inside-out, especially in close ups that reveal stained and broken teeth, as well as blood-spattered skin flaking beneath a thin layer of powder. Though suggestive of ritualistic suicide 'marked by religious ecstasy', the captive woman's bloody 'flowers' (her glistening internal organs) are harvested non-consensually through violence rather than 'offer[ed] up' (Hunter 1998: 160) voluntarily. The euphoric expression on her face is the result of intravenous drugs administered to silence her screams and, as the killer informs us, impose a state of rapture.[9]

Thus, *Flowers of Flesh and Blood*, documents more than the mutilation of a Japanese woman. It reveals a paradoxical tension within postmodern Japanese culture, namely the struggle to construct and maintain an imagined homogenous cultural identity within an increasingly transformative and 'heterogenous present' (Harootunian 1989: 66). This contradictory impulse positions the Japanese social body as a 'body in pain', to borrow Elaine Scarry's term, a body under attack from its own 'regimes of power', its integrity threatened by assaults from 'inside and outside alike' (1985: 53), by a will to nationalism and a recognition of the demands of an increasingly global society.

Exhuming the Past, Dissecting the Present: *Devil Woman Doctor*

The final two *Guinea Pig* films under consideration in this chapter, *Devil Woman Doctor* (*Peter no akuma no joi-san* 1990), directed by Tabe Hajime, and *He Never Dies* (*Senritsu! Shinanai otoko*,1986), directed by Kuzumi Masayuki, share *Devil's Experiment*'s and *Flowers of Flesh and Blood*'s fake documentary structure, as well as the films' depiction of the tortured and disarticulated human form to advance a socio-political critique of a transforming Japanese culture. Unlike the two *Guinea Pig* films discussed above, however, Tabe's and Kuzumi's contributions to the notorious series mix gore with dark humour in a fashion that inevitably evokes comparisons to Sam Raimi's *The Evil Dead* films (USA, 1981-93), as well as Troma Studio's most extreme productions, like *Redneck Zombies* (USA, Pericles Lewnes, 1987) and *Tromeo and*

---

[9] Coincidentally, as in *Devil's Experiment*, the last organ removed from the captive woman is an eye, which the killer fondles lovingly as he sucks it clean of blood. While lacking the visceral impact of the eyeball piercing sequence in Satoru's film, the dislodging of the woman's eye in *Flowers of Flesh and Blood* possesses a metaphoric power that justifies its status as the film's ghastly denouement. For the killer, and the multiplicity of cultural imperatives for which he stands, the eye represents the quintessence of female physicality. As the killer in samurai armour states: 'Well, now, for the finishing touch is to take out her precious jewels. Ah, this is the most beautiful thing of a woman's body. This is it!'

Juliet (USA, Lloyd Kaufman, 1996). This combination of the horrific and the satirical proves an effective mechanism for interrogating conceptions of national trauma haunting Japan throughout the twentieth century, from the brutal legacy of Japanese imperialist aggressions in the South Pacific during World War II, to shifting notions of sex and gender roles during the 'bubble economy's' waning years. Understood as a barometer for the multiple social and economic fluctuations endemic to late industrial culture in Japan, *Devil Woman Doctor* and *He Never Dies* reveal a social and national body in mortal conflict with itself.

Tabe Hajime's *Devil Woman Doctor* consists of a series of gruesome set pieces and comical experiments narrated by the eponymous 'physician', a drag queen named 'Peter'. From the film's opening moments, in which a scalpel-sliced doll expels an impossible geyser of blood, to a scene of a reporter hovering curiously above a buffet of cannibal delicacies (including eyeballs, testicles, and vulvas), to a sequence during which four of the 'Devil Woman Doctor''s patients compare their increasingly bizarre ailments, Tabe's film, with its tacky special effects and ridiculous over-acting, defines itself as an explicitly self-conscious text that is not meant to be taken seriously. Though certainly aiming to 'gross out' viewers with its copious depictions of the human body bleeding, exploding, mutating and decomposing, the dialogue accompanying the images renders the events at once comical and critical. Most importantly, *Devil Woman Doctor*'s narration deploys blunt observations and barbed insights to dissect both Japanese history and contemporary Japanese culture. Thus, like a sadistic physician carving her way into a fresh corpse, Tabe's text probes both old and new 'wounds', peeling back layers of flesh to expose the allegorical connections festering like cancers just beneath the surface of the Japanese social body.

By way of illustration, consider the sequence in which a reporter, Kageyama Tamio, attends the inaugural 'tasting party of human flesh', a catered buffet of dishes featuring assorted body parts variously prepared for human consumption. Among the dishes on display are human brains 'pickled in soy sauce and vinegar', jellied eyeballs garnished with cockroaches and flies, severed hands and heads in bowls of crisp iceberg lettuce, sausage-like intestines, boiled testicles, and vaginas in blood sauce, the latter prepared, Kageyama informs us, during menstruation. Anxieties surrounding representations of abject physicality and corporeal violability clearly dominate this scene, but what are viewers to make of the cannibalistic connotations of the 'tasting party'? Interviewing several of the guests in attendance, Kageyama discovers that most are curious about the feast, albeit quite reluctant to sample any of the items on display. Then the reporter questions some of the event's more peripheral attendees. He approaches a cleaning woman who is obviously the 'Devil Woman Doctor' in disguise. Although the blatant conflation of a traditionally female occupation ('cleaning woman') with a conventionally male practice (a physician) raises several compelling questions regarding shifting gender roles in contemporary Japan (an issue with which I will engage more deeply in the pages to follow), it is the cleaning woman's reply to Kageyama's query that the film's director, Tabe, clearly intends his audience to ponder. In response to the reporter's inquiry as to whether or not she has ever 'tried human flesh before', the cleaning woman / 'Devil Woman Doctor' shyly states: 'Maybe my father has eaten some during the war. But I never have.' This answer transforms the macabre 'tasting party' into a forum for evoking cultural anxieties surrounding reports of Japanese war-time atrocities, including acts of cannibalism allegedly committed to fight off starvation. Furthermore, as news and rumours of these crimes did not reach the general public until the mid-1980s, the peak of the so-called 'bubble economy', they represent an unassimilated past distanced from later generations both by the passage of time and by the demands of the post-war 'economic miracle'.

Tabe's intentions here seem both instructive and critical. As Tanaka Yuki notes in *Hidden Horrors: Japanese War Crimes in World War II*, '[t]he current generation of Japanese still do not have a clear concept of the responsibility of their parents and grandparents in relation to the war' (1996: 202). 'This is an entirely different situation,' Tanaka continues, 'from what exists in, for example, Germany, where an acute awareness of the role of the German people in World War II and genocide of Jews and Gypsies continues to be a major factor in political life and memory' (202). Noting frequently, and correctly, that many nations around the globe have lengthy histories of war crimes,[10] Tanaka provides readers with a litany of Japanese atrocities committed primarily in the South Pacific and China. The specific crimes he recounts include the mistreatment of prisoners of war, the testing of biological warfare agents upon living human subjects, and the sporadic practice of cannibalism, an activity for which only two soldiers were actually convicted (132). Additionally, Tanaka reminds readers that those guilty of war crimes are often themselves the victims of war crimes (134):

> The case of cannibalism in the South Pacific clearly demonstrates that some Japanese soldiers were perpetrators of war crimes in their murder, mutilation, and cannibalism of enemy soldiers, POWs, and local civilians, but they also were victims of a war crime in that they were abandoned and starved by their high command. (134)

Thus, '[i]n literal terms, Japanese soldiers were obviously the physical perpetrators of such atrocities', but '[i]n psychological and ideological terms, they were also the victims of an emperor system that legitimised such atrocities' (204), as well as a military establishment that effectively 'cut off' entire platoons from necessary resources in the name of winning the war for imperial Japan.

Although details regarding Japanese war crimes were largely withheld from the Japanese population in the years following the end of World War II, depictions and conceptualisations of the Japanese as a monstrous 'other' inform many western prejudices against Japan. During the 1980s, for instance, US popular culture representations of Japan portrayed the nation as an economic force powered by maniacally-driven labourers that posed a significant threat to US cultural and economic hegemony. As well, US popular culture both preyed upon and exacerbated Orientalist fears of Japan and its ever-increasing economic might as a neo-colonialist force that threatened the illusory notions of 'The American (sic) Way' in their imagined quest to 'buy up' US

---

[10] One need only recall recent U. S. atrocities in Iraq (crimes perhaps best exemplified by the sexual abuse of prisoners in the Abu Griab prison), the genocidal policies carried out in Rwanda and Bosnia, and the U. S. bombing at Mai Lai to note the extent to which such abhorrent behavior continues to this very day.

industry and property. Lost amidst such rhetoric, as Michael Schaller reminds us in his history of late twentieth century US and Japanese international relations, is the extent to which the US not only played a significant role in the creation of the Japanese 'economic miracle', but also depended upon a Japanese national stability to satisfy its own imperialist agenda in East Asia (1997: 96-113).

Similar anxieties surrounding the rise of Japanese economic power, accompanied by representations of monstrosity, permeated the dominant social and political ideologies of other nations across the globe. As Tanaka illustrates, Australia – whose soldiers in the South Pacific during World War II contributed eye-witness accounts of Japanese war crimes – was particularly noteworthy in this regard:

> The reports of cannibalism dovetailed easily with the picture of the Japanese developed in Australian propaganda during the war: that the Japanese were a Jekyll and Hyde-type people capable in a stroke of switching from refined and civilised activity to savagery and barbarity...This view...carried over into the Australian image of the Japanese "economic miracle" in the postwar period. On the surface, Japan is seen as a society to emulate and learn from, especially, in its development of a highly successful business- and technology-oriented society with a consumers-based approach to industrial relations. Yet underneath there persists a belief that the Japanese are somehow different from other cultures and that they would have been easily capable of purely gratuitous cannibalism. (1996: 132-3)

This 'Jekyll and Hyde' motif appears throughout Tabe's *Devil Woman Doctor*. Its most explicit iteration occurs in a brief sequence during which the title character dines with a patient whose body's right half has taken on a life of its own and viciously assaults the very organs and muscles that give it life. Only a fork driven through the hand can temporarily squelch the rebellion. The doctor calls the illness 'Jekyll and Hyde disease' and notes that 'every human being' suffers from some degree of this simultaneously internal and externalising combination of '[c]omposure and violence... [i]ndul-gence and daintiness'. Presented in an overtly slapstick fashion (complete with ample physical exaggerations on the part of the actor portraying 'the patient'), this scene suggests that the ailment afflicting the patient is one with which 'everybody' can relate. It defines the self-combatant behaviour as universal, effecting humans as a species. As such, Tabe seemingly rejects easy stereotypes of the Japanese as a populace culturally predisposed to extreme civility and extreme rage.

At the same time, however, Tabe represents this 'Jekyll and Hyde disease' through numerous darkly-humorous depictions of the Japanese social and corporeal body in conflict with itself. The 'Devil Woman' Doctor, for example, introduces viewers to a dysfunctional contemporary family unit suffering from a disorder that causes their heads and/or hearts to explode when confronted with even the slightest social pressures. In a similarly amusing scene, a *yakuza* boss develops a 'human face shaped malignant tumor' with its own distinct personality. Such contradictory physiologies in *Devil Woman Doctor* parody transformations in Japanese culture struggling with conflicting notions of Japanese-ness. In other words, through representations of the human form in conflict with, or in some fashion escaping the domineering control of, the 'self', Tabe's film exposes Japanese identity – in all of its biological, psychological and national manifestations – as far less cohesive and/or coherent than previously imagined. Verbal assaults challenging the dysfunctional Japanese family's inability to conform to conventional societal and gender roles precede their exploding heads and hearts, positioning their gory fates as allegorical explosions or, in some cases, implosions. Furthermore, by revealing that the *yakuza* boss has found a new profession as a street performer singing macabre duets with the face-shaped malignant tumor on his belly, Tabe foregrounds the performativity of identity, begging spectators to consider what their own individual 'performances' convey to those around them.

If, as Tanaka Yuki suggests, '[w]hat seems to be lacking in Japanese history writing is the kind of work that can bring home to readers how much continuity there is between life during wartime and everyday life here and now' (1996: 214), then *Devil Woman Doctor*, with its references to cannibalism during World War II, its bizarre illustrations of the 'Jekyll and Hyde' paradigm, and its depiction of the Japanese body in conflict with itself, performs a vital function. Likewise, the Devil Woman Doctor, the unlicensed medical practitioner after whom the film is named, may, ironically, be the ideal entity for bringing about such reflection. After all, she is, in her own words, '[a]n underground surgeon' dedicated to examining 'heretical sicknesses where the commonsense of medicine cannot be applied'. Pathologising multiple aspects of contemporary Japanese culture, the Devil Woman Doctor's 'examination histories' are less experiments and treatments than exorcisms of the 'devils' that her patients invariably see in others rather than in themselves.

Image 3: Cannibal Delicacies in *Devil Woman Doctor* (© Ecclectic DVD Distributors)

Butchering Masculinity in Kuzumi Masayuki's *He Never Dies*

Discussing Realism as an aesthetic and political methodology, Bertolt
Brecht remarked that, 'Realism is not what real things are like, but what
things are really like' (Stremmel 2004: 42). In other words, art may be
considered Realist(ic) as long as its mode of presentation both accurately
conveys some element of the complex logics informing human
interactions, and reveals the social, cultural, or political 'realities' of the
world in which the artist and her audience live. A high modernist whose
best known plays frequently abandoned conventional sets, props, and
dialogues, Brecht worked to disallow the kind of fantasy worlds evoked
by the conventional theatre's tendency towards verisimilitude. In the
process, Brecht endeavored simultaneously to entertain his audiences *and*
to stimulate their critical faculties to such a degree that the viewing
experience became an active intellectual engagement with the ideologies
on display. Many directors, from Jean-Luc Godard and Wong Kar-Wai to
Lars von Trier and Tarr Béla (to name just a scant few), have variously –
and, in some cases, famously[11] – deployed 'Brechtian' strategies
throughout their films. In recent decades, similar disruptions of the
traditional viewing experience have become as commonplace as classical
Hollywood cross-cutting and continuity editing. However, when applied
to documentaries, a filmic genre predicated upon the illusion of
conveying a 'reality', such attempts at audience distantiation still
possesses the potential to impact radically the way viewers understand the
artistic creations they encounter. As a result, mock documentaries, in
their subversion of the conventional documentary's verist aesthetics,
stimulate a pronounced intellectual engagement with the very real social
and political ideologies informing the genre's always-already impossible
claims to objectivity.

---

[11] Although I could cite virtually every text by these directors, consider: Jean-Luc Godard's
characters' frequently ruptures the 'fourth wall' through direct address (*Pierrot le Fou* [1965]);
Wong Kar Wai's expressionistic colors and his application of intentionally disorienting
temporal manipulations (*2046* [2005]); Lars von Trier's vacillation between melodramatic
histrionics and explicit minimalism (*Dogville* [2003] and *Manderlay* [2005]); and, lastly, Bela
Tarr's epic dolly shots and elliptical narrative structure (*Sátántangó* [1994]).

Filmed four years earlier than Tabe Hajime's *Devil Woman Doctor*, Kuzumi Masayuki's *He Never Dies* anticipates Tabe's application of verist aesthetics, as well as Tabe's dark humour and socially critical agenda. Kuzumi frames his film with narration delivered by a US scientist who, seated beside a huge globe, adopts a stereotypically academic posture and repeatedly stresses that what we are watching is undeniably 'real'. The text he introduces is the story of a young 'salaryman', Hideshi, and his multiple, inevitably vain attempts at ending his unfulfilling life of deadening routine and virtual invisibility. Retreating from human interactions and vocational responsibilities, Hideshi leads an *otaku*-like existence, surrounding himself with *manga* and *anime*. Importantly, like many of the Devil Woman Doctor's miserable patients, Hideshi wages a gruesome war against his own rebellious physiology; he has become a man who literally cannot die. Progressing from conventional suicidal behaviours, like slashing his wrists and throat, Hideshi soon hacks off his own limbs with a large knife, disembowels himself so that he can pelt a visiting co-worker with internal organs, and, finally, decapitates himself with a pair of giant gardening sheers. Building upon its outlandish premise, the film's combination of exaggerated performances, complex editing, and non-diegetic sound ensures that, by its final sequence during which Kuzumi cross cuts between the closing credits and reverse-motion 'highlights' of the most intense instances of self-inflicted violence, no spectator can possibly confuse what they see with 'what real things are like' (Stremmel and Grosenick 2004: 42).

At the same time, careful viewers can discern an underlying examination of contemporary Japanese culture, or, in Brechtian terms, 'what things are really like' (42), from certain perspectives. To immerse viewers within the waking nightmare that is Hideshi's life, Kuzumi shifts between extreme high-angle black and white shots suggestive of surveillance footage and a myriad of more overtly filmic strategies ranging from non-diegetic sound effects and music to extreme close ups, from slow motion photography to creative editing techniques. Consequently, Kuzumi readily abandons any pretenses towards 'documentary authenticity' in favor of presenting a cinematic spectacle so extreme and, at times, so clumsily constructed that its appeal initially seems limited to audiences composed of spectators longing for over-the-top displays of blood and gore. It is precisely this inconsistent and amateurish approach, however, that renders the film's politics practically transparent. Consider, for instance, the film's central protagonist, Hideshi. Both ineffectual in his coworker's eyes and the continued target of his employers' ire, Hideshi withdraws from his exploitative office job, but his absence goes largely unnoticed. Sequestering himself within his cramped apartment, Hideshi fantasises about his superiors' disgust and worries that he may disappoint his father. In short, he chafes against his position as little more than a superfluous cog in a larger capitalist machine, a status confirmed by an error message that flashes on his computer screen: 'no value'.

Images of impotence recur throughout Hideshi's daily attempts at physical self-destruction, wedding his feelings of uselessness inside and outside of the work place with a larger perceived crisis in masculinity. In an especially revealing sequence approximately half-way through the film, Hideshi imagines a discussion between three young women who work in his office. Lensed as if responding to off-camera questions and choreographed to intensify their comic impact, the women muse about waning notions of traditional Japanese masculinity in a culture dominated by business and industry, as well as the rigid corporate hierarchies such convoluted interpersonal relationships may engender:

> **Girl #1:** You know? How can I say this? It will not be of interest to a person without talent.

> **Girl #2:** There are no attractive men in this company. No men good for anything. I'll never marry a man who works for the company.

> **Girl #3:** But I don't feel good in Japan, do you? It's, how should I say, the complicated human relationships.

Taken together, these comments (whether we understand them as a part of the 'real world' of the film or as a figment of Hideshi's 'imagination') paint an unflattering portrait of life during the height of the Japanese 'bubble economy'. They suggest that the social climate produced by the desire for continued advancement within late industrial capitalist culture threatens to transform the average Japanese 'salaryman' into an individual all but incapable of detaching himself from his socially proscribed role of hard-labouring employee within a carefully established and strictly maintained system of rank and order.

Unlike his more self-assured and sexually dynamic colleague, Nakamura, Hideshi lacks the necessary confidence to initiate romances, or even to establish significant friendships. Rather than exuding charisma, Hideshi walks with his head lowered, mumbling, often incomprehensibly, to himself. The most explicit metaphor for Hideshi's social alienation and interpersonal impotence, however, emerges through Hideshi's inability to take his own life. No matter what he does, he cannot die. Even when he plunges a knife into his midsection, pulls it across his belly, and then finally severs his head in an action immediately reminiscent of the form of Japanese ritual suicide, *hari kari*, Hideshi still cannot die. As the film comes to a close, he is no more than a talking head on his living room table, laughing maniacally as his suave co-worker Nakamura, and Nakamura's love interest, Kyoko, chastise him for making such a mess of his apartment.

Given the scenario described in the paragraphs above, it would be easy to categorise *He Never Dies* as an uneven exercise in dark comedy, or as a special effects extravaganza that focuses primarily on a socially maladapted failure that can't even successfully take his own life. The film indeed conforms to these assessments; however such a narrow analysis merely scratches the surface of this unusual text. We can certainly read the film as a satire (which it is), but what, then, are we to make of the film's ending, in which Nakamura and Kyoko berate Hideshi for his slovenly, blood-splattered abode? Does this sequence merely stress, yet again, Hideshi's struggle against a corporate mindset that continually renders him useless, impotent, invisible, and obsolete? Is Kuzumi's film simply a critique of masculinity in a transforming Japanese culture, or are there larger stakes in this motion picture's engagement with conceptions of an identity undergoing traumatic reorganisation? Might Hideshi's gradual biological and psychological disarticulation advance a radical politics of identity through visual displays of corporeal extremity and disintegration?

As a means of addressing these questions, consider a string of events that take place late in the film. Unable to die no matter how violently he attacks himself, Hideshi phones his colleague, Nakamura. In the course of their conversation, Hideshi convinces Nakamura to pay him a late night visit, interrupting, in the process, the handsome Nakamura's exchange of post-coital tendernesses with the equally comely Kyoko. Nakamura, the antithesis of the socially stagnant and withdrawn Hideshi, arrives at his co-worker's tiny apartment only to discover a pale, gore-soaked Hideshi who, pretending to be a zombie, states: 'I am not the Hideshi of before. No longer the old Hideshi who is always apologizing. No, I am sorry. Not really, but...meet the new Hideshi who will not die.' It is at this point that Hideshi disembowels himself and, laughing hysterically, pelts a screaming, frightened Nakamura with an assortment of tangled, blood-drenched internal organs.

This sequence is vital to Kuzumi's film, for it transforms the reactive, put-upon Hideshi into an *active* agent, a Deleuzian 'Body without Organs' that exceeds binary constructs like 'life' and 'death'; 'internal' and 'external'; 'clean' and 'dirty', or 'sterile' and 'contaminating'. What makes Hideshi unique in a culture of conformity also makes him monstrous, but ecstatically so. As his body resists the physical logics that should logically culminate in his death, Hideshi transforms into an object of 'pure immanence'; he becomes an infinite becoming, 'a singular life' that 'can be mistaken for no other' (Deleuze, 2001: 29). In contrast, Nakamura and Kyoko scramble about Hideshi's tiny abode on their hands and knees, sopping up gallons of blood and complaining about the 'dirt' and 'contaminating' filth. Through these actions, which Hideshi's laughing head watches with a combination of amazement and ridicule, Nakamura and Kyoko firmly position themselves within an ideological framework preoccupied with discipline and order. Additionally, their impulse to clean Hideshi's apartment reifies the notion that the excretions (including the blood) of others violates long established conceptualisations of 'internal' and 'external', ultimately realising what Emiko Ohnoki-Tierney describes as 'people dirt', an 'outside' impurity that, in turn, threatens the sanctity of the 'inside' in all of its multiple forms – i.e., the body, the house, the nation. Freed from such concerns, Hideshi, the 'He' of *He Never Dies*, is finally the character that is the most 'alive'. Through 'pollution' and 'self-mutilation', Hideshi embraces 'an affirmative relation to death in its material existence: corpse and decay' (Menninghaus, 2003: 347). A manifestation of pure immanence in his reconfigured relationship to gore, death, and decay (those most abject of abjections), Hideshi frees himself from the soul-crushing cycles of the Japanese corporate, capitalist machine and its supporting binaries. Consequently, Kuzumi Masayuki's *He Never Dies* advocates the potentialities of an opposition to 'the cosmetic struggle against death's traces', a perspective that offers the possibility – to paraphrase Georges Bataille – of playing in ones own 'decomposition' (347).

Image 4: The body at war with itself in *He Never Dies* (© Ecclectic DVD Distributors)

Chapter Two:
Cultural Transformation, Corporeal Prohibitions and Body Horror in Sato Hisayasu's *Naked Blood* and *Muscle*

I want to make a film which has the influence to drive its audience mad
to make them commit murder.
- Sato Hisayasu

Social (Dis)eases and the Body Horrific

Sato Hisayasu's cinematic vision, particularly as realised in his films, *Naked Blood* (*Naked Blood: Megyaku*, 1995) and *Muscle* (*Kurutta Butokai*, 1989), is often compared by Western critics to that of Canadian-born director David Cronenberg. Though rarely explored beyond the basic acknowledgment that both filmmakers blend 'the visceral, the psychopathological and the metaphysical' (Hunter 1999: 139), this association helps to point out that Sato, like Cronenberg, is a 'literalist of the body' (Shaviro 1993: 128). Accordingly, Sato posits the body as an indiscrete, transformative, and immanent space that reveals the potential for imagining new economies of identity. He is a filmmaker who explores both the abject dread and infinite possibility of the human body in a state of dissolution. This chapter examines Sato Hisayasu's *Naked Blood* and *Muscle* as texts that imagine the human body as an unstable nexus of often contradictory social codes informed by the cultural logics of contemporary Japan. Set within late-industrial landscapes where the flesh is at once agonisingly immediate and increasingly anachronistic, *Naked Blood* and *Muscle* engage both the extreme dread and the 'extreme seductiveness' that, as Georges Bataille reminds us, may constitute 'the boundary of horror' (Bataille 1994: 17). Indeed, it is my ultimate contention that while Sato's *Naked Blood* and *Muscle* engage a multiplicity of territorialising cultural forces, they also revel in intensity until what emerges is a narrative of social and physical corporeality that allows viewers to conceive of an alternative existence that 'no longer resembles a neatly defined itinerary from one practical sign to another, but a sickly incandescence, a durable orgasm' (82).

Locating the films of Sato Hisayasu within a particular cinematic genre is an especially frustrating endeavor. Indeed, even his most commercially accessible works, if in fact such texts can be said to exist, are largely exercises in generic and cultural cross-fertilisation. Though influenced by Western literary and cinematic traditions, Sato's films reveal a myriad of social and political anxieties over the 'appearance' of the Japanese physical and social body. Emerging at the intersection of horror, science fiction, and Japanese soft-core pornography, Sato's films are a veritable mélange of splatterpunk, cyberpunk, and erotic cinema motifs that locate the body as a liminal construction. As a result, it is perhaps most accurate to examine Sato Hisayasu as one of cinema's most famous (infamous?) practitioners of 'body horror' – a hybrid, and thus somewhat more inclusive, category that, according to Kelly Hurley, 'recombines' multiple 'narrative and cinematic conventions of the science fiction, horror, and suspense film in order to stage a spectacle of the human body defamiliarized' (Hurley 1995: 203). A comprehensive term like 'body horror' is intensely appropriate in discussions of Sato's films, where the metaphoric implications of the splattered or transfigured body are central to his aesthetic and political agenda. Though frequently exploring non-human topos of technology's complex role in the social imaginary of Japan's late capitalist political and ideological terrain,

Sato's cinema simultaneously turns on foregrounded images of endangered physiognomies and corporeal disintegration. Even throughout the last ten years, as the circulation of capital, information, and interpersonal communication has become increasingly *invisible* and *electronic*, Sato's films have continued to turn and return to the physical body, in its visible, messy, and all-too-vulnerable splendor, as a site of perpetual contestation. The body in *Naked Blood* and *Muscle* provides a flexible and ever-encodable space that again recalls Cronenberg's cinema, where the body is 'at once a target for new biological and communicational technologies, a site of political conflict, and a limit point at which ideological oppositions collapse' (Shaviro 1993: 133-4).

The Seen and the Obscene:
Sato Hisayasu's *Naked Blood* and the Japanese Body

Naked Blood is perhaps one of Sato Hisayasu's most complex and visually arresting films. The plot revolves around a seventeen year old boy genius named Eiji. Inspired by his dead father's scientific and philosophic aspirations, which included a desire to better the world by helping humanity achieve a form of intensity akin to blinding light, Eiji creates the 'ultimate painkiller' to 'improve the happiness of mankind.' The fruit of his labor is a drug called Myson, a substance that causes the human brain to feel pain as pleasure. Seeking humans upon which to test his creation, Eiji sneaks his elixir into an intravenous contraceptive that his mother (an established scientist) unknowingly administers to three young women. The test subjects include two unnamed women – a vain woman whose 'greatest pleasure[s]' are having an attractive body and wardrobe, and a food-obsessed woman whose 'greatest joy' is eating – and Mikami, a woman who hasn't slept since she was in the fifth grade, when the 'shock' of the onset of menses 'blocked' her 'sleep cycle.' Eiji chronicles Myson's impact by videotaping each woman from a distance, but his anonymity is compromised when Mikami catches him spying on her and confronts him. In part because Myson allows Mikami to experience her disdain for Eiji as attraction, they become romantically involved, and Mikami brings Eiji into her private world by showing him her 'sleeping installation', a virtual reality unit that allows her to experience a dreamlike state by showing her 'the scenery' of her heart.

Inevitably, Eiji's experiment goes horribly awry. The other two Myson test subjects become grotesquely self-destructive: the woman for whom beauty equals 'pleasure' slowly transforms herself into a bloody, albeit orgasmic, human pin-cushion, and the woman for whom eating is 'joy' literally consumes herself in what are undeniably some of the film's most unsettling moments. The narrative's climax occurs when Mikami, with whom Eiji has forged an uneasy yet intimate relationship, first kills her fellow test-subjects, then slices a gaping vaginal-shaped wound into Eiji's mother's stomach and, following a cyber-enhanced sexual encounter with Eiji, kills the young genius by first injecting him with Myson and then cutting his throat. In the film's final scene, set several years after Eiji's death, we learn that Mikami and her young, camcorder-wielding son – also named Eiji – are traveling about the country, spraying the air with a substance that might be herbicide or might be Myson. As Mikami drives off on a motorcycle equipped with a canister and spraying tube ('I think I'll go west today,' she tells her son. 'It hasn't spread there yet.'), the child meets the viewers' gaze and says, 'the dream has not ended yet.'

Controversial both in Japan and in the few Western markets and film festivals in which it was publicly screened, *Naked Blood* continues to provoke strong (if, at times, bewildered) reactions by film critics, movie reviewers and cinephiles, some of whom have left written reactions and thoughts about the film on the various on-line paracinema catalogues and fan-based Internet websites dedicated to the celebration and circulation of 'shock' and 'gore' cinema. Thomas Weisser and Yuko Mihara Weisser, authors of *Japanese Cinema: The Essential Handbook* (1998), *Japanese Cinema Encyclopedia: Horror, Fantasy, and Sci-Fi Films* (1998), and *Japanese Cinema Encyclopedia: The Sex Films* (1998), label Sato's filmmaking as 'bitter' and composed in a 'sledgehammer style' (463), and describe *Naked Blood* as rating 'high on the gross-out level' (417). Similarly, an online fan review called the film 'an incredibly transgressive horror film' (white pongo 2000: para 1), while a reviewer for the Sex Gore Mutants web site, while lauding the film for being 'one of the most depressing movies ever', also characterises *Naked Blood*'s plot as 'raw, existing to frame a raw emotion, not to tell a story' (Gruenberger 2002: para 4). This last observation is not surprising, especially given the film's surreal imagery and complicated storyline, as well as the movie's intentionally disorienting and ambiguous closing scenes that explore the tenuous distinction between what constitutes reality and what represents a part of virtual reality's 'consensual hallucination' (Gibson 1984: 51).

Manipulating audience understanding of what is real and what is imaginary is a popular narrative gesture in films that speculate upon the promises and pitfalls of an ever-emerging cyberculture.[1] What separates *Naked Blood* from many comparable Western films, however, is that *Naked Blood*, as is the case with many of Sato's productions, was not backed by large budgets and extensive marketing strategies. Rather, *Naked Blood* emerges from Sato's work both within and against the Japanese *pinku eiga* cinema, a largely uniform and highly regulated tradition of 'soft core' films that, especially within the subgenres known as *Best SM Pink* or *Violent Pink*, have become increasingly notorious for emphasising partial male and female nudity coupled with narratives depicting 'the rape and brutalization of young girls' (Alexander 2001: para 8).

In other words, unlike Western films with comparable plots, Sato Hisayasu's works arise from a largely low budget cinematic tradition with a distinctly formulaic, yet surprisingly flexible visual iconography. Yet, as I will demonstrate in the paragraphs to follow, *pinku eiga*'s frequently violent and misogynist tropes, coupled with prohibitions against the depiction of pubic hair and genitalia enforced by *Eirin* (Japan's

---

[1] See, among others, such high-profile films as Kathryn Bigelow's *Strange Days* (USA, 1995), Josef Rusnak's *The Thirteenth Floor* (Germany/USA, 1999), Alejandro Amenabar's *Abre Los Ojos* (Spain, 1997) and its 2001 US re-make, Cameron Crowe's *Vanilla Sky*, the Wachowski Brothers' *The Matrix* (USA, 1999) and its two sequels, David Cronenberg's *eXistenZ* (Canada, 1999), and Tarsem Singh's *The Cell* (USA, 2000). The theme of 'illusion' or 'hallucination' versus 'reality' also appears in Sato's *Genuine Rape* (1987), the film from which many of the concepts behind *Naked Blood* eventually developed, and *The Bedroom* (*Shisenjiyou no Aria*, 1992).

censorship body which rules on 'decency' in film), nevertheless allows for the possibility of a critique of dominant cultural power relations.[2] Sato Hisayasu, however, stands out among his fellow *pinku eiga* directors in both his detached, almost ambivalent cinematic vision of postmodern alienation (what Paula Felix-Didier calls the 'exposition of the existential emptiness of modern life' [2000: para 21]) and the extent to which the splattered bodies in his texts function as subjects for political and cultural inquiry. In *Naked Blood*, Sato questions not only the politics of censorship in Japan and the cinematic tradition within, and against which, he toils, but also the impact of changing gender roles and the emergence of virtual technologies in late capitalist Japanese society.

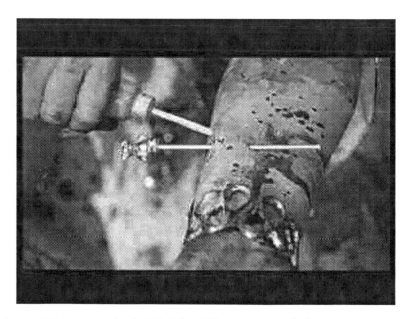

Image 5: Extreme piercing in *Naked Blood* (Courtesy: beyondhollywood.com)

---

[2] Paula Felix-Didier argues that such erotic and pornographic cinema can frequently function as a weapon for interrogating traditional cultural values. See Felix-Didier, P. (2000) '*Cine y sexo en Japón*', in *Film: On Line*, 15 April 2000, para. 3. <www.filmonline.com.ar/40/dossier/40dossier3.htm>.

Decontextualised Lips: Censorship and the National Body

To fully appreciate the ways in which Sato's *Naked Blood* functions as a critique of Japanese censorship policies, though, it is first necessary to explore how these regulations came to be established. In *Permitted and Prohibited Desires: Mothers, Comics, and Censorship in Japan*, Anne Allison locates the origin of contemporary standards regarding what can and cannot be shown on screens in Japan as originating from a nexus of concerns about national identity and the 'appearance' and 'purity' of the Japanese physical and social body. Much of this national focus on appropriate bodily representations, she argues, stems from a reaction to Western Orientalist imaginings of the Japanese biological and social body, particularly as they developed within the nineteenth century:

> It was as a corrective to this Western perception of Japanese 'primitiveness' that the modern laws against obscenity were first imposed: they were a means of covering the national body from charges that it was obscene...in part, acquiring such an identity meant adopting Western standards of corporeal deportment. In part as well, it meant developing a notion of the public as a terrain that is monitored and administered by the state. Thus, the behavior of the Japanese, as state subjects, in this terrain is regulated and surveiled. (Allison 2000: 163)

Of course, policing (and prohibiting) certain modes of behavior and visual representations of the human body and human sexuality, especially in reaction to a perceived 'dirtiness', also functions to 'protect what is "real"' – 'unique to Japanese culture' – from 'outside contamination, from being infiltrated and deformed by Western influence' (164).[3] Some of the most heated debates about censorship in Japan have arisen in

---

[3] It would be a mistake to assume that this reactionary internal and external 'othering' is limited to visual culture. Identities are, after all, constructs with borders that are often reified/ reinforced, sometimes violently so, when exposed as illusory. As such, when cultures come into contact, there are bound to be varying degrees of appropriation, reactionary attitudes and, as Takayumi Tatsumi posits, 'fabulous negotiations between Orientalism and Occidentalism'. See Tatsumi, T. (2000) 'Generations and Controversies: An Overview of Japanese Science Fiction', in *Science Fiction Studies*, *80*, 27:1 (March), 113. It is also important to note that certain behavioral prohibitions related to sexuality were long a part of Shinto mythology. See Allison, 163.

response to the controlled importation and, in several cases, subsequent visual alteration of Western films and other media depicting genitalia and pubic hair. In this complex history of negotiation over cultural value, pubic hair and genitalia have come to resonate beyond their prurient indexical value, signifying a set of privileged discourses embodying questions of cultural authenticity and anxieties about Western contamination.

In *Naked Blood*, Sato operates within and, in some important ways, exceeds the conventions of *pinku eiga* cinema, including the foregrounding of nudity and graphic violence, to illustrate that censorship's function to territorialise 'national and public space according to body zones' is far more important than whether 'covered or uncovered sex organs are prohibited' (Allison 2000: 161) in Japan. By violently altering bodies in scenes that wed conventional signifiers of sexuality (such as moans of pleasure and ecstatic postures) with violent images of the human form turned horrifically against itself, Sato invests the body with the kind of 'radical otherness' that Jean Baudrillard locates at the 'epicenter' of 'terror'[4]; the body is dis-/re-figured in a way that at once exposes (makes 'naked') and explodes (splatters) the social codes that inform its socially prescribed shape and meaning.

Such oppositional politics behind *Naked Blood*'s scenes of body horror is perhaps best illustrated by a consideration of the scene in which one of the most memorable instances of self-cannibalisation in film history is performed by the Myson test-subject who equates joy with eating. Sitting naked upon her kitchen table, her body surrounded by plates and cutlery, she slowly moves a fork and knife into her genitalia, which is carefully concealed by the *mise-en-scène*. As she moans in ecstasy, her arms move in a manner that suggests that she is slicing something. It is at this precise point in the film that the Japanese censors' prohibition against the depiction of human pubic regions is radically and horrifyingly recontextualised and subverted: she slowly raises the fork and the camera focuses upon the bloody, quivering genital lips pierced on

---

[4] See Baudrillard, J. (1990) *The Transparency of Evil: Essays on Extreme Phenomena*. London and New York: Verso.

its tines. It is only at this point, when lips meet lips that the audience fully realizes the extent of her orgasmic, self-destructive action. Her self-consumption continues with a nipple and an eye, too, but it is the woman's consumption of her own labial lips that most viewers will remember long after the film is over.

This scene offers what is perhaps Sato's most explicit example of how the violent dismantling of the human body provides a metaphor for the ways that disciplinary power in Japanese culture both grants and restricts personal expression, maintaining a notion of a cohesive national and cultural identity. By blatantly displaying that which cannot be shown (human genitalia) through a removal of the 'obscene' object from its traditional context, Sato simultaneously shocks his audience and reveals some of the logics at work in contemporary Japanese culture. By revealing, through an ingenious process of decontextualisation, the very corporeal features rendered invisible by national censors, Sato forces his audience to confront the nationalist logics behind contemporary representations of the human body within Japanese visual culture, an image system designed to maintain a specifically 'Japanese' physical and social body free (at least theoretically) from Western, Orientalist notions of embodiment. The politics of censorship and (controlled) nudity in Japanese cinema is laid bare, exposed in a frenzy of the visible that ultimately discloses how the concerns over maintaining a consolidated social body are at once partially informed by, and yet ideally resistant to, Western and other non-traditional concepts of social and cultural identity that inform how the human body is visually portrayed and ideologically invested. The quivering flesh at the end of the fork both *is* and *is not* genitalia; Sato is both reveling in the dangers of the 'obscene' body and playing by the (or maybe creating new) rules. *Naked Blood*, then, pushes and deconstructs the boundaries of what can be seen, both making the logics of cultural negotiation visible as well as contesting them. *Naked Blood* skillfully directs the viewer's gaze, guiding his/her experience of this film about detached characters caught up in extreme events that, within the diegesis, unfold almost completely before the lenses of photograph and video equipment, including the meta-lens of Sato's own camera. As such, the film provides a commentary on bodily experiences, mediated visions and the eroto-politics of the gaze.

Mothers and Sons: Women and Work

Sato's depiction of the splattered body recognises social anxieties accompanying changes and continuities in gender roles and expectations as they relate to contemporary Japan's transforming social and economic landscape. Manipulated by the euphoric effects of Myson, the violence that the vain woman and the gluttonous woman perform against their own bodies can even be understood as a proto-feminist critique of the destructive impact of patriarchal authority and beauty ideals: the women literally self-destruct in a frenzy of body modification taken to near fatal extremes. In addition, *Naked Blood* addresses what Anne Allison describes as cultural apprehensions over the steadily emerging presence of women in the workplace and, by extension, the occasional reconfiguration of domestic space: 'In Japan in the 1990s...domestic labor is losing its moorings. Women are working in greater numbers, for more years, and with less inclination to quit at the point of marriage and motherhood' (Allison 2000: 174). This gendered transformation of the social body finds cinematic articulation in the character of Eiji's mother. It is her position as a legitimately employed scientist, coupled with her son's familial, social, and professional alienation (Eiji, after all, is still a teen and, thus, still under intense pressure to succeed in school), which results in the unauthorised delivery of Myson to the unwitting test subjects. This bodily chaos, engendered by the mother's unwitting Myson tests and mapped across explicitly feminine bodies, seems to suggest that women's participation in what was conventionally a masculine sphere can only result in catastrophe.

This social anxiety over women's transgressions of traditional feminine roles plays out in the oedipal politics at work in Eiji's dysfunctional family. Eiji's desire to become a scientist and develop the aptly named Myson stems from his hope to follow in his deceased (and, thus, 'absent') father's footsteps. Like his father before him, Eiji longs to achieve a form of intensity; Eiji's wish to create a drug to 'improve the happiness of mankind' mirrors his father's quasi-scientific quest for a form of immortality through intensity – 'We'll break through time and space,' his father wrote prior to his disappearance, 'and head for the kingdom of light.' Consequently, it is his anger over what he perceives as his mother's failure to assume the traditional female role and support her husband's 'dream' that Eiji cites as a contributing factor to his emotional distance from his mother. The social implications of her refusal to blindly comply with gender expectations derived from a traditional patriarchal economy are intensified when one considers that Eiji's mother, as a scientist working towards the development of a more effective method of contraception, is in a position to further usurp conventionally masculine cultural roles by literally controlling biological, and by extension ideological, reproduction.

Additionally, throughout the majority of *Naked Blood*, Eiji, like his father before him (and like any member of a capitalist society), is denied the satisfaction he seeks: by consistently assuming the role of voyeur, Eiji's observations are perpetually mediated by technology, either in the form of cameras or virtual reality equipment. This, too, speaks to changing gender roles in Japanese society, given that, as formulated by Allison, 'situating the male subject as viewer and voyeur is not necessarily or unquestionably a practice of scopophilia that empowers him' (2000: 29). Consistently removed from the objects of his desire by cameras and other technological devices, Eiji looks but does not actually reach out and touch. Even his participation in sexual intercourse towards the film's conclusion is mediated by virtual reality goggles that project surreal images upon his retinas, resulting in a conflation of generic signifiers that provides the closest thing to a 'money shot' in Sato's film: the image of Eiji's arterial blood spraying both Mikami's breasts and her euphoric visage.

Technology, East/West Border Crossing and Cyberpunk

Like many Western works of speculative fiction, *Naked Blood* engages
cultural trepidations surrounding rapid increases in technological
development. In its extensive depictions of computers, video equipment,
designer drugs, and virtual reality, Sato's film borrows tropes from the
cyberpunk genre. As scholars like Joshua La Bare and Takayuki Tatsumi
have illustrated, Japanese science fiction and its Western counterparts
have existed in a strange state of symbiosis in which each tradition
borrows from the other, with various Orientalist and Occidentalist
consequences. The scope of this ideological cross-fertilisation is quite
extensive, however even a perfunctory survey of Western and Japanese
cyberpunk texts reveals the degree to which these traditions inform one
another. William Gibson's novel, *Neuromancer* (1984), and Ridley
Scott's film, *Blade Runner* (1982), are merely two examples of well-
known Western cyberpunk texts that are particularly rich with Orientalist
imaginings of Japanese culture as simultaneously mysterious, seductive,
apocalyptic, and technophilic. When these motifs find their way into
contemporary Japanese science fiction, a recursive pattern of cultural
inflection occurs, in which Japanese works of speculative fiction
simultaneously perpetuate and condition operant tropologies. Certain
familiar motifs emerge, but they are frequently invested with cultural
codings that often confound Western viewers. Thus, while many Western
cyberpunk narratives tend to adopt a largely cautionary, if not outright
pessimistic view towards the conflation of the 'human' and the
'technological', the 'extrapolative tendency' in Japanese science fiction
'seems more oriented towards enthusiasm for the benefits or potential
consequences [of technology] than for any social changes likely to be
caused by that technology' (Hull and Siegel 1989: 262).

    The cross-cultural transfusion of science fiction tropes extends
back at least to post-World War II Japanese importations of 'a huge
variety of Anglo-American cultural products' (Tatsumi 2000: 113),
including numerous literary and cinematic works of speculative fiction. In
turn, this new and, given Japan's steady re-emergence as a global

economic power, increasingly expansive consumer base impacted how numerous Western and Japanese authors and filmmakers imagined the shape and content of multiple genres, especially those dealing with the fantastic. Takayuki Tatsumi describes this symbiotic relationship in 'Generations and Controversies: An Overview of Japanese Science Fiction, 1957-1997':

> Given that science fiction is a literature reflecting the frontiers of techno-capitalism, it was inevitable that Japanese writers of the 1960s would follow the original literary examples produced by the Pax Americana in the West. In the 80s...a revolutionary paradigm shift took place: Anglo-American writers began appropriating Japanese images as often as the reverse, while Japanese writers came to understand that writing post-cyberpunk science fiction meant locating the radically science fictional within the semiosis of 'Japan'. Of course, Anglo-American repre-sentations of Japan appeal to readers largely by distorting Japanese culture, much as the Japanese people in the 50s and 60s...unwittingly misread their Occidentalism as genuine internationalism. (113)

To this day, science fiction and horror texts emerging on both sides of the Pacific frequently reflect complex economic, cultural, and historical tensions. Analysing representations of human (and posthuman) embodiment within these texts provides a method for gaining insight into identity politics on the local, national, and trans-national level.

Furthermore, in both Japanese and Western science fiction, the dominant tropology of scientific extrapolation provides compelling insight into larger societal concerns related to technological advancement. If, as Elizabeth Anne Hull and Mark Seigel argue, modern Japanese industrialisation occurred 'as a defense' against Western 'exploitation' (1989: 262), then the cyberpunk aspects of *Naked Blood* reveal not only cultural concerns over the extent to which technology has impacted and/or may impact how Japanese people view both their own bodies and their relationship to the larger social body, but also a compelling ambivalence, on the part of Sato as an artist, towards the infusion of technology in society. As Thomas Weisser and Yuko Mihara Weisser have noted, 'electronic tools and media gadgets' are crucial props in many of Sato's films. 'Besides being critical of... "dehumanizing pop culture"', they argue, '[Sato] is fascinated by it' (1998: 463). The extent to which *Naked Blood* exemplifies this ambivalence is evidenced when one considers how technological advances constitute both a destructive force (Myson – the ultimately destructive pain killer 'tested' upon unsuspecting human guinea pigs) and a potential solace (the 'sleeping installation' – the only way that, given her permanent insomnia, Mikami can attain the rest she needs). Technology, then, functions paradoxically in Sato's film. Despite its destructive effects on the various characters, Myson was seemingly created with the best of intentions. In contrast, Mikami's virtual reality 'sleeping installation', like Eiji's ever-present video camera, provides yet another barrier to conventional interpersonal contact, thus heightening the film's theme of postmodern alienation.

Going Too Far: Intensity and the Body Horrific

Sato Hisayasu's *Naked Blood* weds horror with science fiction, or, more specifically, splatterpunk with cyberpunk. As such, this conflation of the biological and the mechanical reveals the oppressive exercise of those systems of disciplinary power that endeavor to control how people think and act. While acknowledging the tyrannical and alienating potential of video, pharmacological, and virtual technologies, *Naked Blood* does not completely disavow the possibility that these technologies may provide alternatives to traditional notions of identity. True, Myson's side-effects have disastrous results, and often what characters see and remember is presented as mediated by lenses and screens, including those containing filmed or recorded images. Nevertheless, it is also possible to understand the mixture of the physical and mechanical in *Naked Blood* as revealing a space where holistic, humanist notions of corporeal (and, by extension, social) embodiment collapse. As Michael Ryan and Douglas Kellner suggest, 'technology represents the possibility that nature might be reconstructable' (1990: 58). In this sense, then, Sato's film explores what Scott Bukatman calls 'terminal identity', that 'unmistakable double articulation in which we find both the end of the subject and a new subjectivity constructed' through technology and media (Bukatman 1990: 9). Thus, *Naked Blood*, like that hybrid cinematic genre known as body horror, challenges the very notion of limits, exposing the borders mobilised to delineate genres, bodies, and nations as not only artificially constructed, but far more permeable than previously imagined.

Consequently, a discourse of corporeal and psychic intensity informs both the film's plot and presentation: from Eiji's father's quest to achieve immortality through becoming light to the narrative's collapsing of pain into pleasure and sexuality into violence; from Eiji's desire to attain 'eternal happiness' to Sato's aforementioned use of corporeal mutilation as a springboard for political inquiry. The multi-generational, (father-son-grandson [?]) pursuit of eternity through intensity (the name 'Eiji', we are told, means 'eternity's child') runs parallel to the violent, orgasmic destruction of the human body, that most basic locus of societal controls. Images of apparent limitlessness – oceans, static-filled screens, the blinding light of the sun or of bulbs burning through celluloid – correspond with gruesome instances of corporeal destruction that, in the quintessential splatterpunk tradition, evokes the notion of 'going too far' (Skipp and Spector 1989: 10), of re-imagining physiology as a 'field of immanence' (Deleuze and Guattari 1987: 157) that rejects technocratic control over the subject. As Georges Bataille notes in his ruminations upon the power that rests within visual representation of the physical body (in this case the eye) punctured and slashed, horror 'alone is brutal enough to break everything that stifles' (Battaille 1994: 19).

In its exploration of intensity as a discontinuous and non-totalisable phenomenon, Sato's film advances an oppositional politics. It is in these moments that Sato reveals the potential of imagining an identity outside of culturally prescribed parameters, or, at the very least, gestures towards the potential for the conceptualisation of such a space. In their quests for eternal happiness, a philosophical (and biological) mission to literally discover 'the blinding flashes of lightning that transform the most withering storm into transports of joy' (69), Eiji and his father embody those 'impulses' that Georges Bataille describes in his essay, 'The Use Value of D. A. F. de Sade', as having 'social revolution as their end' in that they 'go against the interests of a society in a state of stagnation' (100).

This is not to suggest that *Naked Blood* is by any means an exclusively progressive body horror film. Although *Naked Blood* advances an oppositional politics of identity, the film does not necessarily end on an optimistic note. In the film's final moments, when little Eiji tells us that 'the dream has not ended yet' and raises his camcorder to follow Mikami's progress as she rides her motorcycle westward, the audience feels a palpable sense of dis-ease well in keeping with the discomforting tone of the film's previous seventy-five minutes. Social theory has long contended that 'the growth of civilization requires simultaneously the restraint of the body and the cultivation of character in the interests of social stability' (Turner 1992: 14-15); texts that render human corporeal and social formations indiscrete – displaying, in the process, the various ideological veins and cultural sinews that keep the fragile, and yet alarmingly resilient, physiognomies intact – disturb, if only momentarily, this 'stability'. Confronting heterogeneity – that first step towards attaining Bataille's 'durable orgasm' – is a messy business. Sooner or later you're bound to get some on you.

'Lunatic Theater': Sato Hisayasu's *Muscle*

While *Naked Blood*'s powerful social critique illustrates Sato Hisayasu's acute understanding of Japanese splatter films as an instrument for serious socio-cultural excavation, it would be short-sighted to overlook the important visual and ideological groundwork Sato set forth several years earlier in his hour-long homoerotic horror film, *Muscle*. Proffering a less subtle, and thereby more pointed, critique of Japanese censorship practices, *Muscle* occupies an interesting position in Sato's *oeuvre*. A melding of *pinku eiga* tropes with the horror genre's visual and narratological motifs, *Muscle* anticipates the extreme images and spectacular storylines that have become a staple of Sato's increasingly unorthodox cinematic vision. Specifically, *Muscle* advocates the contestation and collapsing of filmic and socio-cultural limits through an explicitly self-conscious probing of their very parameters and the social mechanisms frequently mobilised to police them. *Muscle* is also one of

Sato's more overtly experimental works, its dominant aesthetic defined by the collision of meticulously crafted scenes intended to frustrate conventional viewing strategies through a filmic discourse oscillating between spectator engagement and estrangement. In other words, Sato's film by turns immerses the viewer within an atmosphere of visceral carnality, and distances her through markedly theatrical sequences that foreground the work's artifice. Such an approach prepares the audience for the film's larger, meta-cinematic dialogue with Pier Paolo Pasolini's *Salò, or the 120 Days of Sodom* (Italy, 1975). Allowed into Japan by Japanese Customs and subsequently "rubber stamp[ed]" (Weisser 1989: 24) by *Eirin*, *Salò*'s critique of the abuses of power had a profound influence upon Sato's development as a filmmaker. While clearly a 'loving salute' (467) to Pasolini, Sato's *Muscle* has more expansive aims, namely interrogating the narratological and socio-political efficacy of aligning Sade's libertines with 1940s fascism. Consequently, a close reading of *Muscle* reveals Sato to be a director far more invested in exploring Sadeian body politics as a mode of ontological terrorism – and, thus, as potentially liberating – than in merely deploying them as a simple and ultimately ineffective (and inaccurate) metaphor for totalitarianism.

As a film that takes the aesthetic and ideological implications of cinematic representation and reception as its primary focus, *Muscle*'s deceptively spare and intractably linear narrative may surprise some viewers. However, it is the plot's minimalist settings and largely straightforward action that affords Sato's meta-filmic exercise the foundation from which to launch the text's larger interrogations of the intersections between visual prohibitions in Japanese cinema and the liberating potential inherent within images of corporeal excess. Beginning with a highly-stylised montage of muscular male bodies lensed in close-up and medium shots, the well-toned physiques glistening beneath flaring theatrical spot lights immediately evocative of flash photography, *Muscle* chronicles the sexual and biological transformations of Ryuzaki, an editor for a body-building magazine titled – appropriately enough – *Muscle*. Entranced by the sinuous build of a male model named Yukihiro Kitami, Ryuzaki embarks upon a sexual relationship that takes an unexpected turn when Kitami turns sadistic, randomly slicing Ryuzaki with the blade of a small pen-knife during their bouts of passion. These sessions cause Ryuzaki to feel as if '[s]omething inside' him had simultaneously 'crumbled and exploded', and he impulsively severs Kitami's right arm during a photo-shoot.

After spending a year in prison for his assault upon Kitami, Ryuzaki returns to his apartment, happily discovering that a fellow editor at *Muscle* has preserved Kitami's severed arm in a narrow glass canister. Additionally, Ryuzaki reveals that his time in prison has culminated in two obsessions: (1) finding and confronting the now one-armed Kitami, who has become a notorious yet elusive hustler; and (2) obtaining and viewing a copy of Pier Paolo Pasolini's final film, the adaptation of the Marquis de Sade's *Inferno*-esque novel, *Salò* (a film mislabelled throughout *Muscle* as *Salo: The 100 Days of Sodom*). Ryuzaki's dual quests, combined with his relationship with Chida and Yoko, a young and sexually adventurous couple, result in his taking a job in the ticket booth of Lunatic Theater, an underground cinema specializing in obscure and controversial titles, including a retrospective of the films of Pier Paolo Pasolini (sans *Salò*). Unable to locate Kitami or view a copy of *Salò*, the latter endeavor frustrated both by Japanese censorship codes and the destruction of an imported video cassette at the hands of a cynical long-haired hustler, Ryuzaki becomes increasingly frustrated. In retaliation for the destruction of the video cassette of *Salo*, Ryuzaki beats the long-haired hustler to death with a metal pipe. Later, when he returns to his apartment, Ryuzaki finds both an invitation to a "Masquerade" at Lunatic Theater, as well as a stocking to be worn over his head. At the masquerade, Ryuzaki finally encounters Kitami. Kitami beats Ryuzaki, who readily welcomes any torture Kitami wishes to dispense, but when Kitami threatens to sever Ryuzaki's arm, Ryuzaki takes Kitami's sword and blinds himself so that he may 'forever see [Kitami's] body the way it was when [they] met'. The film ends with Ryuzaki and Kitami on a pier at dawn, waltzing in a manner reminiscent of the young Italian soldiers dancing during *Salò*'s closing sequence.

Most of *Muscle*'s erotic encounters conform to conventional *pinku eiga* aesthetics and prohibitions. Even during the film's most erotically-charged moments, the characters' genitalia remain safely hidden beneath tight undergarments, while objects ranging from spittle-wet mouths, to a samurai swords' handle in silhouette, to Kitami's severed arm, variably function as visual surrogates for those conspicuously prohibited portions of the human anatomy. Indeed, *Muscle*'s narrative repeatedly broaches concerns surrounding the politics of film censorship. Ryuzaki's desire to view Pasolini's *Salò*, for example, is aggravated by his having been incarcerated during the film's brief theatrical run that, given the work's explicit content, is not likely to be repeated. 'I want to ask you something,' Ryuzaki writes to a friend living in Italy. 'I want to see "Salo", the last film Pier Paolo Pasolini made. But it's not showing here, and there are no plans to bring it out on video either'. Similarly, Ryuzaki's inability to view the videocassette of *Salò* his friend subsequently mails him speaks to *Eirin*'s rigid guidelines and procedures: 'They can't transfer uncensored films,' Ryuzaki explains when asked if he has been able to convert the videocassette into a viewable format.

Additionally, Sato's use of low key and chiaroscuro lighting effects throughout *Muscle* adheres to traditional *pinku eiga*[5] and horror film motifs. By carefully brightening certain portions of the frame while confining others to shadow and darkness, Sato enhances moments of erotic tension and dread, often within the very same sequence. Consider, for instance, not only the 'sadistic' sexual encounter that precedes Ryuzaki's severing of Kitami's arm, but also Sato's depiction of Ryuzaki's surprisingly violent assault. In the former scene, Sato illuminates Ryuzaki and Kitami's erotic encounter in low key lighting, a technique frequently deployed in horror films to heighten tension, and in conventional 'love-making sequences' to amplify sexual intensity while, paradoxically, obscuring the sexual act. Thus, the dominant *mise-en-scène* casts the actors' bodies almost entirely in silhouette. With the same graceful fluidity of motion that accompanies his practiced affectations

---

[5] Though heterosexual sexual practices dominate much of *pinku eiga*, homoerotic content is by no means implicitly or explicitly absent from the genre. Examples of such films include Nakamura Genji's *Beautiful Mystery* (*Kyokon densetsu: utsukushii nazo*, 1983), as well as Oki Hiroyuki's *Melody for Buddy Matsumae* (*Matsumae-kun no senritsu* 1992) and *I Like You, I Like You Very Much* (*Anata-ga suki desu, dai suki desu*, 1994).

before the erratic flashing bulbs of photographers' cameras, Kitami, the model/sadist, exaggeratedly wields a thin phallic penknife above Ryuzaki's recumbent form, periodically lowering the blade to inflict a series of tiny incisions in his lover's flesh. Each successive slash makes Ryuzaki writhe and grunt, his physical contortions simultaneously evocative of pain and pleasure. In keeping with the majority of the events depicted in Sato's film, this coupling is highly stylised. Much of the sequence, for instance, transpires behind a thick white lamp that Sato conspicuously foregrounds in the center of the shot, providing an extra obstacle to obfuscate the shadowy bodies that comprise the ultimate locus of the viewers' gaze. This image links the apportioning of light with corporeal intensity, a conceit that becomes increasingly important as the film progresses. What's more, the scene's frustration of traditional spectatorial pleasure compels viewers to reconsider their expectations as they actively engage with the visual and aural components of Sato's cinematic composition.

In the latter scene, Sato prefaces the sudden severing of Kitami's arm with a montage depicting Kitami posing beneath the flood of light emanating from Ryuzaki's arrangement of professional-grade lamps and reflectors. Following hard upon the events described in the paragraph above, the sequence of images leading up to Ryuzaki's assault resonate with an orgasmic intensity obviated by Ryuzaki's declaration that Kitami's sudden 'sadism' educed a state of psychic excess ('[s]omething inside me crumbled and exploded at the same time'). Here, too, light takes on a vital thematic weight, as the lamps' brightness temporarily blinds Kitami, leaving him vulnerable to Ryuzaki's aggression. Sato's editing likewise contributes to the climactic assault; the unsheathing of the sword with which Ryuzaki dis-arms the disarming Kitami transpires in a brightly illuminated close-up, immediately followed by a series of rapid-fire cuts that culminate in a highly stylised representation of the arm's violent dismemberment that weds the viewer's perspective with the inverted POV of one of Ryuzaki's camera's view-finders. By lensing Ryuzaki's graphic crime of passion as at once disorienting and ejaculatory, Sato suggests that understanding the motivations behind his characters' actions may require his audience to adopt new ways of seeing.

Furthermore, this sequence builds upon its predecessor in its appeal to an almost hyper-kinetic presentation that requires the film's viewer to become more acutely aware of not only what they *can* see, but, perhaps more importantly, what is *withheld* from easy view or, quite possibly, hidden in full sight.

The film's climactic sequence at Lunatic Theater also capitalises upon the apportioning of light and shadow/darkness, albeit in a manner that, given the scene's setting on the stage of an empty movie house, structures the inevitable conflict between Ryuzaki and Kitami as a deliberately 'performative' event (en)acted to call attention to the philosophical concepts informing their dialogue. Transpiring before an intentionally sparse background in the form of a large white movie screen and edited so that the viewer's perspective alternates between long, full and medium shots, the sequence combines an overtly affected, stage-like remove with the intimacy of classical Hollywood-style continuity editing. As a result, Sato disallows spectators the comfort of a stable viewing position. The empty movie screen further heightens the spectator's awareness of *Muscle* as an aesthetically- and technologically-coded material object, amplifying the degree to which one must actively engage with Sato's counter-cinematic text. Additionally, accentuated by the prominent use of spotlights both to divide action within the frame (a practice most noticeable in long shots), and to emphasise specific verbal and physical interchanges (usually during full and medium shots), the sequence takes on a persistently disruptive, over-determined theatricality. Hence, Sato's manipulation of lighting effects maximises the immediate dramatic impact of some scenes while, paradoxically, rupturing the verisimilitude of others. Rarely does Sato's lighting result in the creation of an exclusively 'realistic' *mise-en-scène*. It is within these less naturalistic moments that Sato's radical approach to cinema in general, and genre filmmaking in particular, becomes most apparent. A gesture immediately reminiscent of the works of avant-garde filmmakers like Maya Deren and Stan Brakhage and 'new wave' directors like Jean-Luc Godard and Oshima Nagisa, this cinematic variation upon the Brechtian alienation effect is intensified by other modes of mechanical distortion. These practices include: the insertion of severely canted camera angles that literally turn the audience's perspective (and viewing experience) on its side, the almost refrain-like repetition of specific shots and actions, and the deliberate imposition of seemingly irrelevant objects (a lamp, a chair) between the camera's lens and the object of the camera's gaze.

Sato Hisayasu's *Muscle*, then, raises three crucial, ultimately interconnected questions. First, what socio-cultural perspective, if any, does *Muscle* challenge? Second, given *Muscle*'s persistent inter-textual referencing of Pasolini's *Salò*, how does Sato's filmic consideration of Sadeian excess anticipate *Naked Blood*'s preoccupation with orgasmic intensity? Lastly, in what way might Sato's film offer an alternative to Pasolini's correlation of de Sade's eighteenth century libertines to fascist ideologies?

Terrorising the Imagination: Sato's Sadeian Excess

Sato references Pier Paolo Pasolini's *Salò* repeatedly in *Muscle*, both by having characters specifically mention the film, and through multiple compositions clearly intended as visual citations of the Italian director's controversial final feature. The invitation-only masquerade at Lunatic Theater, with its distanciating long shots, recalls the expansive, cavernous interiors of the chateaux in the fictional 'Salò Republic'; Riyuzaki and Kitami's stiff, silent waltzing in one of the film's earliest scenes, and again in its closing shot (as previously mentioned), deliberately echo the final image in Pasolini's film. To analyse the logics behind these inter-textual references more completely, an understanding of the social and political critiques informing Pasolini's adaptation of one of the infamous Marquis' most difficult novels is required, as is a careful evaluation of philosophical agendas informing Sato's protagonists' behaviours.

In defense of his decision to film *Salò*, Pasolini writes that his film should be read as a 'cinematographic transposition of Sade's novel *The 120 Days of Sodom*' (2004: para 2). In keeping with this description, Pasolini explains his approach as one that, despite temporal – and, as such, sartorial and geographic – displacements, nevertheless adheres 'faithful[ly]' to 'the psychology of the characters and their actions':

I have added nothing of my own…Even the structure of the story is identical, although obviously it is very synthesised (sic). To make this synthesis I…was able to reduce…certain deeds, certain speeches, certain days from the immense catalogue of Sade' (para 2).

While cinematic adaptations of sprawling literary texts often require extensive compression or consolidation, reducing Sade's libertines and their violent lusts with a historically specific moment (and its iconography) is a perilous maneuver. The libertines' effectiveness as fictional entities resides as much in their exaggerated anatomies as in their 'monstrous' cruelties and their resistance to metaphors that limit their signifying potential. In *Salò*, however, Pasolini – in his own words – recognises his work as presenting:

…an immense sadistic metaphor of what was the Nazi-Fascist 'dissociation' from its 'crimes against humanity'. Curval, Blangis, Durcet, the Bishop – Sade's characters (who are clearly SS men in civilian dress) behave exactly with their victims as the Nazi-Fascists did with theirs. They considered them as objects and destroyed automatically all possibility of human relationship with them. (para 4)

Gary Indiana, in his BFI monograph on Pasolini's *Salò*, elaborates upon the Italian director's 'cinematographic transposition', seeing it as a meditation on power that 'condenses' the novel's 'mayhem to credible proportions', even if its tone frequently resounds with a 'pedantic moralism' in the process (2000: para 10).

As critics such as Georges Bataille, Angela Carter, and Matthew Coniam note, however, readers far too frequently and reductively dismiss de Sade's writings as constituting little more than a vile strain of 'monstrously' violent and misanthropic pornography, a gesture no doubt facilitated in large part by the depictions of the often 'extreme' carnal events catalogued within his novels. In his essay, 'The Trouble with de Sade,' Coniam insightfully targets Pasolini's *Salò* as one of contemporary cinema's 'most careful and important' (2001: 127) adaptations of de Sade's work. At the same time, he is quick to acknowledge that *Salò* is also perhaps contemporary cinema's least successful adaptation of de Sade, especially when it comes to capturing the libertine and potentially revolutionary spirit of the notorious French author's pornographic satires. For Coniam, Pasolini's film differs from Angela Carter's interpretation of de Sade's magnum opus as the work of 'a sexual guerilla whose purpose is to overturn our most basic notions of these relations, to reinstitute sexuality as a primary mode of being' (Carter 2001: 21-2). Likewise, it fails to understand de Sade's tales as fictions set in purposefully ambiguous locales and populated by exaggerated grotesques that nonetheless invite readers to indulge 'in irresponsible, undeserved license' (Coniam 2001: 128). As Coniam correctly notes, Pasolini's film is 'the complete negation of every idea that Sade ever put on paper' (129). As Coniam states, '[w]hat Pasolini has in fact done [in *Salò*] is take de Sade's fantasies and not only made them "real" but made them answerable, by locating them in actual historical experience' (128):

> Pasolini's Sadeans have their own faces, while Sade's inevitably have the face of the reader. And further, they all look ordinary; rather ugly, stupid and weak. Thus Pasolini denies us any vicarious endorsement of their pleasures; the very effect that Sade wants and encourages. (129)

Thus, virtually eliminated from Pasolini's *Salò* is de Sade's rejection of not only a plurality of political arrangements, including totalitarianism and fascism, but also the multiplicity of potential sexualities and sexual conjunctions including, even as they most blatantly exceed, most conventional notions of eroticism frequently deployed in the service of that most insidious of all masquerades: heteronormativity.

These differences between de Sade's libertines and Pier Paolo Pasolini's all-too-human metaphors for the genocidal cruelties of 1940s Italy are important to note, especially when it comes to the orgiastic possibilities imbedded in Sato Hisayasu's *Muscle*. As one of the hustlers attending the climactic masquerade at Lunatic Theater remarks to Ryuzaki, '[e]verything is an illusion...like in the movies.' Indeed, films by directors eager to relegate meaning to simple binary models (for example: *Salo*'s libertines as embodiments of Fascist ideologies; the bodies of the victimised men and women as metaphors for the targets of genocide) can limit experience. It is for just this reason that *Muscle*'s action unfolds either outside of movie theatres or in front of empty movie screens. Despite Sato's obvious admiration of Pasolini as a sexually liberated social critic with an enticing visual style, the destruction of the imported video cassette of Pasolini's final film, coupled with Ryuzaki's previous inability to attend one of its few screenings, ultimately frees Ryuzaki, like de Sade's libertines, to define his sexuality and desire on his own terms. Hence, anticipating *Naked Blood*, *Muscle* promotes identity (and the human body itself) as infinitely (re)codable, surpassing the parameters of a 'normal'ising culture. Attending Lunatic Theater's masquerade is voluntarily, and the erotic potentialities enacted within the cinema at once resemble and extend Ryuzaki's quest for corporeal intensity. '[T]he domain of eroticism' that Sato's *Muscle* finally posits is one that, in the words of Georges Bataille, exposes viewers to a model of identity formation that comprehends '[t]he whole business of eroticism' as obliterating 'the self-contained character of the participators as they are in their normal lives' (Bataille 1957: 24). The film, therefore, resists the compulsion 'to limit ourselves within our individual personalities' (24); in the process, *Muscle*, like *Naked Blood*, embraces an ecstatic intensity that positions physical disfigurement as a model for corporeal and ideological re-configuration.

Image 6: *Muscle* – video box art (© Strand Releasing)

Chapter Three:
Ghosts of the Present, Spectres of the Past: the *kaidan* and the Haunted Family in the Cinema of Nakata Hideo and Shimizu Takashi

Spirited Vengeance

Long a staple within Japanese literary and dramatic arts, the *onryou*, or 'avenging spirit' motif, remains an exceedingly popular and vital component of contemporary Japanese horror cinema. Drawing on a plurality of religious traditions, including Shintoism and Christianity, as well as plot devices from traditional theatre (for instance Noh theatre's *shunen-* [revenge-] and *shura-mono* [ghost-plays], and Kabuki theatre's tales of the supernatural [or *kaidan*]), these narratives of incursion by the spectral into the realm of the ordinary for the purposes of exacting revenge continue to find new articulations, as well as new audiences, courtesy of visually arresting and internationally acclaimed *shinrei-mono eiga* (ghost story films) by directors such as Nakata Hideo's *Ringu* (1998) and *Dark Water* (*Honogurai mizu no soko kara*, 2002), and Shimizu Takashi's *Ju-on: The Grudge* (2002). Like the myriad of cultural texts from which Nakata and Shimizu draw their inspiration, including now 'classic' *kaidan* such as Shindo Kaneto's *Onibaba* (1964) and Kobayashi Masaki's *Kwaidan* (1965), these recent revisions of the 'avenging spirit' trope continue to relate tales of 'wronged', primarily female entities who return to avenge themselves upon those who harmed them. The targets of these angry spirits' rage, however, are often multiple, and careful analyses of the focus of the spirits' wrath, as well as the motivations behind their actions, provide valuable insights into the historical, political, gendered, and economic logics informing current socio-cultural tensions between nostalgic imaginings of a 'traditional Japanese' past and the equally illusory threat and/or promise of an ever-emerging technological, global, and postmodern Japan. Consequently, the impact of late industrial capitalism on the various (re)constructions of the 'family' in contemporary Japan constitutes one of the chapter's primary concerns. In particular, since both *Ringu* and *Dark Water* feature heroines who are also single mothers, this chapter examines the extent to which Nakata's female protagonists function as aesthetic and cultural barometers for highly contested comprehensions of gender and gendered behaviours in Japan. As well, these cinematic heroines – and the ghosts they confront – provide compelling analogies not only for Japan's protean economic and familial landscape, but also for emerging neo-conservative ideologies that threaten to re-imagine the notion of equal rights for men and women from a more 'conventionally Japanese' perspective. Furthermore, although Nakata depicts the exorcism, or even temporary placation, of these 'avenging ghosts' as nearly impossible, containment is frequently depicted as achievable, if only (as is most conspicuously the case in *Ringu*) through a process of eternal deferment.

Similarly, Shimizu Takashi's *Ju-on: The Grudge* (2002) extends the *onryou* motif in important new directions. The initial 'big screen' re-imagining of Shimizu's two 1998 straight-to-video precursors, *Ju-on 1* (*The Curse*) and *Ju-on 2* (*Curse 2*), *Ju-on: The Grudge* is a curious filmic hybrid, combining carefully chosen aesthetic trappings of Western – particularly US – horror films with visual and narrative tropes long familiar to fans of Japanese horror cinema. Such a mixture of filmmaking approaches seems appropriate when one considers that Shimizu Takashi is, by his own admission, largely influenced by US 'splatter' movie icons like *A Nightmare on Elm Street*'s Freddy Kruger and *Friday the 13th*'s Jason, as well as 'an alumnus of the Film School of Tokyo' where he flourished under the tutelage of 'horror maestro' Kurosawa Kiyoshi and *Ringu*'s scriptwriter Takahashi Hiroshi (Alexander 2004: 14-6). This meshing of US and Japanese influences is crucial to understanding not only the film's significant appeal in Western markets, but also Shimizu's aesthetic as a director of cinematic horror. Additionally, this visual combination is important since physiological, social, and narratological hybridity, as well as the interstitial spaces from which such hybrids emerge, inform not only *Ju-on*'s content, but how the film posits changes in the institution of the family as at once the result of, and a barometer for, larger socio-cultural transformations.

Of course, tales of horror and monstrosity have long concerned themselves with the notion of hybridity in their exploration of those regions where categories fail to maintain their integrity. Ghosts, for example, are by their very definition liminal entities negotiating the supposedly unbridgeable gulf between the world of the living and the realm of the dead; likewise, monsters are perpetual scramblers of social codes, often troubling the nebulous, perhaps oxymoronic distinction between the 'human' and the 'animal', or the 'human' and the 'non-human'. By combining, in his own words, 'an American and Japanese style' (Macias 2003: para 18) of horror cinema, Shimizu creates a hybrid of the US slasher film and the Japanese *kaidan*. Rather than a single, individual ghost returning to seek revenge, *Ju-on: The Grudge*, through a web of primarily non-linear, episodic narratives, confronts viewers with a mother and 'housewife', Kayako, and son, Toshio, who were slaughtered by their delusional patriarch, Takeo. Restless, Kayako and Toshio haunt both the house in which they died – a geographical location that can be read as a microcosm of a Japanese culture in transformation – and the lives of those mortals unlucky enough to enter their abode. The murdered mother and child are at once ethereal and corporeal; they are not merely ghosts, but not fully monsters in the term's most conventional sense. As liminal, hybrid entities demanding the attention of those they encounter, they are perhaps the most appropriate models for exploring a radically transforming Japanese culture in which tensions between an undead past and the unborn future find articulation in the transforming family of a haunted present.

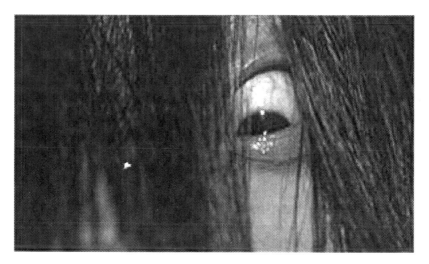

Image 7: Sadako's furious gaze in Nakata Hideo's *Ringu* (© Tartan Video)

Monstrous Transformations: Single Mothers, the Return of the Oppressed, and the Fear of National Disintegration

In his edited volume, *Japan Pop!: Inside the World of Japanese Popular Culture*, Timothy J. Craig notes that in Japan, '[e]conomic development' has produced 'new social conditions', including 'urbanization, consumer cultures, changing family structures and gender roles, and lifestyles and values that are less purely traditional and more influenced by outside information and trends' (2000: 16). One could safely articulate a similar observation regarding many of the world's nations, but one of the more interesting aspects of contemporary Japanese culture is the varying degrees to which US ideologies and popular aesthetics, especially in the years following the end of World War II, have had a deeply rooted and curiously expansive impact upon Japanese social formations. From the profound influence of late capitalist economic philosophies, to the sometimes difficult reassessments of long-held ontological categories of individual subjectivity, Japan's contemporary transformations (and the internal resistances that have arisen – and continue to arise – in the face of such significant changes) reveal the often traumatic socio-political contortions accompanying US colonialism in all of its various imperial and aesthetic manifestations.

One such Western influence takes the form of the Japanese constitution created in 1946. Still a highly contested document, this post war text has had an extensive impact upon gender roles in contemporary Japan, reconfiguring the multiple ways in which the nation's populace imagines the sex- and gender-based apportioning of social and cultural roles, as well as the impact of conventional and emerging conceptions of masculinity and femininity. As Catherine Makino notes, the constitution 'helped reshape life for women' (2005: para 3) in Japan. One such change for women came in the form of marriage reform. Specifically, the new constitution stipulated that:

> 'marriage would be solely based on agreement of husband and wife, who had equal rights. Before then women were not guaranteed civil rights or legal rights. They were not allowed to vote or own property. Although husbands could file for divorce, wives could not'. (para 3)

Coupled with the sometimes radical social and cultural transformations that accompany 'most industrial societies' undergoing 'restructuring from an industrial to postindustrial economy' (Ueno 1994: 23) – a shift that inevitably impacts divisions of labour both within and outside of the domestic sphere – the position of women in Japanese society invariably impacts the dynamics of male-female relationships. This is not to suggest that contemporary Japan is by any means a meritocracy in which men and women occupy positions of absolute equality; as in most industrialised nations across the globe (including the US and the UK), sexual discrimination persists, resulting, as Roger J. Davies and Osamu Ikeno remind us, 'in important social problems: sexual harassment, inequality in the work place, and so on' (2002: 67-8). Robert C. Christopher anticipates Davies and Ikeno's sentiments when he states that 'male dominance' remains 'an overwhelming reality in professional and public life' (1984: 67). In other words, although '[t]oday there are powerful women in the government', and despite the fact that 'women have also recently gained much clout outside the home', females 'at university and management level in Japan are still paltry compared to the west' (Bornoff 2002: 61).

Despite traditionalist voices bemoaning the collapse of the pre-war 'extended family' and ideological shifts that seemingly privilege 'egoism' (a distorted mode of 'individualism') over the triumvirate of 'family, community, and the nation' (Makino 2005: para 7), marriage and reproduction have ceased to represent a 'woman's sole option' (Ueno 1994: 38). Thus, re-imaginings of the Japanese family have consistently accompanied the frequently extreme economic transitions occurring in Japan over the last half-century, including its 'miraculous' economic recovery and subsequent recession. In numerous instances, the family has steadily 'become a micro-corporation' in which '[f]athers have been known to sacrifice their families to their business, and a recent trend is that mothers spend a great deal of time in the office or at night school and children do so with their classmates in private "after-schools" (*juku*)' (Kogawa 2005: para 8). In other instances, financial pressures and the spread of feminism have combined to lessen the stigma surrounding divorce, though single mothers continue to struggle against patriarchal authority in the form of destructive prejudices and restrictive legislation. As Sonya Salamon reports, when it comes to employment practices, employers are frequently ill-disposed toward married women, and even more so towards mothers. As a substantial consequence of a divorce rate that has been on the rise since the end of World War II, single mothers experience descrimination on an even wider scale, leading at least one major sociological inquiry to recognise that single mothers constitute what is quickly becoming a form of 'invisible poverty in Japan' (1986: 133). What's more, Salamon's study illustrates that this 'intergenerational poverty' not only 'formed within a nexus of capitalism' that necessitates certain familial reconfigurations, but also reflects the presence of profound 'problems' embedded deep within both contemporary and so-called 'traditional' Japanese 'societal structures' (133).

As is often the case in transforming capitalist cultures, the aforementioned post-war shifts in economic and, by extension, familial dynamics have not transpired without resistance from Japanese desirous for a return to what they perceive as – to borrow a term from reactionary US politicians – 'traditional family values'. In June 2004, for example, several government officials proposed constitutional revisions aimed at reducing the impact of a distorted and US-influenced individualism upon what was once perceived as a more communal socio-political paradigm. As such, a recent report on Japan's morphing social and cultural landscape drafted by Morioka Masahiro, 'a ruling party member in the House of Representatives' (Makino 2005: para 7), declared that '[i]t is shameful that Japanese people no longer think much of family, community and the nation, and that some of them even insist on having a system of retaining separate family names…The constitution must ensure that protecting family is the foundation of securing the nation' (para 7). While Morioka's contention that Japan no longer perceives value in social institutions like the 'family' or, indeed, the 'nation' resounds with a remarkable degree of alarmist hyperbole, his rhetoric proves illuminating in that it reveals the extent to which concerns over recuperating a lost sense of 'Japaneseness' inform the larger popular imagination. As well, it exposes the recurrent allure of ideological configurations that link conceptualisations of the family as a cohesive social unit with the re-establishment of a nationalist fervor that was once perceived as vanishing amidst unrelenting social change.

Here, too, an analysis of recent Japanese horror cinema provides valuable insights into the assorted perspectives constellating around the morphing sex and gender roles that accompany a period of economic, social, and cultural transition. In the following pages, this chapter analyses two films by the noted Japanese director Nakata Hideo, positioning these *kaidan* tales as key texts for mapping crucial socio-cultural anxieties. *Ringu* follows the exploits of Asakawa Reiko, a reporter and recently divorced single mother who briefly reunites with her former spouse (a university professor) to uncover the secret behind a cursed videocassette that, once viewed, kills its spectator in seven days. A similar conceit informs the plot of Nakata's *Dark Water*, in which Matsubura Yoshimi, a mother in the midst of a psychologically trying battle over the custody of her six year old daughter, must come to terms with her own history of parental abandonment while defending both her child and herself from the restless spirit of a young girl who, left unattended by her parents, drowned in a water tank atop the block-style tenement in which she lived. Indeed, the motif of drowning plays an important role in both films, allowing viewers the opportunity not only to experience two contemporary manifestations of the 'avenging spirit' theme, but also to engage with a metaphorical interrogation of the 'return' of a 'repressed' societal configuration that, like the spectral entities that haunt these popular narratives, refuses to die quietly.

'Dead Wet Girls': Nakata Hideo's *Ringu* and *Dark Water*

In a recent interview on US National Public Radio (NPR), noted Japanese cinema scholar Grady Hendrix contributed to a discussion of Japanese horror cinema's international popularity by describing texts like *Ringu* and *Dark Water* as tales about 'dead wet girls' (quoted in Ulaby, 2005) seeking revenge for past injustices. Clearly intended as a humorous over-simplification designed to enhance public interest in the recent wave of popular *kaidan* or *shinrei-mono eiga*, as well as the inferior Hollywood remakes they inevitably spawned, his reference to 'dead wet girls' is illuminating. Hendrix's recognition both of the theme of water and of the angry ghost's gender is crucial, especially when interrogating the social resonances haunting some of the darkest corners of Nakata Hideo's best known works. Each based on a popular novel by the successful horror writer Suzuki Koji, an artist that *Publisher's Weekly* describes as 'the Stephen King of Japan' (2004, para 1), *Ringu* and *Dark Water* stand out as two of the best known contemporary Japanese horror films. As the motion picture most frequently cited as the text responsible for initiating global interest in Japanese and other East Asian horror cinemas, *Ringu* has received copious critical attention, ranging from studies that read the film as a thinly disguised postmodern fable about the cultural impact of emerging communication technologies, to discussions of the film as a cult text that has elicited an expansive fan base due, in large part, to *Ringu*'s popularity on Internet newsgroups.[1] *Dark Water*, on the other hand, has been largely overlooked by film scholars, though it, too, spawned a Hollywood remake in 2005. Viewed together, both *Ringu* and *Dark Water* – with their focus on single parent households, recovered pasts, and wetness as a metaphor for illness and decay – provide valuable insights into a transforming contemporary Japanese culture.

As many horror fans around the globe well know, *Ringu*'s plot involves an urban legend of a cursed video tape that proves all too real for a reporter named Reiko, her potentially psychic son, Yoichi, and her ex-husband. The tape's images are as surreal as they are frightening, and once viewed, the spectator(s) has seven days to live before the stooped, drenched, and vengeful apparition of a young woman in funereal white appears and frightens the hapless viewer(s) to death. When a series of teenagers mysteriously die, expressions of abject terror contorting their once youthful features, the resourceful reporter becomes determined to solve the mystery behind the allegedly cursed videocassette. Retracing the deceased teen's final weeks, Reiko soon locates the videocassette at a resort on Izu peninsula, watches it, and then answers a ringing phone that, she believes, indicates that her life will end in one week. Rattled, Reiko turns to her ex-husband for help; together, they attempt to decipher the video's images and eventually trace its origins back forty years to a psychic woman, Samara, whose supernatural talents and uncanny predictions elicit the violent derision of a room of angry male reporters. Afraid for her mother's life, Samara's daughter, Sadako, kills one of the reporters with a single thought. Consequently, Samara kills herself, and soon Sadako, too, meets an untimely end when the primary scientist studying Samara's abilities pushes Sadako into a well. Hoping to put Sadako's anger to rest, Reiko and her ex-husband find the well into which the young girl's body was cast and, after some tense moments, succeed in recovering her remains. Hopeful that all is now well, Reiko and her ex-husband return to their daily activities. Sadako's wrath, however, has not been satisfied. Before long, her ghost emerges from a television screen,

---

[1] For an insightful analysis of this phenomenon, see Hills, M. (2005) 'Ringing in the Changes: Cult Distinctions and Cultural Differences in US Fans' Readings of Japanese Horror Cinema', in McRoy, J. *Japanese Horror Cinema*. Edinburgh: Edinburgh University Press, 161-74.

and, in a particularly terrifying scene, frightens Reiko's ex-husband to death. Perplexed, Reiko reviews the recent events, discovering that the tape her ex-husband viewed was a copy of her version. It soon becomes clear to Reiko that the curse can only be avoided by creating a copy for another person to view. Realising that her son has brought the curse upon himself by viewing the tape while she was distracted, Reiko telephones her father and informs him that she has a copy of a tape she would very much like for him to watch.

Similar in subtle ways to *Ringu*, Nakata's *Dark Water* immerses viewers within the melancholy life of Matsubura Yoshimi, the mother of a six-year-old girl named Ikuko and the former employee of a publishing house for which she proofread what she describes as 'extremely graphic and sadistic' fictions. Enmeshed in a divorce proceeding and a bitter custody battle, Yoshimi is determined to provide for her daughter and demonstrate her parenting abilities to attorneys hired to decide whether, given her history of mental breakdowns and familial disruptions, Yoshimi should continue to be Ikuko's primary caretaker. After an exhausting search for affordable housing, Yoshimi rents a small apartment in a run-down block-style tenement located near the kindergarten her daughter is scheduled to attend. Yoshimi and Ikuko move in, only to discover a small, mysterious red backpack bearing the name of a missing child (a kindergarten age girl named Kawai Mitsuko), as well as a rapidly spreading water stain slowly bleeding its way through Yoshimi's bedroom ceiling. As the story progresses, Nakata builds a mood of quiet dread tinged with a palpable sadness. Yoshimi, herself the child of divorced parents, finds herself consistently reminded of her fear of abandonment stemming from an incident when her own mother failed to pick her up from school. Yoshimi's own quest for a job to provide a decent life for her daughter exacerbates the pain evoked by this memory, especially when she arrives late to her daughter's school, only to discover that her soon to be ex-husband picked up Ikuko moments earlier. On the verge of a mental collapse, Yoshimi meets a sympathetic lawyer, Kishida, who assists her by asserting the legal pressures necessary to get the dripping stain on her ceiling fixed. Yoshimi's daily life appears to be improving, but soon Mitsuko's restless spirit reappears and viewers discover that not only did she drown in the water tank atop the apartment complex in which Yoshimi and Ikuko live, but that the spirit will not find peace until the cycle of abandonment and loneliness completes its round. In a harrowing climax, the apartment building weeps cataclysmic tears from every crevice, corner, and ceiling as Yoshimi symbolically adopts Mitsuko's ghost by clutching the phantom of the long lost girl to her chest, much to her biological daughter, Ikuko's, heartbroken dismay. Nakata's film, however, does not end here. In a remarkably restrained and poignant epilogue, Ikuko, now ten years older and possessing only fragmentary recollections of her tempestuous childhood, returns to the apartment she shared with her mother in the dilapidated housing block. In their former apartment, Ikuko and Yoshimi share a few tender moments, but when Ikuko inquires as to whether she may once again live with her mother, Yoshimi falls silent and Ikuko realises that Mitsuko's spirit still resides within the building. Yoshimi apologises for the fact that they cannot be together, and when Ikuko turns her head quickly in hopes of catching a glimpse of Mitsuko's spirit, her mother disappears. Saddened, Ikuko walks home alone beneath a clear blue sky.

Perhaps one of the most immediate comparison viewers may draw between Nakata's *Ringu* and *Dark Water* concerns the central protagonists' marital and, by extension, socio-cultural statuses. In each case, the heroine struggling against supernatural forces is the single mother of a young child; *Ringu*'s Reiko is divorced, and *Dark Water*'s Yoshimi is in the midst of a divorce. These respective situations inform not only the mothers' relationships with their offspring, but also the extent to which the restless spirits succeed in insinuating themselves into their lives. In *Ringu*, for example, Reiko and her ex-husband's frantic quest to determine the origin of the haunted videotape renders their son, Yoichi, vulnerable to Sadako's viral-like curse. Although early in the film Yoichi expresses curiosity about the existence of a cursed videocassette, Reiko – who is clearly coded as Yoichi's primary caretaker – is ultimately unable to police her son's every waking moment. As a result, she cannot prevent Yoichi from viewing the sinister images on her copy of the cursed tape and, as the film closes with a high angle extreme long shot of her car on a lonely stretch of highway, Reiko finds she must telephone her father and attempt to obtain his unwitting assistance in freeing her son from the otherwise sure death awaiting him.

Similarly, *Dark Water*'s Yoshimi, in her scramble to find housing, employment, and sympathetic legal council, leaves her daughter, Ikuko, vulnerable to the sporadic, yet increasingly threatening machinations of Mitsuko's troubled spirit. Equally distressing for Yoshimi is the fear that Ikuko may experience a sense of isolation and abandonment akin to the emotional pain she suffered as the child of divorced parents struggling against economic pressures in a culture clinging to communal ideologies privileging 'conventional' pre- and immediate post-war family structures. Yoshimi's anxiety heightens when Ikuko's school principal remarks upon Ikuko's strange behavior, a condition that isolates her from her fellow classmates and that, in the principal's opinion, stems from domestic instability: 'I...hear you are divorced. That must be affecting her. We see this a lot with children of divorced parents.' What's more, when Yoshimi inquires as to the purpose behind a wall of children's drawings depicting a little girl in a yellow raincoat and holding a red bag reminiscent of the scarlet backpack that frequently accompanies the increasingly uncanny encounters with Mitsuko's ghost, the school's principal explicitly links Ikuko's troubles with Mitsuko's disappearance:

> As a matter of fact, she [Mitsuko] used to behave oddly, too. However, in Mitsuko's case her mother abandoned her. Just got up and left one day. You never heard of her? The girl who disappeared two years ago: Mitsuko Kawai? She was one of our kids here.

The principal's allegation that Mitsuko's mother abandoned her young daughter resonates deeply with Yoshimi, who, as we learn from *Dark Water*'s opening sequence, habours heartrending memories of waiting alone at her own kindergarten for her divorced mother's belated arrival. Such moments position Nakata's film not only as a text concerned with the myriad economic and social dilemmas accompanying transform-ations in the Japanese family, but also as a work that addresses how such alterations may engender traumatic cycles of abandonment and neglect that could have catastrophic consequences for successive generations.

The ghosts that haunt Nakata's *Ringu* and *Dark Water*, then, assume two distinct, yet ultimately interconnected forms. Firstly, they are supernatural beings, conforming to the vengeful spirit (or *onryou*) motif by imposing their phantasmic distress upon the living. Secondly, they are culturally-coded entities in that they function allegorically, their demises inextricably linked with social transformations and the anxieties that often accompany such changes. Consider, for example, the scene in *Ringu* in which a roomful of exclusively male journalists' vehemently reject Samara's uncanny psychic abilities and apocalyptic predictions. The men are threatened by more than Samara's possession of a knowledge that exceeds that of the patriarchal scientific community; it is her ability to vocalize this knowledge and, thereby, insert herself into the realm of public discourse that evokes a virulent fear from the male audience. It is this incredulity turned into fear and anger over Samara's skills that evokes Sadako's demonstration of her even more powerful, and consequently more threatening, mental acumen: her ability to kill with a single thought. It is thus fitting that Reiko's scientist ex-husband, though instrumental in the discovery of Sadako's corpse, cannot break the curse that provides a posthumous outlet for Sadako's prematurely silenced rage; it is finally the investigative journalist, Reiko, who uncovers the simulacral secret of the young Sadako's technologically inscribed vengeance – the cursed videocassettes representing a mode of mass communication that the psychic mother's and daughter's male persecutors, given their violent rejection of the very notion of a woman's will made at once increasingly present and increasingly pervasive (and increasingly abject), would have found too terrifying to even imagine. Like Samara, a lone maternal figure whose prediction of a volcanic eruption had the potential, if heeded, to save many from certain death, Reiko's discovery of the logic behind the cursed videocassette may very well allow her not only to save her child (an action Samara's suicide precluded), but also the lives of countless others, if only through a process of eternal deferment. It is no mere coincidence that the first to view the viral video will be Yoichi's grandfather, a clearly patriarchal figure. Hence, to break a contemporary cycle of literal (within the film's diegesis) and figurative (socio-cultural) fear, tragically and historically repressed woman must forever be acknowledged, their silenced voices perpetually recognised if never fully understood. What these women should never be, Nakata's film suggests, is forgotten or ignored. Such willful negation takes place at one's own risk.

Likewise, to allay the sodden, restless spirit at the heart of *Dark Water*, Yoshimi, the film's heroine, endeavors to sever a cycle of perceived abandonment and neglect by exchanging her living daughter, Ikuko, for the ghost of a dead child, Mitsuko. This substitution transpires during the film's torrential climax, in which the deteriorating block-style apartment building in which Yoshimi and Ikuko reside floods as if drowning in the bitter tears of countless lamentations. This deluge packs an emotional charge that is at first terrifying, then heart-breaking. In one particularly effective sequence, Yoshimi, endeavoring to flee her supernaturally drenched environs, grabs her daughter's arm and splashes her way down the darkened, leaking hallway. She enters the building's cantankerous lift, and frantically mashes the button for the building's lobby. With an incredibly assured command of visual (mis)direction, Nakata orchestrates the film's *mise-en-scène* so that it alternates between varying close-ups of Yoshimi's panicked face, POV shots that allow viewers to glimpse through the lift's thin rectangular window as the mechanism ominously rises rather than descends, and extreme close-ups of Yoshimi's finger jabbing frantically at the lift's array of numbered buttons. As the lift reaches the floor directly above Yoshimi and Ikuko's apartment, a POV shot reveals a darkened, water-logged hallway. The shot recalls a moment from earlier in the film, during which Yoshimi catches a fleeting glimpse of Mitsuko's spectral form seemingly walking out the door of the apartment in which, we discover, she once lived with her father. Approximating Yoshimi's POV, this shot likewise reveals the shadowy image of a young girl walking out into the hallway. The child-sized figure turns and, calling for her mother, races towards the lift as it jerks to a stop and it's doors slide open. The child, Yoshimi soon realizes, is Ikuko. Next, in perhaps *Dark Water*'s most chilling moment, Nakata cuts to a medium shot of Yoshimi and then slowly dollies in to a close-up of her face as she turns her head to see who, or what, is in the lift with her. A reverse shot reveals her companion to be Mitsuko's long drowned

corpse, its flesh slipping off her decaying skeleton in damp chunks as she
extends her arms and lurches forward, an infant's wail emerging from her
darkened, gaping maw. Rather than running away, Yoshimi cradles
Mitsuko in her arms. In a powerful medium-long shot, the lift's doors
close, separating Yoshimi and Mitsuko's ghost from Ikuko's screaming,
tear-streaked face.

As powerful as any scene in Nakata's breakthrough international
sensation, *Ringu*, this sequence from *Dark Water* likewise deploys
elements of the Japanese *kaidan* to advance a consideration of shifting
socio-cultural codes. As alluded to earlier, *Dark Water*'s narrative
engages the impact of economic transitions on both conceptualisations of
the Japanese family as a social construct, and on the social support
systems (or significant dearth thereof) available for single parents in
general and single mothers in particular. It is also a sequence that raises
several important questions. Given not only the film's focus on the multi-
generational ramifications of divorce and the decline of the traditional
Japanese extended family, how are viewers to understand Yoshimi's
rejection of Ikuko in favor of Mitsuko? Additionally, what is the function
of the film's mysterious epilogue which transports the film's spectators
ten years forward in Yoshimi and Ikuko's lives?

To address these queries, let us first consider in some detail the
film's puzzling *dénouement*. Following the title card that alerts us to the
passage of time within the film's narrative, we meet a sixteen year old
Ikuko dressed in her high school uniform and accompanied by two
friends. As they walk home from school together, they pass the
kindergarten Ikuko attended when she was six. A lone, seemingly
forgotten child sits on the ground awaiting the arrival of her parent, an
image that immediately recalls both Yoshimi and Ikuko's loneliness and
reiterates – if only momentarily (for the lone child's parent soon arrives)
– the film's cyclical theme of abandonment. Though we quickly learn
from Ikuko's own words that she can barely remember the brief time she
spent living with her mother while her parents were in the process of
obtaining a divorce, the child's momentarily disheartened visage has a
profound emotional impact on Ikuko. She parts ways with her friends and
walks to the apartment building she shared with her mother ten years

earlier. From the exterior, the building appears even more dilapidated than in previous external shots; the interior of her mother's apartment, however, appears virtually unchanged, as if time has stood still within its modestly decorated walls. Yoshimi does not seem to be home, and so Ikuko quietly looks around, finally picking up a photograph in a silver frame from her mother's bedside table and studying it for several seconds. Ikuko pauses as she is about to leave, then turns to find her mother standing several feet behind her. Ikuko and her mother reminisce. We learn not only that Ikuko has been living with her father, but that the father has remarried and now has children by his second wife. Ikuko also reveals that she had no idea that her mother was still living in the apartment and, kneeling before her, asks if they can live together once more. Yoshimi sadly apologises to Ikuko, stating that living together would be impossible. Nakata then presents us with a powerful medium shot of Ikuko on the right side of the frame and, behind her, the blurry image of Mitsuko in her yellow rain slicker. Ikuko spins around quickly to catch a glimpse of Mitsuko, but there is no one there. When she turns back to her mother, Yoshimi, too, has vanished. In the film's closing shot, we see a very long shot of Ikuko walking away from the decaying apartment building that looms huge and menacing behind her. The sky above, however, is blue and free of clouds for the first time in the entire film.

Dark Water's closing moments are filled with ghosts. However, conspicuously absent, save for the shot of Ikuko and Mitsuko described above, is the mood of fear and dread that saturates the majority of the film. Nakata eschews the chiaroscuro lighting effects and ominous music generously employed throughout the film's previous eighty-plus minutes to evoke fear in the spectator in favor of a brighter, though by no means intensely lit, *mise-en-scène* and a softer, melancholy piano score. Although ten years has passed, Yoshimi appears not to have aged at all; even the apartment's seemingly unchanged décor suggests an uncanny timelessness within the apartment's walls. Yoshimi's decision to become Mitsuko's surrogate mother despite the presence of her own biological child represents one potential, if ultimately limited, approach to breaking the cycle of individual and cultural anxiety accompanying both the increasing emergence of single parent families in late capitalist Japan, as well as the transforming roles of women in the home and workplace. In a gesture similar to the logic of eternal deferment with which *Ringu*'s Reiko displaces Sadako's technologically-mediated fury, *Dark Water*'s Yoshimi elects to heal the wounds of the present by literally and figuratively embracing the residue of a traumatic past in the form of Mitsuko's ghost. However, rather than affecting change through the recognition of a traumatic past, as Reiko does, Yoshimi's attempt to placate Mitsuko's lonely, mournful rage, disallows her from living effectively in the present. For all practical purposes, Yoshimi transforms herself into an entity as elusive, wraithlike, and insubstantial as the spectral being she clutched to her chest in the lift a decade earlier. Thus, Yoshimi's sudden appearance – and sudden disappearance – within the apartment she once shared with Ikuko mirrors Mitsuko's phantasmic presence. In this regard, Yoshimi differs radically from Ikuko, who is very much alive and, as the film's closing shot suggests, free from the confining parameters of the crumbling edifice that stands as a bleak if fading reminder of a past she has actively left behind in favor of a living present and potentially bright future.

Image 8: Cycles of neglect: a young Yoshimi awaits her mother's arrival in Nakata Hideo's *Dark Water* (Courtesy: beyondhollywood.com).

Hybrid Moments: Cinematic Symbiosis and Familial Mutation in
Shimizu Takashi's *Ju-on*: *The Grudge*

The symbiotic relationship between US and Japanese cinema is perhaps the most creative and consistent in the history of motion pictures. Of course, at the epicenter of any discussion of this topic looms the presence of legendary director Kurosawa Akira, whose *Stray Dog* (1949) and *High and Low* (1963) remain vital experiments with the primarily US style known as 'film noir', and whose more canonical works, such as *The Seven Samurai* (1951) and *The Hidden Fortress* (1958), have been famously remade in the US as *The Magnificent Seven* (USA John Sturges, 1960) and *Star Wars* (USA George Lucas, 1977) respectively. When one factors in such epic Japanese-US co-productions as *Tora, Tora, Tora* (Richard Fleischer and Fukusaku Kinji, 1970) and *Gojira 2000* (Okawara Takao, 1999), as well as the increasingly prevalent interconnections between Japanese anime and Western science fiction texts, one soon discovers that even a cursory investigation of this phenomenon could fill an entire volume of film scholarship and, most certainly, exceeds the scope of this project.

Recognising the debts that these two crucial film industries owe to one another, however, is critical to this essay's project. At the very least, it allows us to advance some preliminary theories as to why Shimizu Takashi's *Ju-on: The Grudge* has so quickly garnered a modest cult following in the US and other Western markets – as evidenced by the Hollywood remake, titled *The Grudge*, starring *Buffy the Vampire Slayer*'s Sarah Michelle Gellar and helmed by Shimizu Takashi himself. If, as Shimizu claims, US horror film series like *Friday the 13th* and *A Nightmare on Elm Street* have impacted his conceptualisation of cinematic horror, then might *Ju-on: The Grudge*'s international success be a result of Shimizu's skillful weaving of the visual logics behind what Vera Dika and Carol Clover call the 'stalker cycle'[2] with filmic sequences

---

[2] See Dika, V. (1987) 'The Stalker Film, 1978-81', in Waller, G.A. *American Horrors: Essays on the Modern American Horror Film*. Urbana and Chicago: University of Illinois Press, and

and narrative motifs often associated with Japanese cinema? By acknowledging the hybridity informing Shimizu's technical approach to cinematic horror, including his manipulation of *mise-en-scène*, we gain critical insight into a larger socio-cultural economy of fear predicated upon anxieties over the illusory integrity of the Japanese social body. As Marilyn Ivy notes, this imagined wholeness is fundamental to modern, and pre-modern, perceptions of cultural and national identity. The Japanese social body, for Ivy, is a hybrid social entity that frequnelty denies the complex amalgamations that constitute it:

> The hybrid realities of Japan today – of multiple border crossings and transnational interchanges in the worlds of trade, aesthetics, and sciences – are contained within dominant discourses on cultural purity and nondifference, and in nostalgic appeals to premodernity: what makes the Japanese so different from everybody else makes them identical to each other; what threatens the self-sameness is often marked temporally as the intrusively modern, spacially as foreign. Although those discourses are being altered by the effects of advanced capitalism they have proved remarkably resilient as they haunt the possibilities of a postnationalist consciousness in contemporary Japan (1995: 9)

Ivy's overarching motif of 'haunt'ing, both in the above quote and throughout her book, *Discourses of the Vanishing: Modernity, Phantasm, Japan*, is instructive in that it represents, and contributes to, a discourse of a returning repressed. Moreover, whether that which is sublimated and/or temporarily contained takes the form of a potentially nation-effacing globalism, or the increasingly important role of women who 'manage the home (even when they labor outside)' (Allison 2000: 174), horror cinema marks the ideal forum for the metaphoric expression of concerns over an indiscrete (or hybrid) national, social, or corporeal body.

The grainy opening montage of Shimizu Takashi's *Ju-on: The Grudge* reveals this latter concern over the shifting role of women in the home, a location which serves as the epicenter of the *onryou*'s unquenchable rage. Beginning with establishing shots of a seemingly anonymous residential street, followed by low angle shots of a vine-clad

---

Clover, C. (1992) *Men, Women, and Chainsaws: Gender in the Modern Horror Film.* Princeton, New Jersey: Princeton University Press.

house, Shimizu then cuts to a rapid, disorienting montage. The images that flash across the screen range from extreme close-ups of a mouth gnawing bloody fingertips, the blade of a box-cutter clicking slowly out of its plastic casing, and Kayako's lifeless eyes framed by streaks of blood, to medium and full shots of a crazed Takeo turning about slowly, the young Toshio drawing pictures of a long-haired woman on a sheet of paper before scampering away to hide in a closet, and a black cat screeching as it is grabbed roughly by the back of its neck. Intentionally disorienting and confusing, these images allow the audience a privileged, if ultimately incomprehensible, glimpse into the violent act that has most likely resulted in the eponymous grudge, a 'curse' that, as the film's title sequence tells us, originates when one 'dies in the grip of a powerful rage', and then spreads virally, killing all those with whom the spirits come into contact and, in the process, birthing new curses. It also anticipates the film's larger organisational logic, a tangled and non-linear narrative that, in its episodic construction, resembles the horror *manga* of Ito Junji, particularly the vignettes that comprise his anthology, *Flesh-Colored Horror* (2001), or that punctuate his larger collected series, *Tomie* (2001) and *Uzumaki* (2002-2003).

The motivation behind Takeo's murderous assault, we eventually learn, is his psychotic anger over Kayako's suspected adultery; while the film's narrative makes it clear that the wife died at her husband's hands, exactly how Toshio met his fate is left vague. Toshio is described only as having 'disappeared', but from the film's first extended vignette, it is clear that both mother and son haunt the site of the carnage presented in the film's opening sequence, as well as the lives of those who move into, or even temporarily visit, the home. This premise reveals a palpable masculine anxiety associated with a rapidly transforming social landscape and its impact upon long established gender roles, a dread exacerbated by the culture's 'strong patrilinear emphasis', as well as women's paradoxical role as 'both a source of danger to the norm and the very means of perpetuating that norm' (Martinez 1998: 7). If, as Susan Napier argues, Japanese men '[c]onfronted with more powerful and independent women...have suffered their own form of identity crises' (2000: 80), then the core of Shimizu's film is the ultimate nightmare for a phallocentric culture: the patriarchal paradigm assaulted at its very foundations. Central to *Ju-on: The Grudge*, then, are those social transformations linked with the radical changes in the socio-cultural landscape that followed the bursting of the economic bubble in the early nineties – an implosion that has resulted in not only transforming notions of gender roles, but also what cultural theorists like Hayao Kawai identify as the collapse of the 'Japanese-style extended family' (1986: 303) and the rise of domestic violence (306). One can read the fragmented, impressionistic opening montage as illustrative of a profound social disorientation, but one can also comprehend the sequence's implied violence as emblematic of a larger compulsion to re-establish and/or maintain a regime of masculine dominance.

Of course, similar 'gender trouble' has long informed Western horror cinema, and so Shimizu's occasional appropriation of visual tropes from US slasher films of the late seventies and early eighties seems fitting, particularly given both the often neoconservative agendas of such texts[3] and the shifting alignment of the spectator's gaze. This is not to suggest that apparently ideologically recuperative productions lack the potential, in spite of themselves, to advance progressive political perspectives. As Douglas Kellner notes, even the most 'conservative' horror films not only 'put on display both the significant dreams and nightmares of a culture and the ways that the culture is attempting to channel them to maintain its present relations of power and domination', but also expose the 'hopes and fears that contest dominant hegemonic and hierarchical relations of power' (1995: 111). Nevertheless, the US horror film icons Shimizu cites as inspirational (*A Nightmare on Elm Street's* Freddie Kruger and *Friday the 13th's* Jason), as well as the slasher film/ 'stalker cycle' sub-genre from which they arise, are veritable repositories of 'repressed body anxiety[ies]…erupting with a vengeance' (Dery 1997: 233). In this sense, even if these films from which Shimizu borrows seemingly promote a certain political or ideological agenda by 'punishing' certain behaviours (for instance, sexual promiscuity, or drug

---

[3] See Sharrett, C. (1993) 'The Horror Film in Neoconservative Culture', *Journal of Popular Film and Television*, vol. 21 no. 3, 1993, pp. 100-110.

use) while 'rewarding' others (chastity, self-reliance, the willingness to resort to violence when necessary),[4] it remains possible also to view these texts as engaging in 'an unprecedented assault on all that Bourgeois culture is supposed to cherish – like ideological apparatuses of the family and the school' (Modleski 1986: 158).

As with the US horror tradition that influenced Shimizu, it is possible to interpret *Ju-on:The Grudge* as both conservative and progressive; in this way, Shimizu's film exposes a myriad of the socio-cultural anxieties that permeate Japan's increasingly hybrid, transitional culture. At times, the film's articulation of an apparent nostalgia for disappearing 'traditions' in the face of an emerging 'modern' socio-economic climate resonates with a conservative ideology that borders on the reactionary. A somber, Ozu-like meditation on generational differences and the collapse of the extended family finds expression in the disquieting image of a neglected elderly woman sitting passively near her own feces-soiled bedding, while in other scenes, incompetent social workers and inept law enforcement officers suffer the demonic Kayako and Toshio's wrath. But Shimizu's film also advances a critique of a Japan still very much steeped in patriarchal conventions. While their return to haunt the realm of the living evokes the 'avenging spirit' motif familiar to viewers of Japanese horror cinema, Kayako and Toshio's ultimately uncontainable wrath suggests an irrepressible hostility towards an abusive and antiquated 'official culture, specifically…the norms and values of patriarch[y]' (Creed, 1995: 132). This latter gesture, as Barbara Creed notes, recurs consistently in Western horror cinema, often revealing a 'symbolic', anti-authoritarian hostility towards an inflexible 'social body' (146).

What sets *Ju-on: The Grudge* apart from other works of Japanese horror cinema, and what might be most responsible for the film's international appeal, is the filmic and trans-cultural hybridity embodied by the figures of Kayako and Toshio. Not quite ghosts in the strictest sense of the *onryou* or *kaidan* tradition, but not quite conventional

---

[4] For a more advanced and specific expansion of this premise, see Dika (1987) and Clover (1992).

biological monsters either, this other-worldly, mother-centered family merges a dangerous corporeality (they can physically attack and manipulate their victim's bodies), with an eerie spectral quality without adhering absolutely to one convention or the other. Furthermore, this uncanny mother and son become even more disturbing, as well as less exclusively linked to Japanese horror cinema, when one factors in Shimizu's masterful camera work and brilliant control of the film's *mise-en-scène*.

In keeping with 'classic' and contemporary works of Japanese horror, Shimizu allows tension to build slowly, almost contemplatively, throughout *Ju-on: The Grudge*'s numerous, non-linear episodes. Many of the expected, culturally specific trappings of filmic terror are present: long black tresses framing wide staring eyes, ominous *tatami* shots of sliding closet doors, shadowy apparitions that render their human victims virtually paralysed with fear. However, true to his roots as 'an eighties splatter movie kid' (Macias 2003, para 18), Shimizu also incorporates a slasher/ 'stalker' film aesthetic throughout *Ju-on: The Grudge*, most obviously via the occasional alignment of the viewer's gaze with not only the central protagonist's perspective, but that of Kakayo and Toshio as well. Such compositions and camera movement allows us, by turns, to 'stalk' and 'be stalked', a visual motif almost exclusively applied to what Shimizu refers to as 'splatter movies' or 'monster stories' (para 18). This collision of 'an American and Japanese style' (para 18) creates a cinematic hybrid that appeals to viewers familiar with the visual iconography and cinematography of both Japanese and US horror cinema.

Lastly, by vacillating between limiting what we see and revealing the objects of our fear in groundbreaking ways that separate him aesthetically from other directors, Shimizu creates a text that may very well alter forever the way that some viewers process cinematic horror. By frequently relegating frightening images to the extreme edges of the frame, as fleeting, yet troubling figures glimpsed peripherally but never completely, Shimizu artfully manipulates the audience's gaze, creating the impression that we may have just witnessed a flash of something disquieting – as if from the corner of our collective eye. During other moments, most particularly the climactic sequences that inevitably bring each of the film's episodes to a sudden close, Shimizu culminates our rising dread by propelling us face to face with Kayako and Toshio in all their monstrous alterity. Finally, *Ju-on: The Grudge* is a film that disallows its characters and, by extension, its audience, access to those conventional 'safe spaces' to which people most commonly retreat when the tension escalates or becomes too much to take. Peering through the fingers covering one's face does not distance the imperiled characters from that which is frightening; rather, it forces immediate confrontation with the horrific. Likewise, pulling the covers up over one's head does not provide a buffer zone but, instead, reveals that the monster you most fear has been in the bed with you the whole time.

Image 9: A doomed social worker tends to a neglected parent in Shimizu Takashi's *Ju-on: The Grudge* (Courtesy: beyondhollywood.com)

Covering Adaptations

As notions of transformation (both thematic and cultural) and the variable impacts of trans-cultural generic debt inform the analyses that constitute the bulk of this chapter, I would be remiss if I did not at least acknowledge that the three films examined in the previous pages –

Nakata Hideo's *Ringu* and *Dark Water*, and Shimizu Takashi's *Ju-on: The Grudge* – have each spawned Hollywood remakes that, while meeting with varying degrees of financial and critical success, nonetheless illustrate Japanese horror cinema's influence upon global horror cinema's visual and narratological landscape. As a Western film critic with an avid interest in horror film's shifting tropologies, encountering this 'new wave' of contemporary horror cinema reinvigorated my interest in a genre that had become depressingly stagnant. Aside from a few truly groundbreaking texts, many of which sailed well under the radar of the handful of distributors that fast-track their wares into the majority of multiplexes and chain stores (both retail- and rental-based) world-wide, Western horror cinema at the millennium's cusp had become stuck in a viscous feedback loop of uninspired sequels reiterating the same tired formulae, or mired in a kitschy postmodern self-referentiality that winked a little too obviously at its own cleverness as it simultaneously mocked and celebrated the plurality of clichés their narratives ironically, and inevitably, reproduced. This is not to suggest that the iconography that permeates Japanese horror cinema emerged without recognisable precursors, nor have they elided the market pressures that lead producers and distributors to pressure directors for 'more of the same'. As mentioned earlier, many of the motifs in these films can be traced back (at least) to Japan's *kabuki* and *noh* theatrical traditions. Similarly, as Japanese directors like Kurosawa Kiyoshi, Nakata Hideo, and Shimizu Takashi were weaned, to various extents, upon the works of Tobe Hooper, John Carpenter, and Wes Craven, perceptive audiences can't help but discern traces of these notable Western horror auteurs' visions within the *mise-en-scène* and, to a lesser extent, the narratives of Japan's latest generation of horror maestros.

When *The Ring* (2002), Gore Verbinski's Hollywood remake of Nakata's *Ringu*, opened in theatres across North America, more than a few Japanese horror fans held their collective breath, anxious to see how well Nakata's film (itself an adaptation of Suzuki Koji's 1991 novel) would translate for Western audiences. As Matt Hill's excellent essay, 'Ringing in the Changes: Cult Distinctions and Cultural Difference in US Fans' Readings of Japanese Horror Cinema', illustrates, Verbinski's version met with mixed reactions among internet-based Japanese horror fans, many of which were divided less in terms of the film's artistic merit than in terms of which version they had seen first (2005: 161-75). Many film critics and horror movie fans found Verbinksi's film both compelling and frightening; it grossed over three billion dollars in US box office receipts alone (Internet Movie Database 2006), assuring that a Hollywood-produced sequel would soon follow. As expected, debates inevitably arose over why Verbinski changed certain elements of Nakata's 'original' Japanese version, as if the term 'remake' implies that successful transcultural adaptations should be largely faithful reconstructions rather than a process of re-visioning or re-imagining that allows larger, perhaps even wholesale reconceptualisations of the material based upon social and cultural disparities. Perhaps, then, as the products of Japanese and other East Asian cinemas continue to find themselves queued for eventual Hollywood refashioning/regurgitation, it is time for film scholars to revisit the aesthetics and politics of adaptation, perhaps envisioning such texts as 'covers' (to borrow a term from music criticism), or as 'variations on a theme', rather than merely visual and narratological translations of a 'foreign' text for a 'domestic' market. If Hollywood's dominant economic logics render remakes of successful Asian horror films virtual inevitabilities, perhaps it is time to perceive such adaptations as musicians approach the recreation of jazz standards from their own unique ethno-musicological positions. Doing so may allow filmmakers to assess the new visual and narrative 'arrangements' on their own merits.

That said, this chapter's conclusion turns its critical attention, if only briefly, towards *The Grudge* (2004), Shimizu Takashi's Hollywood-funded reworking of *Ju-on: The Grudge*, a text whose premise and visual style, as mentioned earlier, has been reconceptualised several times for television and theatrical release. Unlike the Hollywood versions of Nakata Hideo's *Ringu* and *Dark Water*, which transport the film's action from Japan to recognisably Western – albeit still uncanny – locations, Shimizu, retaining a substantial degree of creative control over his motion picture franchise, elected to set his film in urban Japan. Although much of the cast, including *Buffy the Vampire Slayer* star Sarah Michelle Gellar and popular character actor Bill Pullman, hail from the US, Shimizu chose to lens many of the film's scenes within the same eerie and disheveled environments that lent his previous *Ju-on* films an air of palpable dread. Clearly, this decision has notable benefits, not the least of which is the ability to capitalise upon the familiar (for Shimizu) geography of Japanese homes and thus, when possible, recreate specific scenes without having to account for architectural differences specific to Western abodes. Likewise, the lack of social and cultural familiarity with which the main (Western) characters that populate Shimizu's Hollywood-backed 'variation on the *Ju-on* theme' must contend serves to heighten their anxiety, turning simple walks into isolating and dread inducing sojourns through crowded, labyrinthine streets and alleyways: 'I went for a walk,' one of the US-raised female characters remarks while voicing her unease to her sympathetic husband, '…and I got so lost and I couldn't find anyone who spoke English that could help me.'

Similarly, everyday events, from the removal of one's shoes upon entering a home ('Even in your own house?' a Western character inquires with a tinge of disbelief) to the observation of an elderly Japanese couple reciting Buddhist prayers, are transformed into exotic spectacles accompanied by conspicuous exposition that, while useful for explaining cultural particularities for many non-Asian viewers, simultaneously functions to exacerbate the Western characters' (and, thus, the Western audience's) sense of discomfort and alienation. This does not necessarily make for a 'poor' or 'ineffective' re-visioning of the *Ju-on* conceit. Indeed, maintaining a Japanese setting avoids the potentially irrevocable alteration of mood and tone that may accompany the transposition of a distinctly Japanese narrative, with its distinctly Japanese cultural resonances, into a variously analogous filmic moment specifically coded for Western audiences. In addition, reworking the source text by populating the narrative with displaced US citizens allows the film to function as a subtle, yet telling critique of US cultural hegemony. At the same time, however, by re-imaging his narrative through the lens of Western characters as 'outsiders navigating their way through an unfamiliar social sphere', Shimizu risks opening his narrative to Orientalist readings of Japan as a 'monstrous other', a strange and estranging environment rendered threatening through its very difference. As such, Shimizu risks transforming the vengeful spirits at the film's core into merely one more manifestation of a culture abjectified through its radical and threatening unfamiliarity. Thus, rather than functioning as the return of a repressed feminine identity or as a creative barometer for social change at the turn of the millennium, the *onryou* of Shimizu's *The Grudge* may be interpreted as constituting the ultimate metaphoric representation of a seemingly irreconcilable alterity. Shimizu risks, in other words, morphing his vengeful spirits – and Japan itself – into abstracted entities, monsters that, in their radical difference, threaten the imagined cultural, psychic, and physical cohesion of the decidedly non-Asian characters with whom Western audiences are invited, if not ultimately forced, to identify.

Chapter Four:
A Murder of Doves:
Youth Violence and the Rites of
Passing in Contemporaray
Japanese Horror Cinema

Bloody Doves

In their invaluable resource, *Japanese Cinema Encyclopedia: Horror, Fantasy, and Science Fiction Films*, Thomas Weisser and Yuko Mihara Weisser use the term 'dove style violence' to describe a trend within contemporary Japanese cinema in which human beings coldly abuse one another with a detached cruelty reminiscent of 'certain species of bird' who, when 'a flock member is *different* or weaker...peck at the weakest bird dispassionately until it's dead' (1997: 21, emphasis theirs). 'Dove style violence', however, has yet to receive the critical attention it deserves, especially in terms of its representation within Japanese cinema in general and Japanese horror cinema in particular. This chapter seeks to address this critical oversight by focusing upon, and hopefully initiating future discussions regarding the bleak, nihilistic, and often graphically rendered motif of *ijime* (bullying) and 'dove style violence' in Japanese horror cinema. Of course, bullying is by no means a specifically Japanese cultural phenomenon, nor is its visual representation limited to works of filmic horror. Nevertheless, representations of 'bullying' and related violence *do* share visual and narratological logics with popular works of contemporary international horror cinema; indeed, considering horror film's predilection for depicting acts of explicit violence, psychological torment, and revenge (a motivation central to numerous 'slasher' and rape-revenge story arcs), this chapter's examination of the deployment of such physical and psychological persecution is one that is long overdue.

In the pages to follow, this chapter positions Iwai Shunji's beautiful (if brutal) meditation on *ijime*, *All About Lily Chou-Chou* (*Riri Shushu no subete*, 2001), as a catalyst for a detailed exploration of Matsumura Katsuya's dark, ultra-violent, and highly controversial *All Night Long* series (*All Night Long* [*Ooru naito rongu*, 1992], *All Night Long 2: Atrocity* [*Ooru naito rongu 2: Sanji*, 1994], and *All Night Long 3: Atrocities* [*Ooru naito rongu 3: Saishuu*-shô, 1996]).[1] As graphic representations of postmodern alienation and the callous mistreatment of others taken to their direst terminuses, both *All About Lily Chou-Chou* and the *All Night Long* series approach *ijime*'s quasi-Darwinian destruction of the weak by the strong(er) through variably intimate and harrowing depictions of the shattered lives of desperate, often jaded or disaffected young people who, as if abiding by the dictates of an inescapable 'animalistic' or 'human' nature, perpetrate acts of deliberate cruelty upon those least able to marshal a defense. In the process, Iwai's *All About Lily Chou-Chou* and Matsumura's *All Night Long* series present viewers with protagonists that embody the most destructive and extreme consequences of an emerging cultural moment informed by, among other social conditions: scholastic competition, economic recovery and recession, and recent shifts in gender codes.

Building from these analyses of the politics of *ijime* and 'dove style violence', this chapter concludes with a detailed consideration of the 'sadomasochistic' splatterfest, *Ichi the Killer* (*Koroshiya 1*, 2001), a film by one of contemporary Japanese cinema's most inventive filmmakers and provocateurs, Miike Takashi. Among Miike's better known films in

---

[1] Since 2002, Matsumura has directed two additional entries into the *All Night Long* series: *All Night Long 4* (*Ooru naito rongu R*, 2004) and *All Night Long 5: Initial 0* (*Ooru naito rongu: Inisharu O*, 2003).

the West, second perhaps only to his much discussed art-house *guignol*, *Audition* (*Ôdishon*, 1999), this hyper-kinetic, genre-bending spectacle offers its audience nothing less than a self-reflexive, ultra-violent *yakuza eiga* / splatter film jacked up on methamphetamines. Throughout *Ichi the Killer*, Miike locates 'dove style' violence as a component of a larger paradigmatic cycle of violence and suffering permeating contemporary Japanese culture. In his tale of Kakihara, the masochistic sadist, and Ichi, the film's eponymous crybaby vigilante, Miike presents a counter-cinematic spectacle that overthrows a multiplicity of ontological regimes, exposing, in the process, the masochistic dynamics informing not only the basest symbiotic exchanges in everyday human interactions, but also the very construction of identity itself.

Ijime and the Popular Imaginary:
Iwai Shunji's *All About Lily Chou-Chou*

In Iwai Shunji's award winning *All About Lily Chou-Chou*,[2] a tall, slender high school student named Hoshino Shusuke[3] befriends an introverted fellow student named Hasumi Yuichi. A victim himself of bullying at his former school, Hoshino returns from a short vacation in Okinawa – during which he almost drowns – with a frightening resolve. His angst aggravated by the collapse of his family's textile enterprise, Hoshino soon physically defeats and subsequently humiliates the class bully. In short order, Hoshino becomes not only class president, but also a mini-tyrant whose brutal reign includes acts of physical violence directed towards assorted 'peers', the blackmailing/pimping of a pretty young girl named Shiori, and the brutal, chaotically-lensed gang rape of Kuno Yoko, a talented pianist whose incredible skill and beauty have elicited the ire of a collection of bitter and vicious classmates. A stunning and complex work

---

[2] In 2002, Iwai Shunji's *All About Lily Chou-Chou* won the C.I.C.A.E. Award at the Berlin International Film Festival, and both the Special Jury Award and the Golden Goblet (for best music) at the Shanghai International Film Festival

[3] In keeping with the name his 'peers' use throughout the film, I hereafter refer to Hoshino Shusuke as simply 'Hoshino'.

described by *Los Angeles Times* reviewer Kevin Thomas as emotionally 'jarring' (para 15) and 'profoundly disturbing' (para 1), *All About Lily Chou-Chou*, though not a horror film in the most conventional sense of the term, contains some of the most unsettling depictions of cruelty, and its consequences, ever recorded. It also explores the multiple social and cultural continuities and discontinuities that inform the destructive, antisocial behaviours of the 'dangerously disaffected' (para 15) characters populating not only Iwai's *tour-de-force*, but also several of the darker, more harrowing works of contemporary Japanese horror cinema.

     As the widespread practice of *ijime*, or bullying, is one of Iwai's primary concerns in *All About Lily Chou-Chou*, a brief exploration of some of the socio-cultural factors behind this pervasive and disconcerting phenomenon is in order. As Sugimoto Yoshio explains in his book, *An Introduction to Japanese Society*, incidents of *ijime*, though faintly declining in recent years, has been 'rampant in schools since the mid 1980s, the very time when Japan's economic performance became the envy of other industrialized nations'(Sujimoto 2002: 127). As we shall soon see, however, its roots may in fact be much older and run far deeper. A collective – rather than individuated – activity (though often one person's agenda emerges as dominant), *ijime* is an all-too-prevalent process by which: 'a group of pupils...humiliate, disgrace, or torment a targeted pupil psychologically, verbally, or physically. In most cases of *ijime*, a considerable portion of pupils in a certain class take part as supporting actors' (127). In this sense, *ijime*, as Sugimoto points out, differs from conventional notions of juvenile delinquency. Rather than being limited to the vile machinations of one or two students dedicated to bringing 'ignominity upon a minority of one' (127), *ijime* is distressingly expansive, with 'a strong group' gaining 'satisfaction from the anguish of a pupil in a weak and disadvantaged position', often out of a 'fear of being chosen as targets themselves' (127). As a social practice, *ijime* remains a significant aspect of contemporary Japanese culture, frequently reflecting the larger culture's 'pressures of conformity and ostracism' (128).

     In *The Japanese Mind: Understanding Contemporary Japanese Culture*, Roger J. Davies and Osamu Ikeno further illuminate some of the motivational factors behind instances of *ijime*. In their discussion of *wa*, or the concept of harmony in Japanese life, Davies and Ikeno note that notions of 'geographical determinism', enhanced by Japan's isolation as a chain of islands, have impacted a myriad of interpersonal and social behaviours, including the practice of *ijime*. As a result, an ideology privileging both hierarchy and community has emerged. In particular, Davies and Ikeno note that:

> [T]he social structure of Japan developed a vertical organization that stresses one's place within the group and in which one's rank or status is clearly distinguishable...Because such a framework includes people with many different characteristics, a form of unity in which all people aim for the same goal is important for the group and is strictly enforced. This strong group consciousness brings about a feeling of "in or out" (*uchi-soto*) (2002: 10-11)

As one might expect, such rigidly dualistic thinking – one is either 'in' or 'out', either a part of 'the group' or 'an outsider' – increases the cultural connotations of 'conformity' and 'ostracism'; consequently, students strive for acceptance as a member of the larger social whole and fear rejection, in which – for often ambiguous reasons – they may be isolated from, or outright rejected by, the majority (Sugimoto 2002: 128). Furthermore, *ijime* frequently assumes 'a "soft" form...damaging victims psychologically' (128). Sometimes misconstrued as 'playful rather than manifestly violent', *ijime* can transpire without capturing the attention of authority figures, and it is not uncommon for teachers and law enforcement to sanction bullying. As cultural anthropologists such as Peter Cave demonstrate, one can link bullying with ritualised traditions that, stemming back to some of the earliest samurai codes, find articulation in cultural practices ranging from the organisation of school clubs (*bukatsudō*) around militaristic ideals, to the construction of the image of the 'corporate warrior' (*kigyō senshi*) during Japan's most successful period of economic recovery (Cave 2004: 412).

Like Fukusaku Kinji's penultimate film and splatter-fest, *Battle Royale* (2000), in which a class of students are fixed with exploding collars, armed with assorted weapons, and placed on a deserted island from which only one class member may leave alive, Iwai Shunji's *All About Lily Chou-Chou* reveals the darker side of a capitalist system propelled by a 'philosophy of individual competition, which sets one person against another' (Williams 2005: 141), and in which a 'winner' emerges only if a 'loser' falls. By chronologically juxtaposing the revelation of Hoshino's victimisation at his previous school and the failure of his family's textile business with Hoshino's rise to power among his fellow classmates, Iwai's film links radical economic transition and generational dissociation with cycles of *ijime*. The abused/victim may, given the right circumstances, become the greatest abuser/victimizer; similarly, the bully's position of power may be less secure than s/he imagines. Importantly, Iwai's *All About Lily Chou-Chou* disallows easy binary categorisations of characters as 'good' or 'bad'; some characters may elicit more sympathy than others, but the motivations behind their actions are seldom, if ever, incomprehensible. Therefore, even though Hoshino's orders – disseminated throughout a complex chain of command – culminate in violent rampages and suicidal leaps, his inner turmoil still resonates powerfully with many viewers. When a crane shot swoops down from above and circles Hoshino's lone figure screaming with a visceral fusion of rage and grief, the image Iwai captures is not that of a heartless bully, but that of an isolated human being in a state of severe emotional turmoil.

The anonymity of the internet, coupled with the appeal of pop star Lily Chou-Chou's ethereal music, provides characters with an ironic form of 'escape' from the routine violence and rigid social hierarchies of everyday life in the 'real world'. In the virtual world, Hasumi Yuichi, the film's central protagonist and a victim of bullying, manages a popular fan-based Lily Chou-Chou web site and discussion board. As on-line Lily 'expert' named 'LilyPhilia', Yuichi finds the community, support, and respect absent from his daily school and family life. However, the refuge provided by the web site, like each of the 'relationships' it enables, is fleeting. Fan postings appear either sporadically or in manic torrents, and although exchanges of ideas and messages of sympathetic encouragement occasionally flicker across his computer monitor, Yuichi must eventually venture outside. When he does, the realm he encounters differs radically from the virtual, idealistic haven in which the only requirement for membership and, thus, acceptance is an appreciation of, or curiosity about, Lily Chou-Chou. Additionally, although his Lily Chou-Chou site at once provides Yuichi with an *otaku*-like retreat from real world confrontations, and functions as a temporary respite from his overwhelming loneliness, such a virtual space is ultimately paradoxical; while the film's many characters construct identities both on- and off-line, and while Yuichi's web site seemingly allows for substantial and apparently heart-felt interchanges, internet relationships effect little to no change in the characters' increasingly hostile material existence. As the elegant crane and tracking shots of individual characters standing alone in expansive green fields and listening to Lily Chou-Chou's music on portable CD players suggest, although Lily Chou-Chou's art and persona permits the recognition of beauty in the midst of socio-cultural dissolution (*aware*), a rudimentary, profound and all-too-real alienation continues unabated. Each character in these memorable sequences is overwhelmingly alone, their isolation rendered even more acute by the breadth of negative space their solitary physiques engender within the *mise-en-scène*.

Given this paradox, 'The Ether', the phrase Lily Chou-Chou fans use to describe the nebulous power and/or mystical essence surrounding the pop idol's art and 'soul', is a particularly appropriate descriptor since many of Lily Chou-Chou's fans experience her music as a kind of opiate through which they reduce the pain of the emotional scars accrued over the course of their lives in a transforming and highly competitive capitalist culture. Like many religions or powerful narcotics, 'The Ether' that Lily fans construct provides the illusion of hope and a sense of something that transcends the grim social realities and hierarchies awaiting them the moment they 'log off' of their computers' internet services or press stop on their portable CD players. In a sequence that makes this dynamic chillingly explicit, the 'real world' and the virtual world of the internet and 'The Ether' collide with a force that momentarily obliterates the façade to which the Lily fans we encounter throughout the film cling. This crash occurs when Hoshino (who, we discover, has been posting on Yuichi's Lily Chou-Chou web site as a Lily fan named 'BlueCat') steals Yuichi's prized ticket to a Lily Chou-Chou concert, a theft that finally pushes Yuichi too far. Creating a diversion by

pretending that he sees Lily greeting some of her fans, Yuichi walks up
behind Hoshino and stabs his tormentor in the back with a knife.
Hoshino's (and Yuichi's) tragic fall brings Iwai's film to a close and,
according to Lily's fans, corrupts 'The Ether'. In addition, although the
film's final scene depicts a troubled Yuichi listening to the piano stylings
of Kuno Yoko (who, earlier in the narrative, reacts to the nightmarish
gang rape at her classmate's hands by personally butchering her beautiful
raven tresses), spectators are left with little reason for believing that
Yuichi and Kuno will connect in a meaningful way. Nor does Iwai's film
close with the suggestion that the practice of *ijime*, which has resulted in
so much anguish, will end any time soon.

Image 10: Hoshino Shusuke screams in abject despair in Iwaii Shunji's *All about Lily Chou-Chou* **(© Home Vision)**

Atrocity Exhibitions: 'Dove Style Violence' and Corporeal Corruption in Matsumura Katsuya's *All Night Long* Series

Thomas and Yuko Mihara Weisser's term, 'dove style violence', is
particularly appropriate in its realisation of a quasi-Darwinian thematic

within contemporary Japanese horror cinema that not only depicts the 'human' as 'animal', but also reveals human interaction as founded upon a logic of 'survival of the fittest'. This perspective underlies many of the capitalist and militaristic discourses that not only informed Japan's economic miracle of the 1970s and 1980s, but also impacted social practices, from education to daily interpersonal exchanges. Additionally, as discussed in the preceding section's analysis of Iwai Shunji's *All About Lily Chou-Chou*, the binary rubric – 'in or out' (*uchi-soto*) – finds regular articulation through the practice of *ijime*, particularly given bullying's privileging of those 'in' the group over the 'outsider', who is often violently ostracised for being deemed too weak for, or somehow undeserving of, a place within the dominant social order. But to what extent is the binary inside/outside, as a discursive construction, operant in contemporary Japanese culture? Additionally, how might notoriously brutal films like Matsumura Katsuya's *All Night Long* series, to which the term 'dove style violence' was initially applied, simultaneously re-inscribe such dualistic thinking while challenging long-held illusions of the corporeal and/or social body as a cohesive formation?

Matsumura Katsuya's *All Night Long* series has yet to receive the intensive critical attention enjoyed by more recent works of Japanese horror cinema, like Nakata Hideo's *Ringu* and *Dark Water*, and Shimizu Takeshi's *Ju-on: The Grudge*. Even the much maligned *Guinea Pig* films explored in this book's first chapter have received more frequent and extensive critiques, even if the vast majority of these explorations have been limited to fan-based internet sites dedicated to Japanese horror cinema. Curiously, it is to the infamous *Guinea Pig* films that Matsumura's *All Night Long* series is most often compared. For example, cultural mythologies or urban legends constellate around both filmic cycles, and in the history of their public reception, the *All Night Long* series resembles the *Guinea Pig* films in that each series' domestic and international reputations were enhanced or, depending on one's tolerance for graphic violence, variably stigmatised by knee-jerk reactions to the films' 'realistic' depictions of the human (primarily female) body graphically dismantled. As well, the *Guinea Pig* and *All Night Long* series benefited from the assorted hype and potentially purposeful misinformation accompanying the texts' circulation through generations of bootleg VHS and DVD copies. As Japanese film scholar Tom Mes notes in his review of *All Night Long 2: Atrocity*, the second and third features in the *All Night Long* series were rumored to have been condemned by *Eirin*, Japan's official censorship board, because of the works' 'unacceptable tone', a highly subjective and nebulous denunciation at best. The extent to which the filmmakers and distributors of the *All Night Long* series contributed to the cautionary discourse surrounding the films is open to question and, unfortunately, exceeds the scope of this chapter's project. Nevertheless, the notoriety the films garnered certainly impacted many spectators' viewing experiences, and the works' straight-to-video aesthetics, especially when viewed in relation to the texts' grim plots, position the works as contentious visions orchestrated to shock those who deem themselves 'up to the challenge' of screening them.

Before commencing upon a reading of the *All Night Long* series and its increasingly nihilistic portraits of alienated youth in 1990s Japan, consider the following plot summaries:

All Night Long (1992): Three socially maladjusted teenagers meet at a train crossing. While waiting for the train to pass, they witness the random murder of a young woman by a male assailant armed with a large butcher knife. The three teenage witnesses include: (1) Saito Shinji – a seventeen year old vocational high school student whose night classes have failed to net him a job at a local airport; (2) Suzuki Kensuke – a nineteen year old man with 'no occupation' and recurring suicidal fantasies; and (3) Tanaka Tetsuya – a meek, intelligent, overworked, and socially awkward (especially around women) '*Eiko-ga-oka* Private School Senior'. The three teens form a loose friendship and agree to meet a few weeks later at Kensuke's apartment for a party to which each must bring a woman as a date. Tetsuya falls for a female student named Riei and seeks the guidance of his classmate, Tamari, an obnoxious young man with a knack for seducing and manipulating women. As the party approaches, Tetsuya's grades begin to plummet, and he soon realises that Tamari, who claims to be preparing a way for Tetsuya to meet Riei, is surreptitiously sleeping with Riei. On the evening of the party, Tetsuya attempts to ask her out, but he ends up humiliating himself when he vomits on her instead. Kensuke has even worse luck. After meeting a woman he believes to be little more than a prostitute, on the night of the party he, too, is humiliated when the woman chains him to a fence outside of a factory, kicks his crotch repeatedly, pours a bottle of cheap champagne over his head, and leaves him stranded and with his pants at his knees. Lastly, Shinji sabotages a young woman's (Yôko's) bicycle, comes to her 'rescue', and they strike up a close friendship complete with stolen kisses backed by a syrupy pop soundtrack. On the night of the party, however, they are jumped by a gang that Shinji once watched set fire to a small animal. This gang beats Shinji, holds him down, and forces him to watch as they continuously rape and batter Yôko. Thirsty for revenge and eager to rebuild their decimated senses of masculinity, Shinji, Kensuke, and Tetsuya arm themselves with a rifle and attack the group of thugs at the thugs' hideout. A bloodbath inevitably ensues, from which only the once docile Tetsuya emerges, psychologically transformed into a ruthless killing machine.

All Night Long 2: Atrocity (1994): The second film in Matsumura Katsuya's dire series bears some striking resemblances to the first. Consider, for example, the main protagonist's character arc; an introverted *otaku* obsessed with building models of overtly sexualised female *manga* characters, Shinichi transforms into a vengeful murderer bent on killing the ruthless rapist bullies whose leader, a wealthy, brutal, and charismatic homosexual, clearly has designs on seducing Shinichi. When Shinichi recruits several 'friends' from the internet to help him defeat this vicious gang of thugs, the film's action quickly spirals into a gore-drenched finale destined to test the collective fortitudes of even the most die-hard horror aficionados. Perhaps the best crafted film in the series, *All Night Long 2: Atrocity* further addresses the themes of *ijime*, masculinity, and violence raised in 1992's *All Night Long*.

All Night Long 3: Atrocities (1996): Sawada Kikuo, a painfully shy employee at a seedy love hotel, spends his days cleaning up used condoms and tangled sheets. A voyeur, he peers through bushes at high school girls humiliating a horribly scarred female classmate, ogles some of the hotel's rutting customers through the slots in the building's ventilation grates (a predilection he shares with an older woman who helps run the establishment), collects pubic hairs from the hotel room's crumpled bedding, and captures flies to feed his assortment of carnivorous plants – the latter a practice that depicts nature as at once beautiful, indifferent, ugly, and deadly. Not long into the film, Kikuo becomes obsessed with a beautiful neighbor, Nomura Hitomi. Taking a cue from a fellow 'Dusthunter'/garbage forager, Kikuo begins collecting intimate items from Nomura's garbage. Among the items he gathers are discarded toothbrushes, blood-soaked maxipads and tampons, strands of hair, and pieces of half-eaten food upon which Kikuo subsequently feasts. As the film progresses, several of Kikuo's fellow workers catch a young woman, Tane Kaoru, stealing from one of the love hotel's clients. Rather than turning her into the police, they drag her into a garbage dump and rape her repeatedly. When one of the workers, a mentally-challenged young man, repeatedly smashes the young woman's head with a jagged piece of concrete, the workers scatter, leaving Kaoru for dead. Kikuo, true to form, secretly watches the sexual assault from a distance. Within seconds after his fellow employees flee the scene, he picks up the wounded woman and conveys her back to his tiny apartment. There, he keeps meticulous records of the brutalised thief's biological functions. When she finally regains consciousness enough to tell him that he is 'just filth!', he strangles and dismembers her. Additionally, Kikuo's attempts to woo Nomura Hitomi fail, and when he realizes that she had become merely another conquest for one of the love hotel's regular customers, he goes on a bloody killing spree.

Shot on video like the *Guinea Pig* films, the *All Night Long* series differs from larger budgeted horror films in that the images possess verist immediacy comparable to home video or television news footage. Such a *mise-en-scène* conveys the illusion of objectivity that Yiman Wang, evoking Raymond Williams, describes as conveying the illusion of 'social experiences that are still *in process*, "present and affective," often not yet recognized as social and political' (Wang 2005: 22). Additionally, 'containing special effects' that, in the words of one enthusiastic reviewer, are sure to 'have any gore fan applauding at the high calibre of graphic talent on show' (Simpson 2005: para 4), Matsumura's films borrow elements from both the *pinku eiga* (pink films) tradition and, especially in the series' first two narratives, the rape-revenge genre.[4] Like many works designated as *pinku eiga*, the *All Night Long* series contains instances of bondage, rape, and humiliation largely directed towards women and, consequently, may lead viewers to dismiss Matsumura's works as merely variations of the sexually-violent patriarchal fantasies that critics like James R. Alexander and Andrew Grossman attribute to the more 'conservative' or 'bridled' works of Japanese soft core pornography (Grossman 2002: para 7). Similarly, given the 'fluidity in the conventional text of the rape-revenge genre' and its ability to explore a 'range of innocence violated – from individual to cosmic' (Alexander 2005: para 7), *All Night Long* and *All Night Long 2: Atrocity* evoke comparisons to films like Meir Zarchi's *I Spit on Your Grave* (1978) and Abel Ferrara's *Ms. 45* (1981). In the first two entries of Matsumura's series, for instance, male protagonists, pushed too far by the callous cruelty of a gang of bullies, seek retribution for the degrading acts perpetrated against them, or against characters with whom they have established personal connections. Of course, the central protagonists'/ ictims' gender sets these texts apart from conventional rape-revenge films, but the narrative trajectories are, nevertheless, quite comparable. This is not to suggest, however, that the *All Night Long* films fit comfortably within such generic categories. As will become apparent through a consideration of the series' first and third installments, Matsumura's cinematic studies of 'the effects of urban alienation' (Mes 2001: para 1) inevitably lead to a filmic deconstruction of the simple

---

[4] Unlike most rape-revenge films, the vengeful parties in *All Night Long* and *All Night Long 2: Atrocity* are male. Furthermore, unlike films such as Meir Zarchi's I Spit on Your Grave (USA, 1978) and Ishii Takashi's *Freeze Me* (2000), Matsumura's series does not take female empowerment as a primary concern.

binary logics that inform the practices of *ijime* and 'dove style violence' in the first place.

As the brief plot summary above suggests, the first *All Night Long* film engages transforming conceptualisations of masculinity during the on-set of the economic recession that followed the bursting of the Japanese economic 'bubble' economy in the late 1980s and early 1990s. Specifically, the themes of failure and impotence permeate the film's action. Each of the three central male characters – Saito Shinji, Suzuki Kensuke, and Tenaka Tetsuya – represents a stereotype of Japanese masculinity, presenting the audience with archetypal figures negotiating their way through a generalised microcosm of contemporary Japan. Moreover, the film's opening sequence locates our three 'heroes' as failures: Shinji is unsuccessful in his attempt to solder together two thin metal bars; Kensuke misses a putt on his portable putting green; and Tetsuya, rushing to make it to class on time, arrives at the subway platform mere seconds after the train's doors have closed and the cars have begun to roll away. In addition, discourses of strength and weakness dominate many of the conversations. Tetsuya's obnoxious mentor, Tamari, for example, states that being homeless, or even a worn-out 'salaryman', is an increasingly common status that, similar to being born female, positions an individual as 'lower' and, thus, deserving of exploitation. 'They look like crummy little worms,' Tamari says, peering down from a second story window, '[t]hat's why I use them. The weak really shouldn't inherit the world.' Additionally, when Tetsuya expresses reservations regarding Tamari's casual remarks about 'using' others for his own purposes, Tamari responds with, '[d]on't worry, I only use females', a statement that reveals a misogynist agenda not surprising in a series so widely cited for its persistently misanthropic content.

Tamari's reference to the 'crummy little worms' to whom he feels superior also provides an excellent example of the quasi-Darwinian consumption of the perceived weak by those who are either physically stronger, or who assume an air of entitlement because of their social or educational status. Furthermore, although women are frequently victimised throughout the series, they are by no means exclusively passive, as Yoshiko, Kensuke's date turned assailant, illustrates:

Yoshiko: (Giggling and handcuffing one of Kensuke's wrists to a chain-link fence.) We're just animals...You don't have to pretend.

Kensuke: Wait! Don't! You've got strange tastes.

Yoshiko: I like this kind of thing. (She pulls Kensuke's pants down to his knees.) Are you ready?

Kensuke: Shouldn't we do this somewhere else and take our time?

Yoshiko: Shut up you pig! (She kicks Kensuke between his legs.) Listen, let me tell you what I hate.

Kensuke: Er...what?

Yoshiko: I hate kids who smell like spent sperm, like an animal. Who don't know what they are doing. Sometimes I find this type here and there, And – did you learn something? Eh? Would you like to learn something more? (She opens a champagne bottle and empties its contents over Kensuke's head.) Humans are not born equal, under-tand? Well, I'll be saying goodnight. Goodnight kid. Enjoy yourself. (Yoshiko walks away as Kensuke screams with anger and shame. Matsumura cuts to an extreme long shot of Kensuke still cuffed to the fence, a factory behind him, its techno-drone overwhelming Kensuke's screams.)

As much an act of self-defense as an act of aggression, Yoshiko's assault on Kensuke demonstrates the 'animalistic' qualities that humans often either sublimate or strategically channel to obtain what they desire. 'We're just animals,' Yoshiko reminds Kensuke as she cuffs him outside of an anonymous factory, a convenient yet effective symbol of late-industrial capitalism in action. Yoshiko, coded as very much *in control* throughout this scene, never denies her own animalistic qualities as she squarely positions herself as stronger than Kensuke, who has taken her for a prostitute and, thus, a lesser entity in his estimation. Likewise, Yoshiko at once infantilises and emasculates Kensuke: 'I hate kids who smell like spent sperm,' she states, 'like an animal.' Similar to Tetsuya, Kensuke represents the notion of conventional masculine identity in crisis; the reference to the smell of 'spent sperm', reminiscent of Tetsuya's nervous vomiting over his potential date, suggests a kind of premature ejaculation and/or impotence in the face of a strong(er) woman, a concern that – as we have seen – informs much of contemporary Japanese horror cinema. Thus, despite Tetsuya's intellectual acumen and Kensuke's wealth, both factors that would have carried significantly greater cultural weight in a pre-recession Japan, Tetsuya and Kensuke signify Matsumura's recognition of anxieties surrounding a shifting social landscape. While far from 'crummy little worms' writhing hopelessly at the very bottom level of the transforming Japan, Tetsuya and Kensuke's respective stations are by no means guarantors of success.

Matsumura provides his audience with one initially promising, albeit ultimately problematic and tragically doomed, relationship in the connection between Shinji and Yôko, the young woman whose bike chain Shinji severs as a means of initiating conversation and proving his resourcefulness. Yet even this relationship's foundation arises from dishonesty and the hierarchical positioning of one person (the rescuer) above another (the individual in distress). As well, Matsumura carefully balances scenes of affection with unsettling instances of disaffection. A date at a waterfront locale affords viewers with one of the film's starkest images, as Shinji witnesses an act of extreme cruelty. Lensed in an extreme high angle long shot conforming with Shinji's POV, a group of young punks stomp upon, and then set fire to, what looks like the battered carcass of a small cat or dog. In keeping with the theme of disaffection, mere moments before Shinji and Yôko fall victim to a vicious assault by the very same gang of miscreants, Yôko articulates her feelings of emotional estrangement: 'I don't feel strong emotions anymore. I don't feel sad. I don't feel mad.' Yôko's subsequent pronouncement, however, that this sense of alienation has begun to ease further amplifies the cruelty of the gang rape, a violation that Shinji, beaten and restrained, can only watch helplessly.

Given the varying humiliations suffered by Tetsuya, Kensuke and, finally, Shinji, one can certainly view the bloodbath with which the film concludes as an act of revenge for the rape Shinji helplessly witnesses. This is certainly the reading privileged by the designer of the film's 'uncut' release from Japan Shock DVD; on the back of the DVD case, amidst gory stills from some of the film's more spectacular moments, is a three sentence plot summary that reads: 'When a female friend gets raped by a gang of criminals, the boys [Shinji, Kensuke, and Tetsuya] decide to hunt them down and revenge the girl' (Japan Shock, 2001). However, although Shinji's murderous rage apparently stems largely from the assault on Yôko, Kensuke's and Tetsuya's roles in the violent attack on the 'gang of criminals', the spectacular event that propels the film to its gruesome finale, seems less an act of focused vengeance than a panicked re-assertion of a specific notion of masculinity, with Kensuke's rifle providing a deadly, if somewhat over-determined, double-barreled phallic symbol. Rather than constituting a moment of retribution, Shinji's rape of the gang leader's drug-addicted girlfriend (who was not present during the assault on Yôko) represents an attempt at violently imposing his masculine dominance over her – a power buttressed by his membership within the more powerful group and her now vulnerable, outsider status. Ultimately, however, when the massacre is over, only Tetsuya, the most conventionally awkward and docile of the trio of characters with whom audiences are asked to identify, remains alive. He exacts a horrible revenge upon the duplicitous Tamari and then wanders through the urban, postindustrial Tokyo streets with a crazed expression, his 'innocence' clearly 'vanished to make way for more disturbing instincts' (Mes 2001, para 3). In the world of Matsumura's initial *All Night Long* film, *ijime* and 'dove style violence' dominate social interactions; in the final analysis, the dominant imperative is one in which everyone must fend for her- or himself.

A related, albeit far more complicated, cultural critique underscores Matsumura's third installment of the *All Night Long* series. Accompanied by a post-colonialist soundtrack of US jets taking off and landing at a local air base, *All Night Long 3: Atrocities* likewise explores alienated, nihilistic youth struggling to survive in a post-recession Japan. Having crafted a film far bleaker in tone than its predecessors, Matsumura deploys a repeatedly claustrophobic *mise-en-scène* dominated by close-ups and tightly composed medium shots. Interior settings are the norm, and as such most of the film's action transpires in small, cluttered rooms apparently located within walking

Understand?

Image 11: Chain-link emasculation in Matsumura Katsuya's *All Night Long* (1992)

distance of one another. From an early depiction of schoolgirl *ijime* that
the film's bespectacled main protagonist, Sawada Kikuo, surreptitiously
observes from behind the leaves of a nearby tree, to a slow tracking shot
of the numerous carnivorous plants that decorate Kikuo's cramped
apartment, Matsumura immerses the spectator within an environment in
which the 'strong' (especially in groups) once again dominate the 'weak'.
As a group of Japanese schoolgirls kick, shove and finally force a timid
classmate with horribly scarred legs to urinate on herself, Matsumura
weds the spectator's gaze with Kikuo's, forcing all who watch the film to
consider their complicity in, as well as their desire to continue, viewing
such spectacles. The director emphasises this spectatorial connection
through frequent cross-cutting between images of violence or pain and
Kikuo's intense stare, a gaze amplified by Kikuo's large round eye-
glasses and his stooped posture, the latter lending his physique the
appearance of perpetually peering in to get a better view. Additionally,
Kikuo's voyeurism extends to his job at a local love hotel, an

establishment where couples rent out rooms for sexual encounters that the congestion of urban life, with its relative lack of privacy, frequently disallows. From repeated shots of the video monitors through which employees keep tabs on the hotel's numerous visitors, to scenes of Kikuo and a female supervisor peeping through the ventilation grates at copulating couples, voyeurism becomes a recurrent motif in *All Night Long 3: Atrocities*. Through his careful yet ultimately subversive direction, Matsumura obscures the viewer's perspective of the love hotel's copulating customers, a practice conforming to *Eirin*'s restrictions on the depiction of genitalia, even as in a subsequent scene a co-worker's amateur mixed-media illustration of a woman's pelvis re-contextualises Kikuo's collection of shed pubic hair.

It is in its obsession with 'filth' and 'waste', both organic and inorganic, that Matsumura's third film ultimately differs significantly from the works that precede it. Kikuo's obsession with abject secretions and corporeal states, from menstrual blood and feces to rotting food and cadavers, modifies the inside-outside (*uchi-soto*) binary repeatedly underpinning the practice of *ijime* and 'dove style violence', as well as wider, nationalist notions of a coherent and possibly inviolable Japanese social body/identity. *All Night Long 3: Atrocities* exposes the copious hybridities that, as the cultural critic Yoshiko Shimada notes, have always existed, revealing the conceptualisation of a Japanese history and culture grounded upon a single 'uniform national identity' (Shimada 2002: 190) as illusory at best. In some instances, Matsumura accomplishes this goal through the subtle yet recurrent implications of a continued US military presence in Japan, from the aforementioned images and sounds of US jets taking off and landing at a local airbase, to the appearance of an 'Uncle Sam' poster gracing the walls of one of the love hotel's corridors. Such representations corroborate Marilyn Ivy's contention that, despite 'nostalgic appeals' to an illusory pre-modern wholeness, '[t]he hybrid realities of Japan today – of multiple border crossings and transnational interchanges in the world of trade, aesthetics, [and] sciences' (1995: 9) remain a persistent and haunting reminder that the Japanese social body has never been as coherent and impermeable as some would like to imagine.

As is the case with many horror films, such larger, socio-national reconsiderations emerge from more immediate, intimate, and visceral portrayals of the human body as porous, leaky and violable. Hence, from the film's earliest moments, garbage in the form of potentially infectious human waste (semen, blood and saliva), trash in perilously thin plastic bags, and towering junkyard mountains punctuate the film's visual landscape. Likewise, for a national audience steeped within a history influenced by symbolic cultural codes that equate 'the inside with purity and the outside with impurity' (Ohnuki-Tierney 1987: 21-2), such images possess the potential to be unnerving, if not overtly repellant. In particular, several of Kikuo's more obsessive behaviors, from his feasting upon Nomura's 'edible' refuse to his incessant sucking upon the mangled bristles of her discarded toothbrush, function as perhaps two of the film's most explicit disruptions of the 'inside'-'outside' distinction. Comparably, Kikuo's obsessive charting of Nomura's menstrual cycle through his collection of her discarded maxi-pads and tampons seems specifically orchestrated to disgust and/or horrify spectators socialised to understand biological and spatial violations of this kind as abhorrent or horrific. This reaction certainly seems in keeping with Emiko Ohnuki-Tierney's sociological study, *Illness and Culture in Contemporary Japan: An Anthropological View*, in which she explores '[t]he symbolic equation...of the inside with purity and the outside with impurity' (1987: 21). The 'outside', Ohnoki-Tierney argues, 'is equated with dirt and germs because that is where the dirt of others is seen to be most concentrated' (21-2). This notion of 'germs' and infection is not only expansive, extending outward to incorporate ideologies informed by the fear of an externalised cultural impurity (also known as 'cultural germs' or 'people dirt'), but also turns inward, where 'germ-sharing' (like kissing or inviting someone to eat from the same bowl) becomes not a threat but, rather, 'an index of social intimacy' (29).

Given this rubric, then, to what extent does Matsumura's third *All Night Long* film's increasing focus upon biological and social contamination, as well as the cultural fears connected thereto, constitute a reconsideration of the rigid, binary division between 'inside' and 'outside'? In other words, how might the third *All Night Long* film locate

Japanese culture (like multiple cultures across the globe) as always-already variably contaminated?

While searching through Nomura's garbage, an intriguing variation on his previously established theme of voyeurism, Kikuo encounters a kindred spirit of sorts in the form of a grubby, self-proclaimed 'dusthunter'. While by no means a 'friendship' in the conventional sense (Kikuo, after all, eventually murders the man without exhibiting as much as a flicker of emotion), their bond nevertheless represents Kikuo's most profound human connection in this dark examination of urban alienation. In a pair of brief soliloquies directed towards our 'hero', the 'dusthunter' elaborates upon his theory behind his unusual vocation. The first of these orations takes place during their initial meeting; the latter homily occurs as the 'dusthunter' assists Kikuo in burning Tane Kaoru's dismembered corpse. Aware that Kikuo's 'experiments' and 'record-keeping' included the meticulously archiving of such 'vital' information as his prisoner's 'nipple circumference', the size of her 'vulva lips', and the length of her 'clitoris foreskin', the 'dusthunter' remarks:.

> rubbish actually contains numerous amounts of information, address, telephone number, if she's single, hobbies, private life, period dates. These dissatisfied women are chasing their dreams. The rubbish hunt is a wonderful fantasy game [...] [When] I was young...what others said was important. But they were just living rubbish. People are just imperfect corpses. As long as they live they will never reach perfection. The corpses are rubbish to burn. Even when they are alive they're still rubbish.

A careful examination of the 'Dusthunter''s discourses on the importance of garbage – the abject detritus through which so much may be inferred regarding an individual's daily habits and personal preferences – raises several compelling ideas regarding not only the previously broached politics of contagion, but also the profound alienation that, ironically, accompanies life within crowded urban cityscapes like Tokyo (or London, New York, etc.). Perhaps most compelling of all, though, is the 'dusthunter''s evocation of a vague 'dissatisfaction', a response to a transforming Japanese cultural edifice and the inevitable societal backlash that reveals tensions surrounding shifts in conventional gender roles.

Furthermore, Kikuo's clinical examination of his fellow humans, achieved through a painstaking cataloguing of their corporeal minutia, reduces the women over which he obsesses to disposable objects for study. At the same time, however, Kikuo's willful collapsing of the long held cultural distinction between 'inside' and 'outside', 'purity' and 'impurity', explodes notions of absolute binary difference. In other words, spectators must, like Kikuo, navigate their way through a world comprised by flexible economies of 'contamination'. Containing several instances of *ijime* and 'dove style violence', *All Night Long 3: Atrocities* offers a despairing perspective upon contemporary life. Matsumura's lengthy exploration of Kikuo's unconventional lifestyle choices reveals an understanding of 'contamination' as an avenue for exploring the potentialities of one's world without falling back upon 'binary categories like black-white, east-west, and *uchi-soto*' (65).

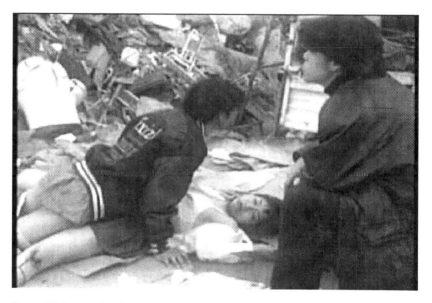

Image 12: Dove style violence in Matsumura Katsuya's *All Night Long 3: Atrocities* (©
Tokyo Shock)

Master and Servant: Inflicting Sadism and Negotiating Masochism in MiikeTakashi's *Ichi the Killer*

A film's opening sequence frequently establishes the work's tone and generates expectations regarding the events to follow. Some films start quietly, following simple opening credits with a momentum that builds steadily as the narrative unfolds; other films virtually explode upon the screen, maintaining a heightened tension throughout the remainder of the film. Miike Takashi's ultra-violent masterpiece, *Ichi the Killer*, opens with a series of off-screen spurts that soon transform into one of the most arresting title sequences in film history.

Fresh from the assassination (which we never see) of a *yakuza* boss named Anjo, Ichi, the film's eponymous antihero, finds his way to the apartment of a hooker receiving a horrific beating at the fists of her pimp. During this unique introductory sequence, Miike cross-cuts between full and medium shots of Ichi voyeuristically peering from behind a potted plant on the apartment's balcony to disorienting close-ups and jerky POV shots of the pimp's fists pounding into the hooker's flesh, raising giant welts and sending blood flying in thick, ropey arcs. As the scene develops, Ichi, clad in a rubber suit with a yellow '1' on the back, masturbates furiously, ultimately losing his balance and making a moderately loud noise that draws the pimp's attention away from his battered 'employee'. As furious as he is curious, the pimp makes his way out to the balcony, but by the time he arrives, Ichi is long gone. However, as an extreme close up of a few of the potted plant's leaves reveals, Ichi has left behind a trace of his presence in the form of thick white semen that drips slowly to the ground. As the semen splashes onto the patio, Miike employs digital manipulation to transform the freshly spilled ejaculate into the film's title.

Ichi the Killer's remarkable opening sequence functions in several ways. Firstly, it introduces us to Ichi, a crybaby vigilante who, programmed by a former cop named Jijii, believes himself the victim of *ijime* and dedicates himself to ridding the world of 'bullies'. He accomplishes this latter task through dazzling martial arts skills supplemented by deadly razors that spring forth from the heels of his boots. A killing machine *extraordinaire*, Ichi is a sadist who, manipulated by an engine fuelled with largely erroneous memories, clearly receives ample gratification by not only personally applying undesired pain upon others, but also – as his title-inducing orgasm illustrates – voyeuristically and enthusiastically observing acts of extreme violence and torture. Secondly, the opening sequence immerses viewers within a world in which the implementation of physical and psychological violence proves a crucial motivator in characters' social and sexual lives. This distribution of power becomes ever more apparent as the film progresses and we are introduced to Kakihara, an up-and-coming *yakuza* whose savage quest for someone to fill the void left by the absence of his former boss/dominator, Anjo, drives him not only to torture and brutalise others, but to seek out a confrontation with Ichi – an encounter that, as we shall soon see, is doomed to frustrate his expectations from the very start. Lastly, *Ichi the Killer*'s opening sequence prefigures Miike's neoconservative deployment of violent images, an approach to filmmaking that conjoins the masturbatory playfulness of 'over-the-top' splatter film aesthetics with a serious consideration of sadism's all-too-real consequences.

In his book, *Agitator: The Cinema of Takashi Miike*, Tom Mes advances a compelling, often brilliant reading of this controversial and frequently censored fusion of two of Japanese cinema's enduring genres: the gangster film (*yakuza eiga*) and the horror film. Mes astutely recognises Ichi's (tor)mentor, Jijii, as 'the film's biggest sadist' (2003: 234). Jijii is, according to Mes, a 'manipulator...who pulls the strings and determines the flow of the other characters' lives either by proxy (through Ichi) or occasionally in person' (234). This point is crucial, for as the sadist behind Ichi's sadism, Jijii annihilates Ichi's initial persona (whatever that may have been) and, in its place, posits a new identity. The Ichi that Jijii constructs finds his primary motivation through false memories of having been a victim of *ijime* (a practice grounded, as we have seen, in the sadistic drive to impose one's power over a weaker individual), and of having been forced to witness the rape of a young school girl, an act of violence by which he believes he was titillated. Consequently, Jijii functions as a kind of Dr. Frankenstein whose 'creation', rather than abandoned and left to find his own way in the world, operates almost exclusively according to his creator's desires. In this sense, Ichi, like the masochistic Kakihara who spends the duration of the film searching for a person to dominate him as his former boss, Anjo, once did, is a profoundly 'rootless individual' (228). Consistently unable to achieve the personal fulfillment they desire, Ichi and Kakihara contribute to a discourse of alienation recurrent throughout contemporary Japanese horror cinema, especially those texts informed by *ijime* and 'dove style violence'.

As Kakihara beholds the gruesome carnage Ichi leaves in his wake, he envisions Ichi as both a threat to his role as a rising force within the Japanese criminal community, and as a possibly ideal replacement for Anjo. In other words, as a ruthless and seemingly remorseless assassin/sadist who leaves a gory collage of disarticulated *yakuza* bodies in his wake, Ichi appeals to Kakihara in that he seems the ideal figure to satisfy Kakihara's masochistic desires. This allure, however, is misguided. As Gilles Deleuze notes in *Coldness and Cruelty*, sadism and masochism derive from two very different impulses. 'In every respect', Deleuze explains, 'the sadistic "instructor" stands in contrast to the masochistic "educator"' because while 'the sadist thinks in terms of institutionalized possession, the masochist in terms of contracted alliance' (1991: 20).

> ...a genuine sadist could never tolerate a masochistic victim...neither would the masochist tolerate a truly sadistic torturer. He does of course require a special "nature" in the...torturer, but he needs to mold this nature, to educate and persuade it in accordance with his special project...Each subject in the perversion (sic) only needs the "element" of the same perversion and not a subject of the other perversion. Whenever the type of...torturer is observed in the masochistic setting, it becomes obvious that she is neither a genuine sadist nor a pseudosadist but something quite different. She does indeed belong essentially to masochism, but without realizing it as a subject...The subject of masochism needs a certain "essence" of masochism embodied in the nature of a woman who renounces her own subjective masochism; he definitely has no need of another subject, i.e., the sadistic subject. (41-2)

Like the bully, or the various social congregations – from high school students to *yakuza* – that frequently comprise cinematic representations of 'dove style violence', sadists find pleasure through enforcing 'The Law'. As a result, sadists reify hierarchical structures founded upon the imposition of their desires and wills against those who do not yearn for such applications. This practice differs drastically from the masochist's craving, which can only be 'satisfied' by never being satisfied. Said differently, masochism, and masochistic desire, depends upon an agreement to inflict pleasure by simultaneously delivering a degree of the pain or humiliation for which the masochist craves, and by establishing an economy of desire founded upon the perpetual delay of gratification or satiation. The 'sadism' implied by the term 'sadomasochism', then, is illusory; it is not the enforcing of the sadist's will, but rather a response to the masochist's desire. The masochist, in other words, is the one in control.

Since their ontological formations are 'entirely different', 'the concurrence of sadism and masochism is fundamentally one of analogy only' (46); hence, the climactic showdown with Ichi for which Kakihara longs is destined to disappoint his masochistic desires. Further, Kakihara's and Ichi's antithetical subject positions allow Miike to frustrate viewer expectations, a consistent directorial practice that has established him as one of the most interesting visionaries in contemporary world cinema. In addition, as Ichi and Kakihara's incompatibility necessarily restricts the degree of satisfaction Kakihara may obtain, Kakihara can only find release through what Tom Mes correctly understands as masturbatory actions (2003: 231), like impairing his own hearing by inserting long spikes deep into his ears to eliminate the sounds of Ichi's unexpected sobs. Reminiscent of his severing of his own tongue in a sarcastic gesture of 'repentence' for wrongly torturing a *yakuza* boss, Kakihara's self-maiming, a process culminating in his suicidal plunge from a rooftop battlefield, amounts to little more than a quick, autoerotic 'fix'. Throughout the film, Kakihara struggles to satiate masochistic desires that, by their very definition, can never be fulfilled.

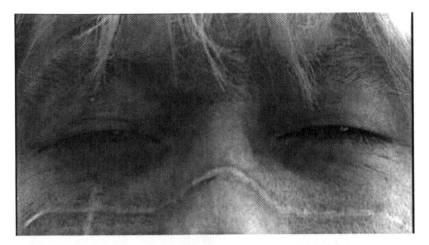

Image 13: Kakihara's stare (© Tokyo Shock)

Cuttings, Slicings, Irresponsible Excisions and the Politics of Excess

At the time of this writing, Miike Takashi remains one of the most prolific filmmakers in the history of cinema, an art form that spans only slightly more than a century. From his earliest straight to video works, released in 1991, to his most recent horror films like *Gozu* (*Gokudô kyôfu dai-gekijô: Gozu*, 2003), *One Missed Call* (*Chakushin ari*, 2003), and *Izo* (2004), Miike has directed sixty-five films. His productivity over the last fifteen years far exceeds the output of most filmmakers, including such notably prolific directors as Rainer Werner Fassbinder and Jean-Luc Godard, with whom he shares a passion for creating works that are not only insightful, but that seem intended to incite spectators. Given many of his works' controversial content, it should come as no surprise that several of his more violent creations, including *Ichi the Killer*, have been released in variously edited versions. For example, some DVD editions of *Ichi the Killer*, including its Hong Kong release and a significantly truncated version available at countless US video and DVD rental stores, remove violent sequences that censors felt were too extreme or unsettling for general consumption. Decisions of this nature constitute an assault to the filmmakers, who have the fruits of their creative labours squashed before they can even be sampled. As well, such censorship marks an attack upon the circulation of knowledge and ideas tantamount to an epistemological assassination.

Here, again, I turn to Tom Mes' essay on *Ichi the Killer*, for his reflections upon Miike's film contain two important observations with which I wish to engage critically. The first of these is his point that:

> [*Ichi the Killer*] as a whole is a completely cohesive unity, in that all of its parts are absolutely crucial to the functioning of the whole. Any attempt at censoring or toning down the violence will have the opposite effect and will in fact make the film more exploitative and thereby undermine its critical stance. Excising scenes of violence, particularly the painful scenes, will harm the symbiosis between the "playful" and the "painful" violence, which forms the basis for Miike's critical approach. (2003: 242-3)

Genre films have long provided directors with opportunities for expressing political perspectives through allegory or through temporal or spatial displacement. As Mes correctly notes, by excising a '"painfully" violent' sequence, like the extremely disturbing scene in which a woman is tortured by having her nipples severed (though, ironically, spectators viewing the un-cut version never actually *see* the severing), censors and distributors that allow for such censorship compromise both the artist's vision and the politics that inform it. *Ichi the Killer* is indeed a very violent film, but as Mes points out, violence and the experience of viewing violence is very much part of Miike's over-arching aesthetic and critical agenda. Miike, in other words, wants viewers to 'think' carefully about what they are watching. He wants them to contemplate both violence's potentially traumatic consequences, as well as their own roles as consumers of brutal images (243). Editing out '"painful" violence' while keeping only the more cartoonish, '"playful" violence' intact constitutes an act of irresponsible excision that, ultimately, has an effect opposite to that intended by the censors. Rather than 'protecting' audiences, such censorship rejects the concept of violence as a social issue worthy of consideration through artistic means and, consequently, reduces the representation and consumption of images depicting the willful infliction of physical abuse upon others to only 'playful' scenes intended, like a roller coaster, to provide immediate, visceral, yet fleeting thrills.

Mes also remarks that the repetition of violence in *Ichi the Killer* aligns with Miike's aesthetic and critical agenda in that it 'underlines [violence's] very futility' (243). I agree with Mes, but would like to supplement his observation with a further consideration of Miike's *oeuvre* in terms of *Ichi the Killer*'s relation to a potentially radical politics of visual excess.

Though best known for his more violent works, Miike is without question one of contemporary cinema's more eclectic directors. The range of genres with which Miike has engaged include: the teen idol action film (*Andromedia* [1998] and *N-Girls Vs Vampire* [*Tennen shôjo Man next: Yokohama hyaku-ya hen*, 1999]); the musical comedy (*The Happiness of the Katakuris* [*Katakuri-ke no kôfuku*, 2002]); the self-reflective deconstruction of popular Japanese horror films and motifs (*One Missed Call* [2003]); *chambara eiga*, or the *samurai* film (*Sabu* [2002]); and the slapstick superhero comedy (*Zebraman* [2004]). These titles and genre categories merely scratch the surface of Miike's staggering output. Similarly, Miike rarely limits his films to the parameters of a single coherent genre. His musical comedy, *The Happiness of the Katakuries*, for example, also adheres to horror film conventions, such as grotesque murders and the depiction of the dead returning to life. Thus, Miike's continual combination and recombination of filmic genres throughout his brief yet hyper-productive career locates him as an auteur whose very output frustrates attempts at labeling him as a certain *type* of director (for example, as a 'horror director'). His range demonstrates his remarkable ability to produce a tremendously diverse body of work that simultaneously contains and exceeds a plurality of genres and genre conventions.

Lastly, *Ichi the Killer*'s depictions of violence in all its 'painful' and 'playful' manifestations contributes to a reconsideration of the very notion of 'borders' and 'boundaries' in both the 'reel world' of filmic representation and the 'real world' that the former simulates. Specifically, the film's relentless display of violence, directed both externally (towards others) and internally (towards one's self), calls to mind the 'transgressive violence of desire' that French cultural theorist Georges Bataille links with the potentialities of 'radical transformation' (quoted in Menninghaus 2003: 367). Seen in this light, the cinema of Miike Takashi in general, and *Ichi the Killer* in particular, contributes to a 'science of [that which] is completely other' (347), a mode of thought allowing for new ways of approaching understandings of human identity and the relation of the self to the physical body and its inevitable trajectory towards death and decay. If one understands mutilated and/or mutilating bodies as flexible arrangements that embrace multiplicity, indeterminacy, and the seduction of extreme physiological configurations, then it is possible to understand *Ichi the Killer* as a text that, while eliciting fear and revulsion on some levels, stimulates the imagination on others. Mutilated and mutilating bodies (including those that, like Kakihara's, undergo sacrificial self-mutilation) are intensive and heterogenous physiologies; they are corporeal formations that hold tremendous promise for those wishing to escape stifling cultural paradigms. Like the variously monstrous bodies populating countless works of horror cinema from around the globe, the masochistic Kakihara can be understood as resisting categorisation through infinite self-creation. Like the Body without Organs described by Gilles Deleuze and Felix Guattari in *A Thousand Plateaus: Capitalism and Schizophrenia*, Kakihara embraces his own 'monstrtous' becoming, rejecting the concept of the group in favor of seeking extreme pleasure through extreme corporeal modification. In the end, his orgasmic plummet from the rooftop is not so much a suicidal leap as one last attempt to 'get off' in a world bounded by ideological structures that all-too-frequently and, perhaps, all-too-sadistically allows for 'alternative identities', if only to the point that forces of 'law' and 'order' can be mobilised to contain them.

Image 14: Kakihara ponders Ichii's grisly handiwork in Miike Takashi's *Ichii the Killer* (© Tokyo Shock)

Chapter Five:
Spiraling into Apocalypse: Sono Shion's *Suicide Circle*, Higuchinsky's *Uzumaki*, and Kurosawa Kiyoshi's *Pulse*

Apocalypse and Transcendence

Akin to the deluge of post-war *daikaiju eiga* (giant monster films) in their depiction of contemporary civilisation under assault or in ruins, Sono Shion's *Suicide Circle* (*Jisatsu saakuru*, 2002[1]), Higuchinsky's *Uzumaki* (1997), and Kurosawa Kiyoshi's *Pulse* (*Kaïro*, 1997) engage a complex history of annihilation and reconstruction. At the same time, these ominous yet captivating cinematic visions contribute, both nationally and internationally, to a recurrent correlation of the Japanese social body with, in Joshua La Bare's words, 'not only apocalypse, but the fact of its transcendence: the finite and, through it, the infinite' (La Bare 2000: 43). Consequently, the events that bring about the 'end of the world as we know it' can be secular (ushered in largely through biological or technological means), or religious (informed by any, or a combination, of

---

[1] Although also released in the US and UK under the title, *Suicide Club*, I elect to use the initial foreign release title, *Suicide Circle*, because it foregrounds the film's theme of recursion.

the multiple faiths practiced in Japan), or both. Following a brief survey of the representation of catastrophic imagery in post-war Japanese horror film, this chapter examines the genre's continued application of apocalyptic conceits as a variable response to a transforming Japanese political and cultural landscape at the dawn of a new millennium.

In *Suicide Circle*, for example, Sono Shion offers viewers a grisly and, at times, darkly humorous depiction of a contemporary Japan plagued by a series of spectacular yet baffling mass suicides. Punctuated by clips of music videos by a pre-pubescent pop group called Desert, an all-girl bubblegum 'band' partially responsible for the epidemic of self-slaughter, *Suicide Circle* presents a biting critique of a culture informed by rampant consumerism, social alienation ironically enhanced by the ubiquity of communications technologies, and gender politics complicated by the simultaneously pervasive and perpetually transitory culture of 'cuteness', or *kawaisa*.[2] Thus, like the film's schizophrenic collision of cinematic tropes and popular culture iconography, *Suicide Circle*'s underlying social commentary far exceeds the parameters of a reductionist logic founded upon simplistic notions of one-to-one causality. Rather, Sono understands Japanese social and national identity as imperilled by a plethora of cultural logics that, 'like leaves which soon…grow into a thick forest of darkness' (Crawford 2003: 307), saturate the country's mass culture (*minshu bunka*). As Sono suggests in a recent interview, an ultimately isolating and fundamentally ahistorical conceptualisation of one's national culture is, in itself, a 'suicidal' posture (309).

Higuchinsky's *Uzumaki* shares Sono Shion's enthusiasm for pursuing more experimental approaches to storytelling. However, the social critique informing the apocalyptic events in *Uzumaki*'s elliptical narrative has a profoundly different ideological 'spin'. Based on Ito Junji's highly successful *manga* series about an isolated town 'infected' by recurring spiral patterns of a supernatural origin, *Uzumaki* borrows from a plurality of secular and religious sources. Higuchinsky eschews

---

[2] See Richie, D. (2003) *The Image Factory: Fads and Fashions in Japan.* London: Reaction Books.

conventional narrative paradigms and 'classical' filmmaking practices (like Hollywood-style cross-cutting and detailed exposition) in favour of a story that is itself a kind of cinematic vortex. In conveying his recursive tale, Higuchinsky melds what Benoit Mandelbrot would describe as the 'fractal geometry of nature' (1982) with a frenetic pacing marked by disquieting moments of Lovecraftian menace. The result is a vertiginous postmodern critique of isolationism and endogamy that posits entropic dissolution as both an 'end' to be feared, as well as a 'means' to potential corporeal and social transformation.

A close reading of Kurosawa Kiyoshi's *Pulse*, in which menacing technological and paranormal forces intersect within a carefully crafted narrative that builds to an apocalyptic finale that is both threatening and promising, concludes this chapter. A work in which Kurosawa juxtaposes congested, alienating urban environments with the high-tech anonymity represented by the internet's seemingly infinite 'non-space', *Pulse* is not only one of the more effective horror films in recent years, but also – like *All About Lily Chou-Chou* (2001), *Suicide Circle*, and a myriad of other texts explored throughout the course of this book – raises vital questions regarding the importance of human connection in late-industrial culture. Thus, although Kurosawa's film culminates in a devastatingly poignant and visually arresting depiction of a world steadily emptied of its human inhabitants, it would be a mistake to read *Pulse*'s apocalyptic climax as unremittingly bleak. To quote Kurosawa in a *Film Comment* article devoted to new trends in Japanese cinema: 'In…my films…you see cities destroyed, and perhaps even hints that the end of civilization is near. Many people construe those images and ideas as negative and despairing, but I actually see them as just the opposite – as the possibility of starting again with nothing; as the beginning of hope' (quoted in Stephens 2002 :36).

Imagining Apocalypse: The Technology of Disaster

As suggested in this chapter's opening sentence, any discussion of apocalyptic imagery in contemporary Japanese horror cinema must begin with a consideration of the importance of *daikaiju eiga* both within their historical context and as a profoundly influential genre for an entire generation of Japanese filmmakers. Among the most immediately recognisable films in Japanese cinema, *daikaiju eiga* provide the perfect arena for addressing numerous social anxieties, not the least of which constellate around the dread of mass destruction, biological mutation, and the environmental impact of pollution resulting from rapid industrialisation. As Japan remains the only nation to have suffered a direct atomic attack, a cataclysm followed hard upon by decades of exposure to US military exercises (including atomic tests) in the Pacific Ocean, the aquatic and aerial origins of the mutated creatures populating most *daikaiju eiga* seem only appropriate, as do the gigantic creatures' intentional, and sometimes incidental, annihilation of major urban centres. Tokyo in particular endures repeated destruction in these narratives, a motif that has received notable critical attention in studies such as Darrell William Davis's *Picturing Japaneseness – Monumental Style, National Identity, Japanese Films* (1995) and Mick Broderick's recent anthology, *Hibakusha Cinema: Hiroshima, Nagasaki and the Nuclear Image in Japanese Film* (1996).

Additionally, the frequent conceit of portraying friction between scientists and the military in *daikaiju eiga* – conflicts that often delay the monsters' vanquishing – seems an ideal plot device for a cinematic tradition emerging from a nation that was at once 'ground zero' for history's most deadly union of science, technology and warfare, and a site of wide-scale industrial, technological and economic development. As Susan J. Napier notes, films featuring Japan's most famous giant monster, Gojira (a.k.a. Godzilla), often convey a substantial 'nationalist twist' (Napier 1996: 240), especially in their message that it is 'American science which brings forth the monster' (240). 'Even more specifically', she adds, 'it is Japanese science, personified by the humane Japanese scientist whose suicide helps destroy Godzilla, which ultimately saves the world' (240). When openly marketed towards children, and thus populated with creatures characterised as friendly protectors of the Japanese islands, *daikaiju eiga* remain creative forums through which very human fears over the very human manipulation of science and technology are projected onto fantastical physiognomies that engage in battle but rarely perish. In their depiction of the simultaneous dread of atomic disaster and trepidation over rapid industrialisation, *daikaiju eiga* resemble American giant monster films of the 1950s, like Gorden Douglas' *Them!* (USA, 1954), in which mutant ants threaten civilisation, and Bert I. Gordon's *The Beginning of the End* (USA, 1957), in which irradiated grasshoppers attack Chicago. Specifically, both cinematic traditions depict a socio-cultural discomfort over 'processes of social development and [scientific, technological, and cultural] modernization' (Jancovich 1996: 2). However, the tropological shift Napier recognises in *daikaiju eiga* suggests that monsters like Gojira and Gamera are ultimately products of Japanese popular culture. Accordingly, these films 'offered [their] immediate postwar Japanese audience an experience that was both cathartic and compensatory, allowing them to rewrite or at least reimagine their tragic wartime experiences' (1996: 240), as well as to confront apprehensions accompanying economic recovery through rapid industrialisation.

In recent decades, *daikaiju eiga* have given way to a proliferation of techno-/body-horror films that literalise the darker side of a process of nation-wide industrialisation largely orchestrated as a result of, and in direct response to, Western (primarily US) military and cultural imperialism. As discussed in my earlier explorations of the *Guinea Pig* films and Sato Hisayasu's *Naked Blood*, techno and body horror films contribute to a discourse of boundary violation and body invasion, graphically enacting, in the process, perhaps the most dreadful apocalypse of all – the perpetual intimate apocalypse of the human body revealed not as a consolidated and impregnable citadel, but as a flexible assemblage that disallows for illusions of corporeal integrity or for ideologies privileging the sovereignty of the human form. In their focus on issues of 'biological privation, technological instrumentality, and the loss of biological control' (Thacker 2002: 111), these works closely adhere to what Eugene Thacker describes as 'biohorror', a union of 'futuristic dystopia produced through science and technology' and 'the violent monstrosities that manifest themselves within the human body' (112).

Given technology's paradoxical status in the Japanese popular imagination, specifically its contradictory role as both a gateway to Armageddon and a means to economic recovery, it should come as little surprise that technology's complex impact upon the social and corporeal body informs much of Japanese apocalyptic cinema in the latter decades of the twentieth century. Perhaps the most prominent example of one such film is Tsukamoto Shinya's *Tetsuo: The Iron Man* (1988), a jarring, visceral motion picture that, set in 'an electroconvulsive Tokyo' (Dery 1997: 270), draws its inspiration from a nightmarishly surreal combination of the *daikaiju eiga* tradition and works of contemporary science fiction texts ranging from William Gibson's novel, *Neuromancer* (1986), to the feature-length *anime* sensation, *Akira* (1988).[3] *Tetsuo: The Iron Man*'s narrative unfolds like a series of hallucinations, a manic and, at times, chaotic visual style that has led numerous reviewers and critics to compare Tsukamoto's anarchic, techno-catastrophic vision with the works of maverick Western filmmakers of postmodern body horror, like David Cronenberg, David Lynch, and Clive Barker. After a 'metal fetishist' with a penchant for violently inserting scrap metal into his flesh is struck down by a 'salaryman' out for a drive with his girlfriend, the 'salaryman' soon discovers that his own physiology is steadily and inexplicably transforming into a grotesque biomechanical hybrid. This new forum not only confounds conventional binaries of human/machine, or organic/technological, but also scrambles traditional notions of gender and sexuality (the 'salaryman', in the course of the narrative, both penetrates others with, and is penetrated by, phallically overdetermined mechanical devices) in ways that have not escaped the attention of critics who read Tsukamoto's breakthrough film as a barometer signalling a larger crisis in masculinity.

Readings of *Tetsuo: The Iron Man* as a panicked reassertion of phallocentrism, or as a homoerotic paean to an increasingly mechanised society, are equally defensible through a close examination of the

---

[3] Susan J. Napier makes a similar argument when she locates *Akira* as occupying an important space in 'a continuum, both in Japan's imagination of destruction and ultimately in Japan's imagination of itself' (2000: 239). Specifically, Napier positions *Akira* as a text that reveals the 'late 1980s' as 'a decade of tumultuous change, both in Japan's conception of itself and its relationship with the rest of the world' (239).

'salaryman"'s progressively radical transformations, as well as the 'electrifying' climactic battle between the 'salaryman' and the 'metal fetishist', both of whom fully transform into heavy metal war machines. However, Tsukamoto's film is perhaps best understood as a text that not only elides a single cohesive exegesis, but that, through its irreducibility, contributes a vital perspective to Japan's cinema of apocalypse. Through the 'salaryman' and 'metal fetishist"'s desire to unite in 'love' so that they may 'mutate the whole world into metal' and, in the process, 'destroy the whole fucking world', the viewer must confront not only the threat of global annihilation, but also the potential for the emergence of new cultural perspectives and identities created by such fusion, mutation, 'love'.

In his essay, 'Metal-Morphosis: Post-Industrial Crisis and the Tormented Body in the *Tetsuo* Films', Ian Conrich insightfully posits Tsukamoto Shinya's 'nightmarish cyberpunk vision' as a tale of 'transformation and incorporation' that locates images of radical biomechanical horror within a larger nexus of machine-age super-hero mythologies, recent urban renewal practices, emerging notions regarding the mechanisation of the body in production processes, and the emergence of new economies of eroticism (including techno-eroticism/fetishism) that confound conventional notions of gender and sexuality (2005: 95-106). Thus, although 'monstrous' hybridity, including the collision of the corporeal and technological, remains a staple of apocalyptic horror films in contemporary Japanese cinema, it would be shortsighted to assume that such works views these ménages as exclusively horrific.

As Sharalyn Orbaugh reminds us, 'some of the most pressing issues' for contemporary Japanese narratives (including film narratives) 'have been questions of legitimacy and illegitimacy..., non-normative forms of reproduction, the hybridity of bodies or subjectivities, and the ambiguous or anomalous incarnations of gender/sex/ sexuality' (2002: 440). Furthermore, it is valuable for viewers of contemporary Japanese horror cinema, as well as readers and viewers of Japanese science fiction, to remember that Japanese horror and science fiction texts frequently differ from their Western counterparts in that the 'other'-ing of the

Japanese corporeal and social body by 'Western hegemonic discourse allows for an exploration of the hybrid, monstrous, cyborg subject from a sympathetic, interior point of view rarely found' in North American and European 'cultural products' (240). Accompanying the horror of the physical body rendered indiscrete in its multifarious hybridity, then, is the notion of the Japanese social body as 'monstrous' both to itself and to an Orientalist Western imagination.

Fashioning Apocalypse: Sono Shion's *Suicide Circle*

Among *Suicide Circle*'s primary themes is the seemingly paradoxical dilemma of alienation and interpersonal dis-communication in an age of proliferating information technologies and 'mass communication'. Infused with allusions to literal and figurative assaults upon Japanese society, the film is a kind of cultural rescue action. It is, in other words, an attempt to direct the audience's attention towards what Sono perceives as an impending dissolution of personal and cultural identity. Hence, the epidemic of self-annihilation driving *Suicide Circle*'s intentionally convoluted storyline provides a powerful, reactionary metaphor for some of Japanese popular culture's more alienating components. In the process of articulating his gruesome, eclectic, and, at times, highly satirical vision, Sono asserts the need for creative individuation and dialogue in a socio-historical moment informed (and mediated) by commercialism, the propagation of vacuous pop idols, and an understanding of national history and social identity that rarely extends beyond the immediacy of the ever-emerging present and the latest pop-culture craze.

  With a complex narrative structure that requires viewers to acknowledge and embrace their roles as active participants in the creation of the film's meaning, *Suicide Circle*'s plot unfolds through strategically placed digressions, frustrating 'red herrings', and the conflation of conventions from multiple film genres, including the splatter film, the police procedural, the family melodrama, the music video, the thriller, the high-camp/cult film, and the pseudo-snuff film. From the film's notoriously grisly opening sequence, in which fifty-four teenage girls dressed in high school uniforms clasp hands at the edge of a subway platform at Shinjuku Station and leap to their deaths beneath the wheels of a Tokyo-bound express train, Sono immerses his audience in a desperate search to discover the motivating force behind an epidemic of mass suicide that threatens to spread beyond one's wildest speculations, consuming an ever increasing number of Japan's youth (including its emerging working and urban-professional classes) in an orgiastic feast of

**Image 15: Promotion photo from Tsukamoto Shinya's *Tetsuo: The Iron Man*
(© Tartan USA)**

wilful self-obliteration. Over the subsequent ninety min-utes, the audience follows the exploits of four central protagonists: Kuroda, a seasoned detective and patriarch of a quietly dysfunctional family; Shibusawa, Kuroda's young assistant; 'The Bat', a young female *otaku* who 'resides' both 'virtually' on the internet and 'physically' within the confines of her dark, cluttered bedroom; and Mitsuko, a young woman whose boyfriend leaps to his death from a window near the top of a tall building. As the film progresses, various clues lead to assorted dead ends, both literally and figuratively. At one point a gang of glam rockers calling themselves the 'Suicide Club' and led by an androgynous figure named Genesis kidnap 'The Bat' and hold her captive in an abandoned bowling alley. Meanwhile, Detective Kuroda, having failed to protect his wife and children from the deadly 'fad' sweeping the nation, responds to his own family's suicide by blowing his brains out. This tragic event strengthens Shibusawa's resolve to discover the truth behind the mass deaths and, in the process, protect Mitsuko, whose own investigation leads her to uncover a collective of prepubescent boys and girls seeking to transform Japan. The collective's unlikely but highly effective plan involves using the all-girl pop band Desert (alternatively – and, as we shall soon discover, importantly – spelled as 'Dessert' and 'Dessret') to incite Desert's many fans to either take their own lives or, if possible, reject an ultimately destructive self-absorption by realising and nurturing their individual 'connection' with other people.

The film's shocking opening sequence in Shinjuku Station not only introduces viewers to Sono's 'audacious' and 'richly rewarding' (Crawford 2003: 306) filmmaking style, but also initiates a series of events intended to recall one of the more tragic episodes in recent Japanese history. Though the over-the-top images of bloody geysers dousing horrified bystanders and thick rivers of gore flooding over the subway station's white tile floor alert viewers early on that the events to follow will most certainly contain graphic material decidedly not for the squeamish, the combination of mass death and mass transportation seem designed to evoke inevitable comparisons with the deadly sarin nerve gas attacks carried out in the Tokyo subway system on 20 March 1995 by members of the Aum Shinrikyo cult. In *Suicide Circle*, despite the rejection of initial speculations that the deaths may be in some way connected via a larger organized faction ('A suicide cult?' the detective in charge of the investigation asks with a dismissive laugh. 'Ridiculous!'), the multiple quests to discover the force behind the rapidly escalating body count propel the plot forward. Additionally, the desire to subordinate one's individual will to a larger, apparently inclusive social or cultural phenomenon – a behaviour evidenced by not only cult members, but by *otaku, hikikomori* (defined below), and avid fans of pop bands – quickly becomes a target for Sono's increasingly expansive social analysis.

In *Suicide Circle*, the character calling herself 'The Bat' most explicitly conforms to popular culture stereotypes surrounding *hikikomori*, an increasingly prevalent social configuration in contemporary Japan. 'Translated literally', Mitsuko Kakiuchi tells us, 'as "those who retreat," *hikikomori* are the frighteningly logical extension of "*otaku*," the buzzword for Japanese teens from last decade... *hikikomori*...retreat from society into complete nothingness, holing themselves up in their bedrooms at their parents' homes and doing anything to fill the hours' (Kakiuchi 2005: para 2). Sono's depiction of The Bat adheres quite closely to Kakiuchi's description; before her abduction by the sadistic self-promoter, Genesis, and his glam rock minions, we see The Bat sequestered in her bedroom, a cramped, refuse-cluttered space lit only by the muted glows emanating from a computer monitor and a murky fish tank. Preferring the fluid anonymity of the internet to interpersonal contact within the solid confines of the physical world, The Bat conducts her own on-line quest for the source of the mass suicides not so much out of an altruistic desire to assist the authorities as out of a yearning to entertain herself by demonstrating, if only to the handful of people with whom she barely communicates, the extent of her computer-assisted research skills.

Indeed, *hikikomori*'s translation as 'those who retreat' is particularly applicable to Sono's representation of The Bat and her primary companion, a fellow *hikikomori* who sits silently by The Bat's side. Additionally, in a brief but important sequence revealing the extent of The Bat's withdrawal from the world, Sono presents his audience with a heart-breaking full shot of the young woman's dishevelled father dressed in a badly wrinkled business suit and seated behind a broken table. A brief but powerful moment suggestive of the economic recession's devastating impact upon the Japanese family, the father pleads before his technophile offspring, calling her by her given name:

'Kiyoko, your dad's tired. Kiyoko, it's not my fault, you know...' In disgust, The Bat slides her bedroom door closed and turns her attention once again to the computer monitor's glow. Convinced that she can ascertain the mystery behind the mass deaths through a relentless scouring of cyberspace's remotest reaches, 'The Bat' so immerses herself within the internet's 'online communities' that her captivation with the 'world wide web' finally results in her all-too-real and all-too-perilous physical captivity, a trauma that could have been avoided were she to engage with the physical world from which she withdraws rather than cyberspace's ecstatic disembodiment.

In *The Image Factory: Fads & Fashions in Japan*, Donald Richie explores the paradox inherent in a culture driven by continual innovations in communications technology. Describing the allure of new products and images in Japan, Richie states that such commodities (*shinhatsubai*) allow for 'a social distraction at the same time that [they] promote a kind of social cohesion' (Richie 2003: 11). Likewise, while acknowledging that such practices are by no means exclusive to Japan, Richie expands his exploration of the embrace of style over, or in place of, substance by revealing the contradiction at the heart of such simultaneously individuating and collective behaviours:

> [I]n a place so status conscious as Japan, self image is important and new image indicators are in demand. All indicate, to be sure, merely how different in a manner everyone else will shortly be. Nvertheless, or consequently, a demand for the new indicator grows and an industry accommodates mass production. This is everywhere true, but Japanese society includes conformism as a major ingredient and everyone wanting to do everything at the same time creates a need which the fad and fashion factories fill. (7)

In *Suicide Circle*, Sono, like Richie, recognises this consumerist cycle by which people define themselves as at once *apart from* the masses, and as *a part of* a larger, virtual, collective identity without which one's personal 'style' would have no meaning. In fact, it is this communal drive to produce an ever-transforming identity through conspicuous consumption that Sono locates as evidence that '[n]owadays...Japan does not have any culture' (Crawford 2003: 309) beyond the ahistorical ephemerality of a mass-marketed popular culture capable of reducing individuals to nameless, faceless cogs in a global capitalist machine, or – as is the case with those characters who take their lives in *Suicide Circle*'s frenzy of mass emulation – to a series of computer-generated red and white dots immediately reminiscent of the colours of the Japanese flag.

Furthermore, the suicides' almost viral proliferation throughout the film reveals the expansive yet, for Sono, ultimately destructive impact of a Japanese popular culture defined by fads and fashions. Teenagers, eager for a way to assert themselves in a society driven by both the allure of the new and the compulsion to 'fit in', form impromptu 'suicide clubs' to which death is the price of admission. Other young people, like those that comprise the murderous glam rock band 'Suicide Club', blindly follow monomaniacal wannabe cult-leaders like Genesis (the self-proclaimed 'Charles Manson of the information age')[4] in an attempt to discover their niche through lyrics that romanticise death ('I want to die as beautifully as Joan of Arc inside a Bresson film...because the Dead shine all night long!') and through the construction of a quasi-Sadean 'pleasure room'. However, it is not merely 'impressionable' teens that fall prey to the suicide fad; several adults are also depicted taking their own lives throughout the film. As Alan Wolfe writes in his essay, 'Suicide and the Japanese Postmodern: A Postnarrative Paradigm', individual self-annihilation provides the ideal model for resistance in a late-capitalist culture defined by 'the endless circulation of increasingly unnecessary consumer goods and images' (1988: 231). Sono explores a very similar notion in *Suicide Circle*: In one scene, for example, Detective Karuda responds to the notion that the suicides are just a 'fad' by warning his fellow officers, '[n]ot a word about a suicide club or kids will be dying all over Japan.' Thus, for Wolfe and Sono, suicide is the ultimate fad in that, like all crazes that soon give way to the next big thing, it 'represents the capacity for the subject to resist without resisting' (229). This is particularly the case in contemporary Japanese culture, where an increasing majority of the population knows only a Japan linked

---

[4] Actually, given the media circus surrounding the 1969 Tate and LaBianca murders, as well as the subsequent protracted Las Angeles trial of Charles Manson and several members of his notorious 'Family', one could argue that Genesis's claim to this title is suspect at best, especially since Charles Manson himself is very much the 'Charles Manson of the information age'.

frequently in the global and national imaginary with the dizzying highs of a prolonged economic surplus followed sharply by the deep lows of a protracted financial recession. Likewise, the atomic desolation of Hiroshima and Nagasaki, while by no means absent from the contemporary consciousness, does not possess nearly the same ontological weight it did for previous generations. A film like *Suicide Circle*, then, engages a very different, 'postnuclear' culture, presenting a social body inflected with a mode of 'modern alienation…anomie, ennui, [and a]…desultory attitude towards nuclear destruction and collective suicide: a cosmic "What's the difference?"' that reflects a 'supremely indifferent' attitude towards 'the possibility of an end' (231).

At once a pernicious 'media tool', a 'symbol' of a 'suicidal' cultural trajectory, and a brilliantly banal metaphor for the effacement of social resistance, the all-girl prepubescent pop band whose inane melodies and discretely revealing lyrics punctuate *Suicide Circle*'s apocalyptic narrative serves a vital role in Sono's social critique. Variably spelled throughout the film as 'Desert', 'Dessert', and 'Dessret', the pop band's transforming moniker is one of *Suicide Circle*'s most compelling, albeit initially perplexing, components. As 'Desert', its most frequent spelling, the band's name connotes desolation and isolation, a beautiful if barren emptiness. Moreover, given both their blatantly commercial appeal and their simulacral interchangeability with any number of similarly composed Japanese pop bands, the name 'Desert' can be understood as evoking Jean Baudrillard's 'desert' of the 'real' (1995), the postmodern phenomenon succinctly described by Slavoj Zizek as 'the ultimate truth of the capitalist utilitarian de-spiritualized universe…the de-materialization of the "real life" itself, its reversal into a spectral show' (2001: para 3). Similarly, as 'Dessert', its second most frequent spelling, the band's name provides a clever commentary not only upon the young girls' readily commodified and consumable image, but also upon their achingly saccharine catalogue of pop hits and, ultimately, their lyrics' seemingly hollow and unsubstantial content. The name 'Dessert', then, at once compliments and expands upon the connotations of 'Desert', a social critique made all the more effective by a humorous sequence in which Sono cross-cuts scenes of multiple, often brutal suicides transpiring across Tokyo with segments from a television advertisement in which the young pop idols cheerfully cavort about a city street while perkily schilling their very own candy bar. Finally, though it appears only once in the film, the spelling, 'Dessret', through its phonetic proximity to the English term 'Death Threat', cleverly alludes to the band's underlying function as a harbinger of destruction.

In addition, Desert/Dessert/Dessret's ubiquity suggests that ultimately, given their enthusiastic reception by a wide cross-section of the film's characters, the band performs a social function akin to that of any fad, including one as extreme as suicide. Consider, for instance, the analysis of Japanese pop bands put forth by Hiroshi Aoyagi in his essay, 'Pop Idols and the Asian Identity'. Reminiscent of Richie and Wolfe's recognition of the inherent contradictions evidenced in the cultural impact of many Japanese fads, Aoyagi explains that carefully designed marketing strategies inevitably co-opt any revolutionary potential that Japanese pop idols may possess. As such, 'Japanese idols...typically depict images that are "fairly standard"', providing the illusion that anyone with enough drive may achieve a similar cultural status and extensive degree of public exposure (2000: 311):

> Playing on young people's social needs, Japan's...pop idols are produced and marketed as personifiers of a typical "girl or boy next door," chosen to become "lucky stars" to represent their generation. Sociologist Hiroshi Ogawa calls them "quasi-companions" (*gititeki-nakama*), who provide their teenage followers with a virtual sense of intimacy...although this companionship is understood to be artificial and impervious, and thus realized only in fantasy, the intimacy it evokes can be as strong as, or even stronger than, that shared among school friends. (316)

In this sense, Desert/Dessert/Dessret's mediated image and vast 'real world' following contributes mightily to Sono's aesthetic and political agenda in *Suicide Circle*. Their flashy if derivative and overtly manufactured façade speaks volumes regarding their role as components of a commodity-driven culture, while their overwhelming popularity provides a forum for an alienated and disconnected populace to experience the illusion of participating in a larger, communal event.

To posit Desert/Dessert/Dessret as an exclusively destructive or isolating force, however, ignores their function as the ambassadors of the prepubescent collective behind the suicides, a group whose 'hatred towards Japan' Sono imagines as 'an angelic beauty' (Crawford 2003: 309). Although many of the lyrics to their ostensibly syrupy ditties can be read as thinly veiled invitations to 'find a match that lasts forever', even if such a quest results in saying 'so long' to life in late-industrial Japan, certain lines advocate a rejection of the isolation that so-called 'communication technologies' can foster in favour of tangible, emotionally-engaged interpersonal relationships. We can find such an ideology championed in the following lyrics from the music video/performance over which the closing credits roll:

> Little did we know
> How little do we really know
> Everyday we're pressing the key
> That executes a million commands
> If only you could say exactly what is on your mind
> And tell me how you really feel
> Maybe I can lend a helping hand
> Scary it's true, but loads of fun, too

In short, Desert/Dessert/Dessret's pop lyrics provide vital clues about the motivations of the 'angelic' children behind the mass suicides, especially their powerful desire to promote external, 'real world' human attachments, exchanges through which people can 'feel the pain of others as [they] would [their] own'. It is this message of 'connection' that characters like Detective Karuda (with his emotional distance from his family and his recurrent obsession with his appearance in mirrors) tragically fail to understand until it is too late. Similarly, it is this contact that the film's suicidal characters only achieve in the most abstracted and ironic of ways: as anonymous, uniform rectangles of freshly-skinned flesh mechanically sewn into gruesome spiralling chains that are eventually wrapped in plastic, packed in nondescript white sports bags, and mysteriously left at the site of numerous suicides.

In contrast, the desire for interpersonal communion informs many of the actions of Karuda's young assistant, Detective Shibusawa, who alone reaches out to comfort Mitsuko following her boyfriend's suicide. If Sono Shion's *Suicide Circle* can be read as espousing even the faintest glimmer of optimism or hope in the face of a seemingly apocalyptic crisis, such an understanding hinges upon the sporadic, yet strategically placed representations of Shibusawa's altruism. Sono provides perhaps the most important representation of Shibusawa's selflessness in *Suicide Circle*'s penultimate sequence, a tense series of tracking and static shots that recall the film's shocking opening. After a multitude of female high school students descend the wide concrete steps leading to a subway platform, a parade accompanied by ringing cell phones playing the refrains of various Desert/Dessert/Dessret tunes, Sono cuts to a medium shot of Shibusawa scanning the crowd for Mitsuko until, in a reverse shot, we see her waiting for the approaching train. Next, in a medium two shot, Shibusawa approaches Mitsuko and grasps her arm to prevent her from potentially leaping to her death. With an expression that vacillates between annoyance and confusion, Mitsuko pulls her arm from Shibusawa's grip and continues towards the platform's edge before looking back over her shoulder at the detective. The camera zooms in quick to a closer shot of Mitsuko, followed by a series of cross-cuts between a close up of the young detective's worried visage and a medium shot of Mitsuko looking sad but determined. As the train arrives, Sono cuts back to a close up of Shibusawa, and then cuts back to a full shot of Mitsuko as she slowly turns, boards the train, and then looks back again at the detective, her body now framed by the closing subway door. Finally, Sono cuts back to a medium shot of Shibusawa watching as the subway cars roll out of the station with a metallic hiss and squeal.

Of course, the wordless exchange described above is an ambivalent conclusion at best. The troubled expressions and abortive gestures throughout the sequence promote this sense of ambiguity. Mitsuko, after all, pulls away from Shibusawa; the subway door ultimately slides shut, separating the protagonists both literally and figuratively. However, it is precisely this indeterminacy that allows viewers to read the film's *denouement* as ultimately hopeful. Although 'cut off' from one another in a geographical space (a subway station) linked throughout the film's diegesis with notions of 'transience' or 'alienation', the fact that Shibusawa endeavours to forge an external/inter-personal connection with Mitsuko implies that a complete surrender to information technology's alienating inertia is avoidable if each person simply reaches out physically and emotionally to those around him and feels 'the pain of others as he would his own'.

Image 16: School girls clasp hands before leaping in front of a subway in Sono Shion's *Suicide Circle* (Courtesy Internet Movie Database)

The spiralling chain of precisely sewn rectangles of skin found at the location of mass suicides need not represent the only form of connection possible in a late capitalist culture in which 'communication technologies' ironically perpetuate isolation; while the wheels of flesh may circle inward to nothingness, they also curve outward toward the possibility of infinite connections that need not conform to those that came before. In other words, while Sono's film may present us with a bleak, apocalyptic vision, the catastrophic events depicted throughout the film need not be viewed as absolutely destructive. Though Sono leaves the audience unsure as to the ramifications of the attempted connection in the film's penultimate scene, Desert/Dessert/Dessret's 'final performance', coupled with their injunction that we – the spectators – should 'live as [we] please', suggests that ultimately breaking free from cycles of self-destruction remains a viable option. The future is in our hands and, in the words of the pop sirens, it is still possible to 'find life again'.

Spirals and Vortices: Higuchinsky's *Uzumaki*

Based on Ito Junji's remarkable *manga* series of the same name, Higuchinsky's *Uzumaki* (also known by the English titles: *Spiral* and *Vortex*, 2000) not only stands as one of the most unique works of contemporary Japanese horror cinema, but also as one of the most original horror films in all of world cinema. Highly experimental in its visual style, and intellectually challenging in its socio-cultural critique and meticulously recursive narrative structure, *Uzumaki* has been described by critics as a 'dazzling' (Sharp 2000: para 6) and 'dynamically rendered' (Macias 2001: 82) work of apocalyptic art. It is also a cinematic vision that, despite humorous moments, intentionally exaggerated performances, and the playful conflation of horror film and romantic comedy tropes, nevertheless concludes with a tone that, compared to Sono Shion's *Suicide Circle*, seems unremittingly bleak. Set in an isolated municipality that functions as a microcosm for modern-day Japanese society,[5] the climax of Higuchinsky's film offers only the faintest glimmer of hope for the future of Kurouzu Town's remaining inhabitants, including the film's optimistic narrator, Kirie, whose careful balancing of Japanese customs with a recognition of the necessity for cultural change provides a potentially valuable avenue for escaping the entropic inertia of socio-cultural isolationism.

---

[5] This comparison is rendered visually explicit when a televised emergency weather broadcast warning of a typhoon's (yet another spiral's) imminent arrival in Karouzu Town graphically represents the impending rain and winds as a red spiral over central Japan.

An admittedly 'strange story' set almost exclusively within the labyrinthine streets of Kurouzu Town – a modest village separated from the rest of the Japanese mainland by large hills, a dark tunnel evoking dizziness and dread in all those that pass through it, and a forbidding expanse of ocean – *Uzumaki* is a counter-cinematic treat for the eyes. At the town's epicentre, as well as the narrative's core, is Dragonfly Pond, a circular pool of water linked with an ancient and obscure mythology that, to echo Patrick Macias's astute observation, is highly reminiscent of the works of H.P. Lovecraft, especially those tales featuring his Cthulhu Mythos, a pantheon of extra-dimensional monstrosities whose alternative logics confound human understanding to the point of driving insane those unlucky enough to cross their paths (Macias 2001: 82). Into this supernatural scenario Huguchinsky introduces the film's two teenage leads: Kirie, whose voice-over narration functions as the story's frame, and Saitou Shiuchi, Kirie's childhood friend/'guardian angel' and an extremely bright student whose daily commute to a school in a neighbouring village initially allows him initially to avoid the destructive impact of the mysterious vortexes possessing his town. It is Shuichi who repeatedly implores Kirie to run away with him and leave their doomed and haunted town behind, even before Shuichi's father becomes one of the vortex's first victims through a grotesque suicide via washing machine. This death is one to which the narrative returns again and again, albeit in ways that provide the film's viewers with subtly alternative perspectives on the gruesome death. Even Shuichi's mother falls victim to the vortexes' seductive, if ultimately nightmarish, allure. Disturbed by her husband's death and the colossal spiral of smoke that fills the sky above the town's crematorium, she soon becomes hospitalised and, in some of the film's most grotesque moments, not only removes her fingerprints and hair, but ends her life by plunging a knife-like shard of broken vase into her ear to remove the vortex she believes resides somewhere beyond her tympanic membrane.

Adding to the film's inventory of surreal, nightmarish events, Kurouzu Town's high school becomes a locus of terror and focus of national media attention as several students slowly transform into large human-snail hybrids called 'Hitomaimai'. Similarly, Sekino, the requisite conceited 'popular' girl, finds herself bedecked with monstrously long curly black hair that inevitably leads to her grotesque demise when these otherworldly tresses wrap themselves around a power line, reducing her to a withered, smoking husk. When Tamura, an investigator who claims to have discovered some vital clues as to the vortexes' origins, dies before he can tell Shiuchi what he has learned, Shiuchi finally convinces Kirie that it is time to leave town. However, before they can depart, Shiuchi becomes possessed by the vortex. His body uncontrollably coiling from ankle to neck, an image accompanied by sharp snapping sounds, he implores Kirie to join him in the vortex: 'Be a vortex, too,' he urges, his eyes two dead grey swirls. Kirie refuses, and the film closes with a series of still shots (some of them paintings) of the town's numerous victims, over which Kirie declares that what we have just witnessed is 'something that happened in her home town.'

Like Kurouzu Town itself, Higuchinsky's *Uzumaki* is in many ways a structure haunted both explicitly and implicitly by vortexes. Even a cursory sampling of spiral imagery in *Uzumaki*'s diegesis reveals the depth and scope of the shape's copious manifestations. Vortexes are located on fingertips, snail shells, mounds of clay rotating upon a spinning pottery wheel, a twirling police officer's baton, the interior of a gun barrel, the helical curves of a spiral staircase, and the spinning of a rotary phone's dial, posters depicting everything from galaxies to cross-sections of the human body. Higuchinsky's intentionally eclectic visual style further inundates viewers with a dizzying array of technical manipulations and skilful editing. For example, in the film's 88 minute running time, Higuchinsky employs: fast motion and reverse motion photography; dissolves and double-exposures; fades to black, white and red; tracking shots; cross-cuts, flash-cuts and jump-cuts; wipes; long takes; POV shots; and hand-held photography. When one factors in Higuchinsky's use of split screen photography, as well as the film's numerous instances of digital manipulation, varying focal lengths, chiaroscuro and low key lighting, and the application of exaggerated sound effects, particularly during the work's ghastlier moments, *Uzumaki*'s unique aesthetic constitutes a kind of visual hyperactivity. As a result, the spectator is never allowed to slip into an optical or narratological 'comfort zone', safely predicting what image will follow the one presently on screen. This is not to suggest that Higuchinsky avoids the familiar logics of classical continuity editing altogether. Indeed, were it not for his periodic observance of such 'standardised' editing practices, his multiple violations of audience expectation would be nowhere near as disorienting as they are. Consequently, viewers would not experience the ontological dislocation necessary to fully associate with the characters' mystification at the supernatural proliferation of spiral patterns.

Furthermore, as the film's action unfolds, the narrative continually cycles back to several key images, often re-visualising them in ways that condition our previous understanding of the scenes in question. As mentioned above, Higuchinsky revisits Shuichi's father's suicide several times throughout the film. The first time we encounter his death, we do not see what his body looks like within the washing machine's tight confines. Later, when Tamura, the police investigator, visits Shuichi and Kirie, Higuchinsky 'shows us' Shuichi's father's suicide from the perspective of a videotape recording made during the fatal incident. Here again Higuchinsky carefully elides a complete or stable visual disclosure of the tragic event, focusing the viewer's attention instead upon a mirror Shuichi's father places in the washing machine, and then cutting to a shot of the investigator's, Shuichi's and Kirie's reaction to the exaggerated cracking sounds one can only assume is Shuichi's father's bones snapping as his body contorts. Tamura returns to this videotape later in the film, rewinding and fast-forwarding to moments that Higuchinsky once again prevents the film's viewers from seeing. Thus, instead of witnessing the bizarre suicide, spectators must either experience it via Tamura's grimaces, or endeavor to 'make sense' of the event through extreme close-ups of the video footage that disallow viewers the necessary context a more removed perspective would provide. Finally, towards the film's conclusion, Higuchinsky again returns to Shuichi's father's suicide, this time from a perspective seemingly aligned with Kirie's gaze. In a POV tracking shot granted 'realistic' immediacy through hand-held cinematography, spectators are finally granted a glimpse of Shuichi's father's body wound snake-like inside the washing machine, a grotesque vision made even more disturbing by the sudden opening of his eyes and mouth, from which a monstrously elongated coiling tongue emerges. In keeping with the narrative's perpetual (and cyclical) deferment of a stable visual referent regarding the vortex's initial victim, Higuchinsky once again removes the potential for an absolute comprehension of events by immediately consigning this first-person perspective to the realm of dream. The opening eyes and curling tongue become aligned with Kirie's unconscious and, thus, Shuichi's father's 'actual' death remains 'unseen'. Lastly, by building upon an economy of frustrated vision amplified by the videotape that obscures as much as it reveals, locating this hand-held POV shot within the realm of fantasy further exploits the film's internal recursive structure, heightening the work's surreal tone.

Engaging in a close reading of the sequence described above provides an avenue by which one might begin to analyse this strange and convoluted film. As Tamura discovers during his investigation into Shuichi's father's suicide (depicted via montage), not only do spirals appear continually throughout nature (from galactic formations, to weather patters, to fingerprints, etc.), but they have been immortalised in art works dating back thousands of years and bridging multiple cultures. In this sense, the chaotic system that is Higuchinsky's *Uzumaki* intersects effectively with works like Benoit Mandelbrot's *The Fractal Geometry of Nature* (1982) and John Briggs' *Fractals – The Patterns of Chaos: Discovering A New Aesthetic of Art, Science, and Nature* (1992). Chaotic, non-Euclidean formations that mathematicians initially pathologised as capable of unleashing a 'gallery of monsters' (Mandelbrot 1982: 3), vortexes are 'scaling', 'self-similar' configur-ations seemingly 'invarient under certain transformations of scale' (18). As such, each successive arc in a spiral functions as a subtle occlusion upon the curvature that precedes it, a 'self-organising' and 'self-similar' pattern ingeniously illustrated by Higuchinsky's persistent return to, and visual/narratological modification of, Shuichi's father's suicide. Additionally, the spiral as image 'appears

on Stone Age structures around the world';[6] an historical detail echoed by
Tamura's research in *Uzumaki*. As John Briggs notes, anthropologists
have long probed the metaphorical potentialities of these fractal images,
understanding them as symbolic of 'activity in the life-giving boundary
between order and chaos' and as 'the ancient symbol for the labyrinth, the
twisted pathway to a journey to the core of being' (1992: 113).

How, then, does Higuchinsky mobilse the image of the vortex in
Uzumaki? In *Seeing Nature: Deliberate Encounters with the Visible
World*, Paul Krafel argues that an expansive dialogue between 'upward
spirals' (or self-similar, scaling fractals that encourage creativity,
multiplicity and regeneration) and 'downward spirals' (vortexes whirling
inevitably towards entropy, dissolution, death) constitute much of the
natural world (1999: 63). Such a conceptualisation intersects productively
with Higuchinsky's film, especially given *Uzumaki*'s abundance of
natural, supernatural, and narratological vortexes. Most of *Uzumaki*'s
vortexes seemingly conform to Krafel's notion of 'downward spirals', as
do the institutions and characters most spectacularly destroyed by the
apocalyptic plague of whirling patterns. In particular, certain socio-
cultural practices – education and the apportioning of gender roles being
the most conspicuous examples – are rendered entropic in their numbing
repetition (that is, in their cyclical constancy), as well as through their
resistance to significant change. Part of Higuchinsky's social critique,
then, targets those deadening socio-cultural systems and ideological
continuities that, if left unchecked or unchallenged, may stifle the
potential for meaningful, or even necessary, modification. In other words,
reading the nightmarish vortexes permeating Higuchinsky's text as
metaphors for institutions and practices linked with the maintenance and
perpetuation of social and cultural power reveals *Uzumaki* as not only a
visually and structurally complex film, but also as a nuanced critical
project. Consequently, rigid conformity in *Uzumaki* can be understood as
a type of vortex, as can the unquestioned adherence to scholastic and

---

[6] Japanese art is no exception. Consider, for instance, the 'eddies and whorls' permeating
works like Hokusai Katsushika's engraving, *Great Wave* (1823-9).

familial conventions, or the perfunctory perpetuation of conventional gender codes.

This is not to suggest that Higuchinsky's apocalyptic vision is exclusively destructive or unremittingly pessimistic. Not all spirals are necessarily downward in their trajectory. As Krafel posits, spirals curve upward as well, and with each ascendant whorl of an 'upward spiral' comes the potential for infinite self-organising variability. As John Briggs notes, '[a] chaotic system constantly mixes things up, creating new directions in which the system can go. These moments of possibility are called bifurcation points by chaologists' (1992: 112). In *Uzumaki,* Kirie, the film's central protagonist and narrator, functions as perhaps the most pronounced example of one such productive bifurcation. Initially, Higuchinsky depicts Kirie as politely resistant to Shuichi's frequent suggestions that they 'run away' together, a cautionary position informed by her desire to remain within the 'comfort' of familiar environs. Only following Shuichi's pronouncement that '[t]his town is finished' – an observation that, given Kurauzu Town's role as a microcosm of Japanese society, may be translated as 'Japan is finished' – does Kirie realise that she must do something to escape the deadening cycles that threaten her very life. When Shuichi finally succumbs to the vortex's simultaneously alluring and horrific force, his body and will twisting beyond his control, Kirie leaves him and, as we are led to assume by her closing voice-over, Kurouzu Town's entropic disintegration for good. Thus, though we can assume that Kirie will most likely adhere to some of the traditional attitudes and practices that have informed her personal development, it is ultimately her optimistic attitude and willingness to not only recognise, but also to create change that allows her to avoid annihilation and quite possibly begin her life anew. As her final words ('[t]his is a story of something that happened to my home town') suggest, Kirie has survived to tell her tale, be that story a narrative infused with the dread of catastrophe or laced, if only in its final moments, with a thread of hope.

Image 17: One spiral among many in Higuchinsky's *Uzumaki* (Courtesy Rapid Eye Movies)

Fade Away and Radiate: Kurosawa Kiyoshi's *Pulse*

In an interview with Patrick Macias, Kurosawa Kiyoshi responds to a question regarding influences upon his cinematic vision by praising the work of Tobe Hooper, the American director of such horror films as *The Texas Chainsaw Massacre* (USA, 1974), *Lifeforce* (USA, 1985), and *Spontaneous Combustion* (USA, 1990). Given Hooper's aptitude for constructing nightmarish scenes redolent with a tension-filled and claustrophobic atmosphere, as well as Hooper's works' overtly politically and philosophically charged agendas, Kurosawa's admiration for Hooper's films should come as no surprise. Throughout horror films like *Cure* (*Kyua*, 1997), *Charisma* (*Karisuma*, 1999) and *Seance* (*Kôrei*, 2000), Kurosawa consistently demonstrates a mastery of the genre; his films deliver plentiful shocks, but not before his deliberate pacing and meticulous compositions submerge audiences within an uneasy sea of escalating expectation and fear. In *Pulse*, his most accomplished work to date, Kurosawa demonstrates the skill of an artist in near total command of his medium. During this exquisitely crafted narrative of ghosts, alienation, and the gradual eradication of human life as we know it, Kurosawa's *mise-en-scène*, with its application of chiaroscuro lighting and muted colours, lures the viewer into an apocalyptic scenario as sad as it is frightening. In the process, he presents a critical dissection of a postmodern Japan that, like the films discussed above, explores the impact of technology upon our lives and the profound alienation that all too frequently (and ironically) accompanies post-industrial capitalist culture.

Summarising *Pulse*'s plot for the purpose of the ensuing analysis presents numerous challenges, not the least of which stems from the density of the film's visuals, as well as its complex individual, yet ultimately intersecting, storylines. From its disquieting opening moments, in which a black screen and the electronic screech of a computer's modem gives way to a brief sequence aboard a lone, largely empty ship motoring steadily through an expanse of ocean darkened by low grey clouds, Kurosawa Kiyoshi conveys a palpable tone of menace and dread that intensifies as the film's plot unfolds. One of the bleakest apocalyptic visions in contemporary Japanese horror cinema, *Pulse* conveys the story of two lonely young adults living in an alienating late-industrial Tokyo, an urban realm where, in a scenario that anticipates Sono Shion's *Suicide Circle*, pervasive communication technologies (from cell phones to the internet) paradoxically enhance the disconnection and isolation the film's protagonists feel. One of the two major characters is a woman named Michi, whose voice-over frames the film's events. Employed by a botanical nursery, Michi volunteers to visit an absent co-worker, Taguchi, to retrieve a disk containing important information for an on-going project. When she arrives at Taguchi's apartment, she speaks briefly with her colleague, who, in the few minutes it takes Michi to locate the crucial disk, commits suicide by hanging himself in an adjacent room. This death variably disturbs the nursery's employees, as does a strange and haunting image they find embedded within the project file: a still photo of Taguchi standing in front of a desk with two computer monitors, one of which reveals a strangely contorted face, while the other displays what appears to be a webpage consisting of an exact reproduction of the very image captured in the still photo. From this moment forward, Michi and her fellow employees experience increasingly bizarre supernatural events, including encounters with ghost-like entities that lead them to become ever-more convinced that '[s]omething strange' is transpiring.

The film's second major character, Kawashima, is a shy economics student whose initial foray into the world's on-line community results in an encounter with a strange web site displaying dimly lit images of shadowy, isolated figures followed by an unsettling invitation: 'Would you like to meet a ghost?' Annoyed, he shuts down his computer and falls asleep, only to awaken when his computer inexplicably boots up and displays the same unsettling images. Kawashima is unnerved by this unwelcome technological intervention, and he soon visits one of his university's computer labs in the hope of learning why his PC has suddenly taken on a disturbing life of its own. It is in the lab that he meets Harue, a female graduate student in computer science with whom he begins an awkwardly tender, yet ultimately ill-fated friendship. During one of his subsequent visits to the university, Kawashima meets another computer science graduate student named Yoshizaki, who has created a computer program in which dots of light drift about on the computer's screen until, when they get 'too far apart', they are slowly drawn together and 'die'. Harue explains that the program mimics human interactions in the real world, an assessment that takes on troubling connotations when thicker, ghostly dots invade the program. In addition, like the employees of the botanical nursery, Yoshizaki and Harue begin to encounter strange otherworldly phantoms. In one crucial scene, Yoshizaki engages Kawashima in a discussion, during which Yoshizaki advances his theory that the world of the dead has reached its maximum capacity and, consequently, these lonely spirits have 'oozed' into the electronic and physical realms of the living in an attempt to find new places to inhabit.

As the film moves towards its climax, encounters with 'ghosts' become more prevalent and the world becomes progressively less populated as people drift into deep, often suicidal despair before transforming into ashy, vaguely human-shaped smudges. These human stains disintegrate into tiny black flakes that whirl skyward, ultimately fusing with the perpetual blanket of low grey clouds. Eventually, Harue abandons Kawashima, and as he wanders through a near empty Tokyo, the film's two narrative lines intersect when he encounters Michi sitting in a broken down car. Kawashima helps get Michi's car restarted, and they, too, begin an awkward friendship as they search for Harue and, later, for anyone who may still be alive. As the film comes to a close, Michi and Kawashima board a ship headed for Latin America, where radio signals supposedly indicate that some human life may still exist. In a poignant scene, Michi watches as Kawashima transforms into a dark stain on the wall and then disintegrates. Unsure of whether she has made the right decision in her choice to continue living, Michi wanders the ship until she encounters the craft's pilot, who reassures her that she has indeed made the correct choice. The film ends with a bird's-eye view of the lone vessel and Michi's final, if cryptic, affirmation that: 'Now, alone with my last friend in the world, I have found happiness.'

Pulse confronts audiences with an ominous vision of an apocalyptic present. Much of the film's emotional impact results from Kurosawa Kiyoshi's direction, especially his construction of the film's consistently evocative if unsettling *mise-en-scène*. Contributing to the gloomy atmosphere that hovers like a pall over virtually every scene is Kurosawa's manipulation of lighting and lighting effects. Chiaroscuro lighting, with its attendant contrast of light and dark, brightness and shadow, dominates the film's compositions; consequently, viewers soon find themselves studying each image, visually probing the darkest regions of the frame with an intensity that only further compliments the impact of those images the director illuminates. As such, audiences soon become aware of their roles as active producers of meaning, scanning each shot in the anticipation of glimpsing the faintest impression of an emerging apparition. Kurosawa's predilection for silhouettes, in both his representation of the spectral entities invading the realm of the living and of human beings reduced to inky shadows on dimly lit walls, illustrates his control over a broad range of darkness and light. In even the lengthiest daytime exterior shots, such as those scenes that take place in the rooftop nursery or, later in the film, on the streets of a desolate Tokyo, the sun is never shown, nor is the sky ever blue. Rather, such scenes further the film's menacing tone through a strategic diffusion of light that creates the impression that the sky is consistently overcast – a thick steam-white glow that obscures far more than it reveals. Thus, throughout the film, the settings go 'far beyond being a simple décor…to the point of becoming characters in their own right, breathing, moving and living, as unpredictable as any of the human characters on the screen' (Mes 2001: para 6).

Kurosawa's compositions are likewise designed to heighten the film's theme of isolation and alienation. When more than a single character occupies a shot or series of shots, they rarely engage in prolonged eye-contact, even when conversing with one another; characters frequently speak to the backs of other characters' heads or look away completely, muttering ambiguous utterances like 'huh', 'hmm' and 'oh', or beginning sentences that end in mid-articulation, a verbal gesture suggestive of a profound degree of distraction and disconnection. What's more, Kurosawa divides his figures in such shots not only through the calculated deployment of negative space (for instance, scenes containing two or more characters are frequently lensed so that their pronounced physical distance from one another accentuates their emotional detachment), but also through the use of strong vertical lines, like doorways and the edges of walls, conveniently located within the sets' geography. These visual arrangements, in turn, strengthen the impact of the rare instances where characters actually reach out to one another or actually make physical contact. However, carefully executed eye-line mismatches invest even these moments with a tone of almost heartbreaking estrangement. So powerful are these compositions that when characters actually touch one another, these otherwise simple and tender gestures resonate with a sadness that, nevertheless, provides a brief respite from the film's dominant images of loneliness and disconnection.

Furthermore, by combining elements of the Japanese *kaidan* tradition with cyberpunk motifs, including the transformation of the corporeal by the mechanical and the 'ghost in the machine' trope popularised by cyberpunk novels like William Gibson's *Neuromancer* (1984) and exceedingly popular science fiction *anime* such as Oshii Mamoru's *Ghost in the Shell* (1995), *Kairo* contributes to dystopian visions grounded upon the paradoxically alienating impact of so-called communication technologies. When Harue, for instance, asks the shy, computer-illiterate Kawashima if he was drawn to the internet out of a desire to 'connect with other people', she responds to his statement, 'everybody else is into it,' with a warning that evokes the drifting electronic dots in her fellow graduate student's, Yoshizaki's, project: 'People don't connect, you know...Like those dots simulating humans. We all live totally separately.' Harue's statement, then, proves a valuable precursor to the critique of technology at work in Sono's *Suicide Circle*; in both instances, attempts at interpersonal communication ironically result in scenarios in which the urge to engage in a mode of technologically-mediated discourse inevitably results in simulated togetherness, a 'union' that is, ultimately, only a veiled form of alienation. Similarly, the suicides in *Pulse* are acts of self-annihilation that almost exclusively occur when another human being is in the general proximity to serve as a witness. As such, one may construe the suicides punctuating Kurosawa's film as desperate attempts at connection that, ironically, sever all ties.

Of course, Kurosawa Kiyoshi is far from the only director reflecting upon the acute alienation many experience living in crowded, late-industrial urban settings marked by the presence of emerging communication technologies in all of their copious manifestations. Directors from Martin Scorsese (*Taxi Driver*, USA, 1976) and Nicholas Roeg (*The Man Who Fell to Earth*, UK, 1976) to Wong Kar-Wai (*Chunking Express*, a.k.a. *Chung hing sam lam*, Hong Kong, 1994) and Tsai Ming-Liang (*What Time Is It There?*, a.k.a. *Ni neibian jidian*, Taiwan, 2001) have famously investigated similar sociological and philosophical terrain. However, what differentiates Kurosawa's film from most works of urban ennui in world cinema, as well as from most films employing tropes from the Japanese *kaidan* tradition, is its ultimate equation of the human with the spectral. In *Pulse*, everyone is a 'ghost', even if their hearts still beat and their lungs still breathe; identity, in other words, is always liminal. Dots of light on a computer screen uncannily mirror social economies of 'real world' disconnection, as do the 'ghosts' inviting internet users to 'meet them'. In a sense, though, the internet has always been an ethereal realm, especially since on-line communities are

largely disembodied collectives in which, as in the 'real world', identities
are continually under construction. *Pulse*'s haunted (and often
emotionally haunting) webcasts are ghost stories conveyed by phantoms,
but much the same can be said of all webcasts, telecasts or films. As
representations of passed or passing events, mediated images are two
dimensional abstractions/shadows through which the absent or dead
'commune' with the living. Many of *Pulse*'s more powerful scenes build
quite explicitly upon such parallels, as this crucial exchange from late in
the film illustrates:

> **Harue:** I always wondered what it's like to die. From when I was really little. I
> was always alone.
>
> **Kawashima:** Any parents or family?
>
> **Harue:** Sure, but they're irrelevant.
>
> **Kawashima:** Right.
>
> **Harue:** That after death you live happily with everyone over there...Then in
> high school it dawned on me. You might be alone after death, too....The idea
> was so terrifying. I couldn't even bear it. That nothing changes with
> death...just right now, forever. Is that what becoming a ghost is about?
>
> **Kawashima:** You can't mean that. It's really bad. What have ghosts got to do
> with us? Besides, we're alive.
>
> **Harue:** (switching on a tiny wall of monitors displaying internet sites
> displaying lone, shadowy figures in dark rooms) Then who are they? Are they
> really alive? How are they different from ghosts? In fact, ghosts and people are
> the same, whether they're dead or alive.

Harue's final observations in this scene illuminate Kurosawa's critique of
the technologies dominating late capitalist culture, particularly the
internet and its paradoxical appeals to creating new, increasingly global
'communities', while privileging anonymity and the mobilisation of high-
tech shadows, like avatars and emoticons, in place of face to face
communication and profound interpersonal relations.

   Pulse's appraisal of modern alienation, however, is even more
sophisticated than the above paragraph suggests. One may comprehend
identities on the internet as liminal simulations, or 'ghosts', but as Harue

suggests, 'ghosts and people are the same, whether dead or alive.' Despite the varying degrees of familiarity a person may feel she has with other human beings, people remain ultimately *unknowable*. Though our bodies are ultimately reducible to meat and bone, our identities are assiduously constructed. As a result, the various 'selves' we 'project' are open to multiple readings, but they remain incomprehensible, irreducible and incomplete. Slavoj Žižek advances a similar critique in his recent book, *Organs Without Bodies: On Deleuze and Consequences.* Comparing human interaction with techno-logical interfaces, Žižek argues that 'we cannot avoid' concluding that when we 'communicate with another person, we get signals from him, we observe his face as a screen, but...we, partners in communication, never get to know what is "behind the screen"' (2003: 118). '[T]he same', Žižek posits, 'goes for the concerned subject himself (i.e., the subject does not know what lies behind the screen of his very own [self]consciousness, what kind of Thing he is in the real)' (118).

Pulse, then, suggests that individual and interpersonal unfathom-ability informs human relationships far more substantially than one may have previously imagined. As Michi's employer at the botanical nursery states when Michi asks his permission to question a co-worker regarding the fellow employee's transparently anti-social behaviour:

> [Speaking with him] might be a waste of time. Words said in friendship with the best of intentions always end up hurting your friends deeply. And then you wind up getting hurt. Is friendship always that way? If that's so, what's left? [...] Who needs friends like that?'

Furthermore, as the discussion between Harue and Kawashima presented two paragraphs above illustrates, a comparable notion applies to that supposedly 'deepest' of all human bonds: the family. A potentially substantial factor in the characters' dismay and extreme isolation, family ties, Harue suggests, have become 'irrelevant'. This perspective echoes Michi's contention, voiced earlier in the film, that endeavouring to contact her absent father in a city as large as Tokyo would be a waste of time, an opinion with which Kawashima, given his response ('Right'), apparently agrees.

While many viewers may find *Pulse* 'despairing', Kurosawa maintains that his apocalyptic vision is also – perhaps necessarily – optimistic in that it proposes 'the possibility of starting again with nothing...the beginning of hope' (2002: 36). A treatise on transience and cycles of change, Kurosawa's film extols the quasi-existentialist benefits of perpetually re-examining one's ideologies and the network of social, cultural, and ontological contingencies one must continually negotiate, even before one interacts with the world in which one exists. As Kurosawa remarks in an interview with Japanese scholar Tom Mes:

> I'm not so interested in the group that surrounds the individual. I'm interested in the values that the individual has come to embrace. For the individual to re-assess those values and understand the way in which those values that he has come to embrace are in fact the forces that have come to oppress him, not something from the outside. (2003: para 31)

Such introspection is never easy. Indeed, as *Pulse* illustrates, it is fraught with its own battery of perils, from abject nihilism to emotionally paralysing despondency, the latter of which ultimately leads to Kawashima's demise. Moving forward while accepting the present and learning from the past, however, is all one can do. Thus, the film's concluding bird's-eye view shot of a lone vessel drifting slowly over an apparently endless expanse of ocean becomes a metaphor for the human condition, a circumstance that exceeds national particularities. Similarly, when Michi's closing voiceover narration informs us that '[n]ow, alone with my last friend in the world, I have found happiness,' we believe her. Like the ship on which she rides, Michi is moving forward with only the vaguest notion as to her final destination and with no assurances as to what, if anything, she might find. Michi is adrift, moving, in transition, becoming; the journey itself becomes the point.

**Image 18: 'Would you like to meet a ghost?' Kurosawa Kiyoshi's *Pulse*
(© Magnolia Pictures)**

Contemporary Catastrophes, Bright Futures

From the atomic and ecological menaces inherent in the plot of *daikaiju eiga* like Honda Ishiro's *Gojira* (1954), to the melancholic postmodern meditations of late industrial urban alienation explored in the preceding analyses of Sono Shion's *Suicide Circle*, Higuchinsky's *Uzumaki* and Kurosawa Kiyoshi's *Pulse*, realisations of apocalyptic devastation have long provided a horrific yet compelling thematic, visual and narratological terrain to which Japanese horror film directors frequently return. At once an end and a new beginning – a representation of death and entropic dissolution, as well as a depiction of rebirth and emergent becomings – cinematic imaginings of apocalypse should continue providing venues for artists eager to frighten their audiences in innovative ways. Additionally, filmmakers and critics will doubtlessly adopt such aesthetic productions as terrifying and entertaining platforms from which they may advance variously explicit (or implicit) social critiques.

Of course, narratives of apocalypse are by no means limited to Japanese horror film; most national cinemas have long-standing traditions of such tales, and given these narratives' function as barometers for social and cultural anxieties, representations of 'the end of the world' should continue to appear on movie screens across the globe. In terms of Japanese cinema, it will be interesting not only to map the continuities and discontinuities within this genre, but also to explore the way these narratives provide insights into the transforming and increasingly pluralistic body that is contemporary Japanese culture. As Kurosawa Kiyoshi stated in a 2003 interview with noted Japanese film scholar Mark Schilling, no one 'can say for certain what kind of future awaits society as a whole' (para 24). However, though 'the future for Japan and the world may well be dark' (para 24), individuals willing to envision the world in new ways need not expire beneath a cloak of gloom and despair. Thus, like the beautiful but poisonous jellyfish iridescently glowing as they float through the rivers and streams in Kurosawa's recent film, *Bright Future* (2003), individuals living in contemporary Japan (or anywhere for that matter) need not perceive the days ahead as irredeemably bleak or ultimately doomed. As Kurosawa explains: 'a bright future is something you make for yourself...You can still have a bright future as an individual, despite what is happening in the world' (para 24).

Chapter Six:
New Terrors, Emerging Trends and the Future of Japanese Horror

Repetition, Innovation, and 'J-Horror' Anthologies

The following pages constitute not only this book's final chapter, but its conclusion as well. I adopt this structural and rhetorical manoeuvre for two reasons. Firstly, the arguments advanced in this chapter provide a critical assessment of the state of the horror genre in Japanese cinema at the time of this writing. As a result, this chapter examines not only the rise of a self-reflexive tendency within recent works of Japanese horror film, but also explores how visual and narratological redundancy may compromise the effectiveness of future creations, transforming motifs into clichés and, quite possibly, reducing the tradition's potential as an avenue for cultural critique and aesthetic intervention. As one might suspect, the promise of quick economic gain – motivated both by the genre's popularity in Western markets, as well as by the cinematic tradition's contribution to what James Udden calls a 'pan-[east-]Asian' film style (2005: para 5) – inform the fevered perpetuation of predictable *shinrei mono eiga* ('ghost films'). Secondly, by examining the emergence of several visually inventive and intellectually sophisticated films by some of Japanese horror cinema's most accomplished practitioners, this chapter proposes that the creative fires spawned by the explosion of Japanese horror in the 1990s are far from extinguished. As close readings

of works like Ochiai Masayuki's *Infection* (*Kansen*, 2004), Tsuruta
Norio's *Premonition* (*Yogen*, 2004), Shimizu Takashi's *Marebito* (2004),
and Tsukamoto Shinya's *Vital* (2004) variably reveal, the future of
Japanese horror cinema may be very bright indeed.

     Given Japanese horror film's appeal in East Asian and Western
markets, it should come as little surprise that producers eager to cash in
on the genre's popularity would soon produce both feature length works
and collections of short films, many originally intended for television
broadcast. After all, such market inundation has obvious precedents.
Consider, for instance, the glut of slasher films that flooded US theatres
in the wake of the success of John Carpenter's *Halloween* (USA, 1978)
and Sean S. Cunningham's *Friday the 13th* (USA, 1990). Largely
conforming to the general tropology informing what Vera Dika and Carol
Clover call the 'stalker cycle' or the 'teenie-kill pic' (1987; 1992),
virtually every major Western holiday soon marked an occasion for
mayhem and carnage. In the majority of such texts, the gory dispatching
of randy young people is followed by the inevitable 'cat-and-mouse'
conflict between the masked killer and the 'final girl', whose combination
of virginal purity and willingness to resort to violence ensures her
survival. Setting aside the copious sequels spawned by *Halloween* and
Friday the 13th, a glimpse at the following titles reveals a formula
stretched to its breaking point: *Prom Night* (CAN, 1980); *New Year's Evil*
(USA, 1980); the New Year's Eve themed *Terror Train* (CAN/USA,
1980); *Happy Birthday to Me* (USA, 1981); *My Bloody Valentine* (CAN,
1981); and *Silent Night, Deadly Night* (USA, 1984). Such market glutting
is by no means exclusive to horror films; nevertheless, the preceding list
proves at once instructive and cautionary when one considers the recent
deluge of Japanese horror tales that have found their way on to Japanese
television and have surfaced in the West as anthologies of short films. In
2005 alone, 'J-horror' collections like *Dark Tales from Japan*, *Kadokawa
Mystery & Horror Tales*, volumes 1-3, *J-Horror Anthology: Underworld*,
and *J-Horror Anthology: Legends* were released in the US. When many
of these narratives recycle the same tropes that viewers have seen time
and time again, they risk alienating the very segment of their audience
that once found the genre a refreshing alternative to Western horror film

traditions. As an exasperated Grady Hendrix remarks in a recent entry on his blog, *Kaiju Shakedown*:

> I mean, after *The Ring, The Ring Two, The Ring Virus, Nightmare, Scissors, Ju-on* 1 & 2, *A Tale of Two Sisters, Dark Water, Kakashi, The Phone, Shutter, Unborn but Forgotten, Into the Mirror, Wicked Ghost, Shikoku, One Missed Call, Horror Hotline...Big Head Monster, Pulse, R-Point, Three Extremes* and on and on, this whole "long-haired-dead-wet-chick" trope is dead. Done. Finished. Must we destroy the planet to save ourselves from this flood of J-horror knock-off movies?... J-horror is dead. Someone, anyone, please get it to lay down and stop moving.

While Hendrix may overstate his case, casually applying the label, 'J-horror' to films from countries other than Japan (six of the nine movies he lists are South Korean productions and one, *Shutter*, is from Thailand) his point regarding the risks of continually depicting similar iconographic images (for example, the 'long-haired-dead-wet-chick' motif) is well worth heeding.

One advantage to this recent proliferation of short films made for television or straight-to-video/DVD release, however, is that the format lends itself, by virtue of the sheer quantity of films produced, to the occasional emergence of narratives that propel the horror genre forwards in innovative if not always revolutionary ways. In the anthology, *Dark Tales of Japan*, for example, Shimizu Takashi's *Blonde Kaidan* distinguishes itself from the collection's other offerings in its critique of Western appropriations and (com)modifications of Japanese horror motifs. In *Blonde Kaidan*'s story of a Japanese director's frustration over Hollywood's neo-colonial capitalisation upon the recent Japanese horror boom, Shimizu's central protagonist pontificates upon not only Western cinema's predilection for remaking films from 'other' cultures, but also what he considers to be Hollywood's fascination with, and insistence upon, heroines with blonde hair. Consequently, in a farcical inversion of 'J-horror' clichés, the filmmaker soon finds himself haunted by a ghostly variation of the *onryou* convention, repeatedly besieged by her ridiculously expansive and resilient flaxen locks. Spectators familiar with Shimizu's work, especially his Hollywood-financed reiteration of his popular *Ju-on* series – 2004's *The Grudge*, starring fair-haired teen icon

Sarah Michelle Gellar – will undoubtedly read this short film as an ironic, self-reflexive indictment of not only the economic factors dominating production concerns both in Japan and abroad, but also Shimizu's own acknowledged complicity in such projects. Japanese producers, like their Hollywood counterparts, have a lengthy and well-documented history of eagerly exploiting popular trends, and the current capitalisation upon the cross-cultural appeal of Japanese horror movies is no exception.

In Shimizu's *Blonde Kaidan*, then, the subject being haunted is nothing less than Japanese horror film as a popular tradition in world cinema. Furthermore, the film's restless blonde ghost, far from merely conforming to the genre's motif of the wronged and vengeful female spirit, assumes a form immediately reminiscent of Hollywood stars like the aforementioned Sarah Michelle Gellar, as well as Naomi Watts, the latter of whom portrayed the resourceful investigative reporter in the 2002 US remake of Nakata Hideo's *Ringu*. As Gang Gary Xu correctly notes, Shimizu's *The Grudge*, with its casting of Gellar as 'an expatriot American social worker' in Japan, could have provided an 'exploration of cultural tensions for Westerners in Tokyo, similar to that revealed in *Lost in Translation* (Sophia Coppola, 2003)' (2004: para 9). That it failed to be anything remotely close to this illuminates the extent to which remaking successful works of Asian cinema has become 'Hollywood's way of outsourcing', a process that saves Western producers from having to pay labourers like 'assistant producers', 'supporting crew', and extensive 'marketing teams' (para 9). In this light, Shimizu's 'Blonde Kaidan' functions as a corrective of sorts, at once foregrounding Shimizu's acknowledgement of the financial pressures driving the (mass) market for Japanese horror films in Western cultures and criticising Hollywood's effacement of 'the original ethnicity, the "aura', the intellectual property' and, last but certainly not least, 'the identity and history of an entire national film industry' (para 9).

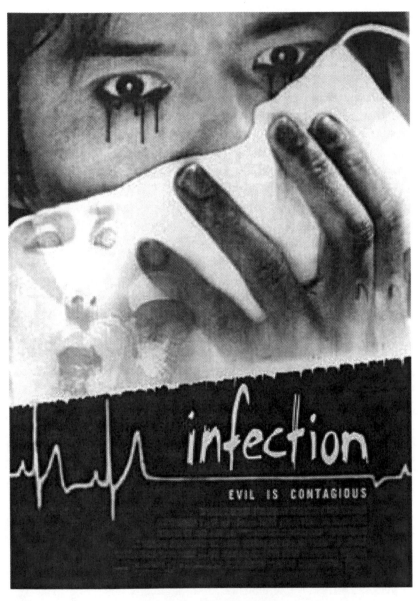

Image 19: Publicity poster for *Infection* (© Tartan USA)

Contagion and Chaos:
Ochiai Masayuki's *Infection* and Tsuruta Norio's *Premonition*

The first two entries in a projected series of feature-length 'J-horror' films directed by several of the genre's most respected filmmakers,[1] Ochiai Masayuki's *Infection* (2004) and Tsuruta Norio's *Premonition* (2004) offer refreshingly thoughtful and, at times, strikingly original variations upon the frantic propagation of retread narratives and all-too-predictable conceits that threaten to dilute the genre. At once contributions to, and variations upon, the plethora of horror films created to accrue quick capital while the genre remains a 'hot' property in domestic and foreign markets, *Infection* and *Premonition* demonstrate that the future of Japanese horror resides in filmmakers' dedication to the potentially hazardous thrills of innovation rather than their adherence to the insipid tedium of clichéd repetition. Each film contains and exceeds the visual and narratological constructs that infuse much of Japanese horror cinema, paving the way for future artists to advance the genre in creative and socially critical directions.

Ochiai Masayuki's *Infection* takes place within a dilapidated urban hospital staffed by a skeleton crew of ethically questionable physicians and under-prepared nurses. Surreal and frequently darkly humorous in tone, *Infection*'s action unfolds slowly at first, though as the film builds momentum, it becomes increasingly clear that Ochiai is more concerned with generating atmosphere and exhibiting gruesome special effects than in constructing a coherent narrative. That said, the events depicted in *Infection* are as gripping as they are sardonic, ultimately referencing a plurality of socio-cultural anxieties with the subtlety of a scalpel slashing across a pulsing artery. When a physician's negligence contributes to a patient's demise, the hospital's guilt-ridden, panicking employees collaborate to shield him. This suppression of culpability results in a chain of successively grisly events exacerbated by the unwelcome arrival, via ambulance, of an internally putrefying man. The

---

[1] At the time of this writing, the release of *Rinne* (2005), Shimizu Takashi's contribution to the J-Horror Theatre series, is imminent.

new patient eventually decomposes into a noxious green gas that, once sucked into the hospital's ventilation system, quickly infects all who come into contact with it. At once claustrophobic in its settings and apocalyptic in its scope, *Infection* is an extensively allegorical text intended to instigate both dis-ease and discussion.

As the preceding plot summary suggests, the material consequences of prolonged economic recession, coupled with extreme fiscal practices like compulsory downsising and the exploitative over-extension of current labour resources, underscores much of Ochiai's film. Likewise, as the film's title suggests, many of *Infection*'s more horrific sequences extend the inside-outside, *uchi-soto* binary discussed at length in Chapter Four. This dread of contagion, which informs popular imaginings of the Japanese corporeal and social body, arises most viscerally and memorably in *Infection*'s numerous graphic representations of corporeal putrefaction. Of course, Japan is far from the only culture embedded with discourses of (im)purity and pollution. As Jonathan Dollimore notes, 'there is no greater human aversion...than that felt towards "those unstable, fetid and lukewarm substances where life ferments ignobly...where the eggs, germs, and maggots swarm"' (2001: 253). The dread of decaying bodies in *Infection* arises from a reaction against, or a wilful disregard of, notions of biological and social permeability. In other words, Ochiai's embattled protagonists – a motley crew made up of doctors, nurses, and patients – reject 'life in its primal reality', disavowing comprehensions of the human form as 'a state of differentiation so excessive that it includes within itself the indifferentiation of death'...the 'stuff of life' that is also 'death gorging life with decomposed substance' (Bataille 1957: 95).

The hospital staff's desire simply to ignore the unwanted patient's putrefying physiology, a rejection of individual and collective responsibility that results in their ultimate inability to contain the infection that spreads from body to body, also positions *Infection* as a text concerned with the return of a ghastly repressed past suddenly bursting forth within the Japanese popular imaginary. As such, *Infection* explores the politics of contagion on both an interpersonal and socio-historical scale. In particular, *Infection*'s negligent staff and morally ambiguous physicians recall the period before the emergence, during the 1990s, of previously suppressed information pertaining to illegal biological and chemical testing performed on Chinese civilians by 'many of [Japan]'s best and brightest doctors' (Barenblatt 2005: xxi) during the war in the Pacific. Like a wilfully overlooked tumour that metastasises into a malignant mass too conspicuous and dangerous to ignore, information regarding the Japanese atrocities during World War II streamed steadily into public discourse, bolstered by the 'high profile class-action lawsuit against the government of Japan' (xvii) recently brought forth by Peize Xu and 180 relatives of some 2100 murdered Chinese. Contested in court from 1997 to 2002, the lawsuit concluded in a verdict 'rejecting compensation claims or an apology even as the judges readily admitted that Japan did in fact kill the plaintiff's family members and enormous numbers of Chinese with germ weapons' (xviii). Japan, of course, is far from exceptional in their perpetration of war time atrocities (as evidenced by Nazi Germany's genocidal legacy and the US's numerous internment camps, to cite merely two examples). Nevertheless, this recent revelation of this suppressed monstrous past, a conspiracy of silence partially enabled, as several history scholars have noted, by the intervention of Western (primarily US) military 'advisors', inevitably affects a reconsideration of the imagined integrity of the Japanese social body. *Infection*'s copious ethical violations and graphic scenes of putrefaction and corporeal disarticulation thus affords viewers a contemporary lens through which the spectres of the past may be confronted, acknowleded and, eventually, exorcised.

Similarly, Tsuruta Norio's *Premonition* aspires to far more than eliciting perfunctory shocks or continuing the creative and intellectual torpor that has sadly resulted from too many recent attempts at replicating the formulas that initially inspired the recent, so-called 'J-horror' boom. This is not to suggest that *Premonition*'s premise is without precedent; based on the *manga*, *Kyôfu shinbun*, by Tsunoda Jirô, and inflected by the familiar Japanese horror film motif of the curse that can only be deferred but never truly escaped, *Premonition* is an emotionally complex and moving study of a husband and wife struggling to come to terms with the loss of their child and the dissolution of their marriage. As the film opens,

Satomi Hideki, his wife, Ayaka, and their five year old daughter, Nana, are travelling home by car from a visit with Ayaka's parents. A university professor obsessed with his research and preoccupied with the fear of failing to secure tenure, Hideki begs his wife to drive back to a pay phone they passed several miles earlier so that he can email his research to his colleagues. As he sits in the cramped confines of the phone booth waiting for his data to upload, he finds a weathered scrap of newspaper with a photograph of his daughter accompanied by a story describing her death in an automobile accident. Confused and understandably sceptical at first, Hideki turns towards the street only to see his wife making her way towards the booth to check on his progress. Behind her, we see the car with his daughter strapped in the back seat. Seconds later, a speeding truck collides head-on with his parked car. Hideki's vehical bursts into flames that quickly consume his daughter's tiny body. As police and rescue crews arrive, Hideki frantically searches for the scrap of newspaper containing the premonition, but it is nowhere to be found.

The narrative then leaps forward three years. Hideki and Ayaka have separated. Unable to reconcile intense feelings of guilt regarding his delayed reaction to the mysterious clipping's otherworldly 'warning', Hideki has suffered greatly. His once promising career as a university professor has crumbled, and he now teaches a class of rowdy, disinterested high school students. Ayaka, meanwhile, has immersed herself in her career, working as a university faculty member studying psychic phenomena and urban legends. Hideki begins to experience premonitions in the form of mysterious news clippings prophesying destruction, and his quest to discover their origin reunites him with his estranged wife. Together, they learn the fate of a young man driven mad by his inability to stem the influx of similar premonitions. As video footage of the young man and, eventually, Hideki's own first-hand experiences reveal, altering the future is possible. However, these attempts culminate in mixed results. For example, Hideki is able to save his wife from a railway disaster, but he cannot prevent the stabbing death of one of his students. Furthermore, attempts at altering possible futures result in radical corporeal transformations, most noticeably the appearance of grey blotches that eventually spread across the individual's entire physique. Over time, these grey blotches take on the texture of aged newspaper, slowly consuming the afflicted person's body until he is reduced to dust. Faced with this scenario, Hideki's grasp on reality becomes increasingly tenuous. In a climactic series of dream sequences, Hideki relives the events surrounding Nana's death. Each re-visitation of that tragic event allows him the opportunity to alter the past. Hideki realises, however, that regardless of his attempts to save his family, one member inevitably perishes. Finally electing to sacrifice himself in his daughter's place, Hideki appears to alter the past, albeit at a price. As the film ends, we find ourselves viewing a scene very similar to the one that opened the narrative. The family car speeds towards its apparently unavoidable collision, the cursed newspaper fragment fluttering through the air as if racing them to their destination. Suddenly, the paper flattens out against Nana's window, displaying its announcement of Hideki's impending death. As this scene suggests, while Hideki may have found a way to save his wife and daughter from a violent demise, his young daughter must now bear the weight of the otherworldly newspaper's endless barrage of premonitions.

The second instalment of Ichise Takashige's 'J-Horror Theatre' series, Tsuruta Norio's *Premonition* articulates a tension between two seemingly incongruous and contradictory fears: (1) the nightmarish potential of a universe in which human relationships and activities are circumscribed by predestination, and (2) the terror of an existence predicated upon randomness and chaos, of a life in which seemingly inconsequential actions may result in both large-scale catastrophes and smaller, personal tragedies. The philosophical conundrum driving *Premonition*, in other words, finds articulation through the film's vacillation between a focus on the dread of foreknowledge ('It's terrifying isn't it,' an enigmatic character ominously inquires of Hideki, 'to see what you write come true?') and a thoughtful reflection upon the anxieties that arise when we recognise that we dwell in a universe driven by chaotic contingencies beyond our absolute control. This tension between an ideological framework grounded upon the possibility of predestination and the ontologically disparate premise of an existence predicated upon the impossibility of knowing the future confronts audiences with nothing less than the terror of being alive. In this sense, *Premonition* can be understood as an existential examination of the limits of human understanding, the inability to predict disasters (let alone prevent them), and, in some ways, the necessity for accepting the horrific as we accept the pleasant and the beautiful. As the sequence of 'what if' scenarios that comprises *Premonition*'s climax illustrates, the existential crisis that by turns paralyses Hideki with grief and compels him to reassess his ability to affect positive change is the same condition that compels humanity to embrace the illusion of order and transcendent meaning through religion and other supernatural narratives, including cinematic horror.

In this preoccupation with chaos as a (self-)organising system, Tsuruta Norio's *Premonition* charts a similar thematic terrain as Higuchinsky's apocalyptic spectacle, *Uzumaki*. The realisation that small-scale, seemingly insignificant decisions (or indecisions) may have catastrophic impacts on a larger scale influences Hideki's actions in several ways throughout the film. Not only does it contribute substantially to his life-shattering sense of culpability and regret ('What if I could have done one thing differently?'), but it also informs his anguish over the potential consequences of interfering with the futures revealed to him by the increasingly overwhelming volume of premonitions he receives. Hideki, having glimpsed a newspaper article announcing his own death, soon finds himself on an all-too-literal deadline reminiscent of that facing *Ringu*'s cursed protagonists. Under the impression that his life is rapidly drawing to a close, Hideki zealously scrawls down as many premonitions as he can. Tsuruta's approach to the trope of a death foretold, however, differs importantly from the 'countdown' faced by the characters in Nakata's *Ringu* who, either by chance or out of desire to prolong the cycle of deaths through a process of eternal deferment, have watched the haunted video tape. Hideki is aware that he will eventually die, but the date and manner of his demise remain indeterminate. As the time and means of Hideki's seemingly inevitable death elide him, his condition can be read expansively as representative of the larger human condition. We are all going to die someday, *Premonition*'s narrative ultimately posits, so what do we do in those moments we are alive? Do we act despite the myriad consequences? Do we remain passive?

Tsuruta directs *Premonition*'s most explicit cultural critique, however, towards the transforming structure of the 'typical' contemporary Japanese family in general, and towards the possibly misguided priorities that frequently characterise the role of the father in particular. Conforming to the stereotype of the excessively overworked Japanese male pressured to achieve material success in the midst of a lingering economic recession, Hideki rarely looks up from his laptop during the film's opening sequence, abstaining from the family 'sing along' much to his daughter's dismay. In keeping with the film's various allusions to the universe as a 'protean' and chaotic system in which every action or 'chance occurrence' can 'bring about macroscopic transformation' (White 1991: 263), Hideki's inability to defer his academic labours initiates the chain of events that leads to his discovery of the scrap of cursed newspaper, his daughter's death, the dissolution of his marriage, and the vocational and financial collapse that, in three years, finds him living alone in a tiny cluttered apartment and working at a job he despises. What's more, Hideki's guilt over his daughter's death is perhaps best exemplified by one of *Premonition*'s most unsettling moments. Haunted by the increasing tide of premonitions, as well as his regret and guilt over the actions (and inactions) that resulted in the dissolution of his immediate family, Hideki awakes, albeit within a dream, to the sound of his deceased child's voice calling out 'Daddy! Daddy!' He stumbles out of bed and follows the sound of his daughter's voice to his apartment door, behind which he encounters Nana's horribly charred form reaching out for him with an unearthly scream. This scene's connotations are obvious: Nana's smoking corpse is the embodiment of Hideki's battered conscience, the nightmare personification of his tragic *hamartia*. It is only through Ayaka's assistance that he is able to engage with the influx of premonitions and come to terms with the trauma of their shared loss. This reconciliation both forms *Premonition*'s emotional core and propels the narrative forward. Fittingly, the film's climactic series of alternate pasts, through which Hideki repeatedly attempts and fails to save his family from roadside tragedy, functions as a kind of metaphorical remasculinisation. Far removed from the workaholic archetype Hideki's behaviour evokes at the film's outset, he sacrifices everything, including his own life, for his family. Thus, though the film's final shot recuperates the Japanese horror film premise of inescapable

Image 20: The horror of knowing. Tsuruta Norio's *Premonition* (Movies Online)

curses, Hideki's selfless recapitulation, made possible through a radical re-appraisal and re-ordering of his priorities, advances a much needed corrective to, or variation upon, constructions of masculinity in contemporary Japanese culture, especially as they relate to negotiating the often incongruent demands of the social and domestic spheres.

Fearful Multiplicities: New Visions, New Directions, and the Future of 'J-Horror': Two Case Studies

Perhaps more than any other recent Japanese horror films, Shimizu Takashi's *Marebito* (or, *The Stranger from Afar*, 2004) and Tsukamoto Shinya's *Vital* (2004) evidence the kind of innovation necessary to keep this vibrant cinematic tradition from falling into a stale cycle of endless sequels and tropological redundancies. Importantly, they accomplish this without deploying the increasingly clichéd strategy of clever self- or poly-referentiality. Thus, *Marebito* and *Vital* rarely partake in the tiresome strain of kitschy, postmodern rib-nudging that has become an all-too-frequent trend within *fin de siecle* horror texts, from Wes Craven's *Scream* (USA, 1996) to Miike Takashi's *One Missed Call* (2003). Shimizu's *Marebito* and Tsukamoto's *Vital* are unsettling narratives that confront audiences with novel re-imaginings of traditionally nightmarish scenarios. What's more, they provoke their audiences with intellectually challenging premises that not only realise horror film's potential for advocating new ways of understanding contemporary cultural transformations, but that also advance a reconsideration of the very 'politics' informing the act of watching horror films.

Haunted by Terror: Shimizu Takasi's *Marebito*

Shot in only eight days during a break in the filming of the US adaptation of *Ju-on: The Grudge*, *Marebito*'s plot is relatively simple. The central protagonist, Masuoka, played by celebrated Japanese filmmaker Tsukamoto Shinya, is a freelance camera operator obsessed with capturing images of fear. These representations of mortal terror, Masuoka reasons, will allow him to break through the banality of his daily existence in early twenty-first century Japan. When Masuoka, armed with with the digital video camera through which he experiences much of the world, fortuitously captures a man's grisly suicide, he soon feels a twinge of excitement that leads him to revisit the scene of the man's violent death. Progressively drawn to the conclusion that the visceral intensity he seeks can only be discovered 'underground', Masuoka soon finds himself wandering through a subterranean labyrinth of darkened tunnels. In this nether world, he encounters a terrified man muttering warnings about the existence of flying Demonic Robots (or 'Deros'), and the spirit of the man whose suicide Masuoka recorded. This latter figure serves as a temporary Virgil for Masuoka's Dante-like excursion. Finally emerging in an impossibly expansive cave containing 'The Mountains of Madness', a direct reference to the monstrous mythology created by the early twentieth century US horror writer, H.P. Lovecraft, Masuoka discovers a beautiful but bruised young female chained to a rock. He brings the woman back to his apartment, where he studies her carefully and concludes that she is not human. He names her 'F', and soon the denizens of the subterranean realm from which she was taken hunt Masuoka down and demand her immediate return. However, Masuoka's understanding that 'F' requires a steady diet of blood to survive, coupled with his willingness to procure this 'food' for her on a regular basis, convince the underground entities of his ability to properly care for 'F'. Masuoka eventually tries to acclimate 'F' to life in human society, but when his attempts prove unsuccessful, he elects to sacrifice his life for hers. Slicing his mouth open with a razor, he allows her to feed on the blood pulsing from his lacerated flesh and then accompanies her back to the rhizomic subterranean tunnels from which she came, and where, as Masuoka remarks, he has 'no need for human words.' The film ends with the same image with which it began: Masuoka's terrified eyes as captured by his digital video camera. Now, however, the camera is in 'F''s hands. Shimizu holds on the image of Masuoka's horrified gaze, cutting out the film's soundtrack for several beats before the final credits roll. This strategy is very powerful, leaving the viewer to contemplate the meaning in Masuoka's eyes without the benefit of the traditional, frequently non-diegetic aural cues that have become a staple of the horror genre.

Tsukamoto Shinya's performance in *Marebito* capitalises upon his iconographic stature as an *avant-garde* director concerned with the various interpenetrations of the biological and the technological. Specifically, it links Shimizu's *oeuvre* with Tsukamoto's. The result is a fusion of aesthetic and critical perspectives perhaps best realised through

Marebito's amalgamation of cyberpunk and gothic tropologies. Copious scenes of industrial culture and technological mediation permeate Shimizu's film, as do explicitly sanguine images of vampirism and Lovecraftian references to seductive yet monstrous (or seductive *because they are monstrous*) dimensions abutting our own. *Marebito*'s dominant *mise-en-scène*, then, repeatedly gothicises technology even as it exploits technology's mediation of the gothic. Stalking through a postindustrial urban environment with his camera poised to capture images of fear, Masuoka is a variation upon such gothic figures as the 'mad scientist' or the 'psychotic voyeur'. References to Victor Frankenstein, the horror genre's prototypical irresponsible father-figure, abound. Similarly, horror film fans will likely notice the parallels between Shimizu's obsessed documentarian and the Mark Lewis character of Michael Powell's *Peeping Tom* (1960). What's more, Shimizu filters many of the film's traditionally gothic moments through a myriad of technological apparatuses, from the miniaturised screen of Masuoka's cell phone to his wall of high-definition computer monitors. By linking these high-tech items with gothic horror, Shimizu echoes post-industrial anxieties articulated in earlier Japanese horror films like Tsukamoto's own *Tetsuo: The Iron Man* and Sono Shion's *Suicide Club*.[2]

Shimizu's direction likewise foregrounds digital video as an emerging medium through which directors and cinematographers may graft new aesthetic criteria onto established genres, including horror. Noticeably distinct from 35mm film stock in its current inability to replicate the 'graininess' and variable focal lengths generally attributed to celluloid's visual 'texture', digital video nevertheless allows for vast flexibility in terms of image rendering. Thus, the image clarity digital video affords ranges from expressionistic colour and light saturation to higher-definition, deep-focus photography. In addition, Shimizu carefully staggers his digital video camera's varying resolutions for dramatic effect. In the process, he creates a documentary feel that heightens the action's immediacy while contributing to a meta-discourse on the politics

---

[2] *Marebito* similarly glosses: Luis Buñuel and Salvador Dali's *Un Chien Andalou* (1929), Fukui Shozin's *964 Pinnochio* (1991) and Roger Corman's *Little Shop of Horrors* (1960).

of viewing in an age of technological mediation. Hence, *Marebito*'s most visceral and unsettling sequences recall the notorious video-based *Guinea Pig* films discussed in Chapter Two, as well as Western horror fare, from John McNaughton's *Henry: Portrait of a Serial Killer* (USA, 1986) – in particular the sequence in which Henry and his homicidal roommate, Otis, watch a slow motion replay of a murder they videotaped – to mock-'found-footage' classics like Ruggero Deodato's *Cannibal Holocaust* (Italy, 1980) and Daniel Myrick and Eduardo Sánchez's *The Blair Witch Project* (USA, 1999).

Where *Marebito*'s digital video aesthetic breaks exciting new ground, however, is in its extension of the conceit of *the reproduced image as authenticated vision*, a trope deployed famously, albeit far less frequently, by Michael Powell in the aforementioned *Peeping Tom*. Consistently conflating Masuoka's POV with the image on his digital video camera's LCD screen until the perspectives become not only interchangeable but indistinguishable, Shimizu posits Masuoka's POV as a product of technological mediation. In other words, Masuoka's camera becomes a prosthetic eye that at once enriches and circumscribes his vision. In addition, Shimizu's copious digital manipulations during the film's editing include the occasional dissolution of the film's image via pixilation, an effect that results in an innovative disruption of conventional viewing pleasures through a 'counter-cinematic' foregrounding of the work's artifice. Similarly, Shimizu reiterates this embrace of cinema as a technological construct in his overt use of painted backgrounds during one of *Marebito*'s signature moments: Masuoka's discovery of the Lovecraft-inspired 'Mountains of Madness'. The scene's composition evokes a strain of heightened theatricality in cinema that audiences can trace as far back to the late nineteenth century 'trick films' of the magician-turned-special-effects-pioneer, Georges Méliès. This embrace of the fantastic through a reminder of cinema's inherent two-dimensionality further obviates the art form's mendacity.

These gestures, taken collectively, comprise merely one component of Shimizu Takashi's larger exploration, in *Marebito*, of the horror film's continued allure. Indeed, the film's preoccupation with the process of variably viewing and interpreting the world around us reveals

Shimizu's obsession with engaging not only the forces that compel us to consume cinematic texts depicting horrific events and scenes of physical trauma, but also the very cathartic release that makes film and other art forms appealing, and quite possibly indispensable, in the first place. The correlation between 'F''s blood consumption and her increased (though by no means complete) acclimation to human society is not simply a convenient plot device. Masuoka literally feeds 'F' blood and carnage to sustain her most vital systems, but is this not what humans do figuratively everyday in a media(ted) culture saturated with, and ideologically buttressed by, images of corporeal trauma? To this extent, Shimizu provides his audience with an initial gesture towards an archaeology of horror. By identifying horror film as a cultural product in a manner that avoids the trite self-referential game-playing of far too many works of 'postmodern' terror, Shimizu, in short, recognises the power that images (including those generally deemed 'abject' or 'horrific') have upon contemporary culture. Through the fabrication, consumption, and perpetuation of visual representations of the body as a sight of biological crisis in the visual arts, we – as viewers – devour ourselves; we cannibalise ourselves through images. Moreover, these framed and otherwise occluded depictions evidence a socially constructed desire to codify and categorise our 'selves' and, perhaps more importantly, 'others'.

Masuoka's quest to experience intensity through an encounter with 'unspeakable' fear should not, however, be understood as an exclusively negative quest, but as a potentially liberating sojourn that frees him from narrow, dualistic convictions. It is, in Masuoka's own words, a kind of "mad'ness that drives him to seek out alternatives to his existence within an alienating postmodern terrain. Like the decentred network of rhizomic subterranean tunnels reminiscent of Borges' 'garden of forking paths' (1964: 19) in their unexpected and possibly infinite bifurcations, mortal fear's intensity is, for Masuoka, a way of breaking free from 'all that stifles' (Bataille 1994: 19). Shimizu likewise articulates this privileging of an ideological position grounded upon an embrace of multiple corporeal and cultural possibilities in his broaching, and eventual dismissal, of what Francois Lyotard calls 'modernist grand narratives'

(1984). Throughout *Marebito*, Shimizu and the film's screenwriter, Konaka Chiaki, have characters discuss a plethora of all encompassing explanations for inexplicable phenomena – from 'hollow Earth' theories to the potential existence of a 'universal unconscious' – only to conflate (and, thus, possibly equate) them so that a multiplicity of absolute rationalisations are acknowledged as possibilities even as the text elides the emergence of a 'superior' or 'absolute' explanation. This gesture towards irreducibility and interstitiality is further evidenced in the scene in which Masuoka, having entered the 'passageway of terror' and descended into the 'underground' tunnels for the first time, passes the rubble-strewn remains of a long buried building with a dented metal door. Partially illuminating his surroundings with the small light fixed atop his digital video camera, Masuoka comments: 'The underground development was a reminder of the second world war. This must be one such war time memorabilia.' Moments later, however, Masuoka adds: 'The underground development of Tokyo was not just from the second world war. It must have been done throughout history, connecting new tunnels to old ones.' Following closely upon Masuoka's assertion that the 'fear of the unknown compel(led)' him to investigate this netherworld in the first place, the reference to the second world war as a contributor to the subterranean tunnels' construction, coupled with Masuoka's subsequent remarks designed to lessen the correlation between the hellish labyrinth and a specific historical period, locates horror both as an emotional state and as a film genre that resists simple elucidation.

As the Escher print gracing the wall behind Masuoka's work station implies, nothing is as straight-forward as it may seem, no matter what stories we tell ourselves to momentarily stabilise our position in a universe that remains well beyond the human mind's capacity for understanding. Determinism in its myriad forms (biological, social, etc.) may provide 'answers', but when it comes to comprehending intense ecstatic physiological and psychological states like fear or mortal terror, these solutions pale in the shadows of infinite alternatives. Consequently, although references to World War II as contributing to contemporary Japanese horror cinema's iconography may be appropriate at times, by no means are such works reducible to this single easy reading. Japanese horror film, as a persistently viable artistic tradition, may very well touch upon fears that run 'deeper' than most socio-historical analyses can excavate. Japanese horror film may also provide a barometer for emerging cultural climates.

Image 21: Publicity poster for Shimizu Takashi's *Marebito* (© Tartan USA)

Correspondingly, terror and horror need not signify a moment of culmination or death; such intense states can also provide points of entry, as well as lines of flight, for those seeking experiences beyond those acknowledged or endorsed by the status quo. Masuoka, after all, voluntarily returns to the underworld with 'F' at his side, surrendering control (via his digital video camera) to a figure that not only confounds gender- and familial-based classifications (Masuoka treats 'F' as a pet, a daughter, an infant, and a wife), but also surpasses binary categorisations of human/non-human. Masuoka's final line of dialogue identifies him as having entered a realm in which he has 'no need for human words.' Closer to attaining his goal of touching the infinite through horror, Masuoka now occupies a space beyond the parameters of dogmatic verbal/linguistic structures. No longer confined by systems of referentiality, he embraces liminality in all of its potential dread and promise.

Posthuman Striptease: Tsukomoto Shinya's *Vital*

Like *Marebito*, Tsukomoto Shinya's recent film, *Vital*, embarks upon an interrogation of the politics of 'seeing'. In particular, it provokes a critical consideration of the ideologies and desires informing simultaneous enticements by, and anxieties over, the unknown, a subject position largely responsible for the horror genre's effectiveness and survival. Formally, however, *Marebito* and *Vital* are quite distinct. Where *Marebito* embraces digital video as an emerging medium, Tsukamoto modifies his trademark avant-garde approach to shot composition and editing by deploying a surreal *mise-en-scène* that is by turns coldly clinical and conspicuously sensuous. The result is an atypically restrained approach to his *oeuvre*'s principle preoccupation: the perils and promises of the human body's practical and ontological status in a high-tech, increasingly posthuman environment. A visceral variation on the 'camera-stylo' premise[3], Tsukamoto's camera becomes a tool that, to paraphrase Jean-Luc Godard's maxim,[4] functions simultaneously as a microscope and a telescope through which artists can explore the visible universe and humanity's role in it. The camera, then, is a mechanism for dissection and reflection, a means for peering 'deeper', looking 'closer', seeing 'anew'. As Tsukamoto notes in the interview on the Tartan Asia Extreme DVD:

> pictures of stars in our universe and pictures taken through a microscope are very similar. It depends on what scale you're using. We usually think of our bodies as one unit. When we use the measure of our human bodies, the universe is huge. The microscopic world is tiny. I thought I was looking at the very same thing except for the way we look at them. The most obscure thing in the universe can be seen if we keep looking through a microscope at the samples in a classroom. We won't get exact answers, but we'll get some kind of answer. (2005)

Echoing the discourse of fractal geometry and chaos theory in his conjectures regarding repetition through scale, Tsukamoto locates cinema as an avenue through which humanity may search for our place in the universe. Furthermore, through the central protagonist's, Takagi Hiroshi's, variably penetrating and sympathetic gaze, Tsukamoto redeploys the 'amnesiac recovering memories' motif as a mechanism for understanding the world as a sequence of *lensed* objects in both the term's verbal and adjectival sense. Consequently, *Vital* grotesquely externalises our oldest 'internal' mysteries and obsessions, providing a meditation upon human connections and disconnections.

    One of Tsukamoto's most restrained films, *Vital* offers a deliberate yet energetic exhumation of the human body in all its base

---

[3] For a fuller articulation of the *camera-stylo*, see Alexandre Astruc's "The Birth of a New Avant-Garde: *La Camera-stylo*" in Graham, P. (1968) *The New Wave: Critical Landmarks.* Garden City, NY: Doubleday, 17-23.

[4] See the transcript of Henri Behar's interview of Jean-Luc Godard conducted at the 1995 Montreal Film Festival. In this insightful dialogue, Godard states that: '…at the beginning, cinema was a tool for study. It should have been a tool for study - for it is visual, and very close to science and medicine. The camera has a lens, like a microscope, to study the infinitely small, or like a telescope, to study the infinitely distant. Having studied that, you could then convey it in a spectacular fashion' (para 14).

corporeality. Similarly, in its depiction of Takagi Hiroshi's search for the traumatic 'truth' of his past, *Vital* functions as one of Tsukamoto's most 'human' films. In the wake of a devastating automobile accident, Takagi Hiroshi discovers that he has lost both his memory and, though he does not recall her, his lover, Ooyama Ryôko. This violent collision of the corporeal and technological, an event immediately evocative of his earlier cyberpunk masterpieces, *Tetsuo: The Iron Man* and *Tetsuo 2: Body Hammer*, seemingly reawakens Takagi Hiroshi's slowly waning interest in human physiology, and he soon embarks upon his first semester of medical school. While dissecting a cadaver for a course on human anatomy, Hiroshi, in response to a strangely familiar tattoo he finds on the cadaver's arm, begins to recover what he believes to be memories of his forgotten past. As these snippets of salvaged time increasingly destabilise his perception of what constitutes reality and fantasy, Hiroshi becomes more and more engrossed in questions of identity, both in relation to the woman on the dissection table in the school's pathology lab, and in terms of 'who he really is'. Discovering the cadaver to be the body of his deceased girlfriend, Ryôko, Hiroshi's approach to the cadaver also transforms from a dispassionate clinical detachment to a maniacal preoccupation with discovering possible alternative causes of the cadaver's death, an obsession that alienates most of his classmates. One important exception, however, is Kiki, who seems drawn to Hiroshi despite finding his erratic behaviour unsettling. Throughout the film, Kiki finds her erotic desire for Hiroshi variously compromised by Hiroshi's obsession with the dead Ryôko. Nevertheless, Kiki alone dares to accompany Hiroshi on his anatomical, sexual, and emotional journeys of (self-) discovery.

   Vital's complex engagement with notions of posthuman identity and the all-too-human will to romanticise our base corporeality extends themes with which Tsukamoto's films have engaged since 1988's *Tetsuo: The Iron Man* and, before that, *Adventures of Electric Rod Boy* (*Denchu Kozo no boken*, 1987). Specifically, *Vital* underscores Tsukamoto's paradoxical fascination with and fear of increasingly technologised environments. A pathologisation of, and critical foray into, the corporeal as a mythical repository for an imagined spiritual configuration, or 'soul',

Vital poses crucial questions regarding the motivating forces behind paradigms that invest the biological with the transcendental, ultimately asking why people conflate these seemingly antithetical realms. As such, the film investigates the plurality of narratives we tell ourselves to sustain and perpetuate this illusion. Two moments from *Vital* emerge as especially noteworthy in this regard. The first is the scene when Hiroshi and his classmates initially encounter their anatomy class cadaver. The anatomy instructor's words reveal a culturally inscribed respect for the dead and their posthumous contributions to the advancement of human knowledge:

> Medical history stems from wanting to understand the body's mechanism. Dr. Sugita Genpaku was amazed by the similarity between Dutch anatomical texts with his texts. So he worked on translating them. Eventually Kaitai Shinsho was published in 1774 in Tokyo. Trust your own eyes. This is a key point, whatever the century. The truth is there for you to see. You must embrace this concept. As students of medicine you are very privileged. You have the opportunity to explore the bodies before you. Treat them with respect at all times, We owe thanks to them and their families.

For the anatomy instructor, the inert flesh through which the students learn their craft remain entities deserving dignity and 'respect'; at the same time, he understands the cadavers as 'bodies' ripe for exploration. Indeed, it is through a meticulous understanding of the body's geography and ecology, the instructor posits, that one 'may come to know the body's mechanism.' Additionally, Tsukamoto uses this moment to advance the theme of vision and its inherent subjectivity: 'Trust your own eyes. This is the key point, whatever the century. The truth is there for you to see. You must embrace this concept.' Of course, as we shall soon discover, differences in vision can be greater than previously imagined. *Vital*'s very narrative twists and turns upon this relativist axis. That said, reducing *Vital* to a treatise on relativism compromises Tsukamoto's larger cinematic inquest into the tensions between modernist, holistic notions of 'human' embodiment and an emerging postindustrial technoscape in which moving beyond simple dichotomies like 'human'/'mechanical' and 'living'/'dead' may reveal new ways of imagining identity in a world that is, in Tsukamoto's words, 'somehow ambiguous as to whether it's reality or a dream' (2004).

Another important sequence locating *Vital* as a film concerned with conceptualisations of corporeality, as well as the assorted lengths to which humans will go to invest the body's material existence with culturally- and historically-coded constructions of a transcendent 'humanity', transpires early in Hiroshi's graduate studies. In a meticulously composed montage of professors advancing theories regarding what it means to be a sentient entity, Tsukamoto cuts between depictions of faculty members from multiple academic disciplines (lensed as if from a student's POV) speculating on the metaphysical connotations of being alive, and medium shots of an attentive Hiroshi:

SHOT ONE: A Biology professor standing before slides depicting human ova. The professor states: 'The ovum, a product of almost pure chance. By means of cellular growth, divergence and migration creates an organism.'

SHOTS TWO and **THREE:** The film's amnesiac pro-agonist, Hiroshi, listens (**SHOT TWO**) as a different doctor lectures on head injuries: 'This person experienced trauma to the frontal lobe section. This area is responsible for personality and memory.' Tsukamoto then cuts to SHOT THREE, in which the lecturing physician gestures towards a large illustration of the human cranium. The doctor continues: 'From this we can conclude the following: human character is not a constant.'

SHOT FOUR: A neurologist lectures while tapping his chalk nervously against the classroom's blackboard: 'The brain and spinal cord form the central nervous system. Nerve cells are concentrated in this area. I wonder, then, where the soul lies?'

SHOTS FIVE and SIX: A psychology professor sits on his desk as he discusses Freud and the subconscious: 'Beneath this, however...there is the vast realm of the subconscious.' Tsukamoto then cuts to another medium shot of Hiroshi listening intently. The camera dollies in to accentuate his immersion. In a voice over, we hear the professor as he remarks: 'It is here that our suppressed desires can cause deep mental conflict as they strive to realise themselves.'

This diverse panoply of theoretical postures ranges from the scientific, or 'secular', to the philosophical, psychological, or 'religious'. This contestation between the body and mind has been a primary concern for Tsukamoto throughout his career and reveals strains of a latent humanism in Tsukamoto's aesthetic vision. This recuperative inertia is by no means rare in works of postmodern body horror, or in the genre's not-so-distant cousin, cyberpunk. Representations of the human body as a site of cultural and ontological contention clearly permeates contemporary Japanese horror cinema, from the notorious *Guinea Pig* films, to Sato Hisayasu's keenly subversive *Naked Blood* and *Muscle,* to the apocalyptic scenarios in recent works by Higuchinsky and Kurosawa Kiyoshi.

What sets *Vital* apart from other horror films, however, is more than Tsukamoto's persistent return to the human body's abject materiality, a thematic recurrence that, paradoxically, necessitates serious reflection upon the master-narratives we fabricate (and advocate) in response to our inescapable mortality. What differentiates *Vital* from other genre-bridging works of filmic terror is Tsukamoto's recognition of the 'human condition' as a liminal state. Moreover, Hiroshi's amnesia, like his often tenuous grasp on 'reality', makes him the ideal protagonist for this narrative. In the tradition of Voltaire's *Candide* and other variations on the trope of the 'impartial observer', Hiroshi brings the illusion of objectivity to Tsukamoto's exploration of human mortality. Hiroshi's cool precision and initially impassive demeanour in the medical school's pathology lab, rather than conveying a callous perspective, discloses a profound and very 'human' desire for meaning that steadily intensifies until it erupts in melodramatic bursts of emotional hyperbole. Thus, far from conveying an attitude of ghoulish prurience, Hiroshi's expressions of childlike wonder as he cracks his cadaver's chest plate and exposes the nexus of organs below suggests a complicated relationship towards the corporeal at once accentuated and compounded by his collection of finely detailed charcoal and ink drawings reminiscent of illustrations by both the Flemish anatomist Andreas Vesalius (1514-1564) and the Swiss surrealist H. R. Giger (1940 -). Like these European artists' meticulous renderings of human physiology, Hiroshi's sketchings stress the human body as mechanistic in its complexity.

Tsukamoto's accentuation of the body's mechanics in *Vital*, then, depicts human physiology as at once cold and sensuous, discretely material and warmly erotic. Extending important conceits that have long dominated his *oeuvre*, the human and posthuman (or variably biomechanical) entities populating Tsukamoto's filmic universe persistently blur assumed distinctions between the 'human' and the 'non-human'. However, it is our base corporeality, in all of its porous fragility, which remains, for Tsukamoto, the most recurrent site of horror. The reasons for this include not only the body's propensity for undergoing radical biological transformations, but also its locus as the ultimate target for, and last point of resistance against, the circulation of disciplinary power in many late capitalist cultures, including Japan's. The larger implication of Tsukamoto's focus on the human form, then, includes the potential for viewing it as an apparatus for resisting oppressive ideologies through an embracing of the processes of adaptation and change that have always comprised our inexorable organicism. Thus, the primary concern of Tsukamoto's film is nothing less than the very ontology of fear. In this sense, *Vital* and *Marebito* might be considered companion pieces. In foregrounding human physicality through an almost clinically orchestrated *mise-en-scène*, *Vital* dissects – or at least purposefully agitates – those sickly logics most fundamental, or *vital*, to our comprehension of the human *as* (and *apart from*), the 'other'. For this reason alone, Tsukamoto Shinya's *Vital* (like Shimizu Takashi's *Marebito*) is not only an important contemporary Japanese horror film, but an indispensable contribution to world cinema.

Conclusion

In short, as the excitement generated by recent works of contemporary Japanese horror cinema remains high, influencing motion pictures and other popular culture productions across multiple national and international markets, one must not take pronouncements of the genre's impending demise too seriously. At the same time, filmmakers concerned about the genre's immediate viability must guard against redundancy, both in terms of the iconography deployed to evoke fear in spectators, and in terms of the film's storylines; narrative reiterations without innovation may not only decrease viewer interest, but jeopardise the chances of more inventive texts reaching receptive audiences eager for more novel approaches to the horror genre. If the works explored in this chapter are any indication, Japanese horror cinema remains not only a vital cultural barometer and catalyst for critical inquiry, but also provides new ways for imagining the future of cinematic horror around the globe

Image 22: Tartan Asia Extreme DVD box art for Tsukamoto Shinya's *Vital*

Works Cited and Consulted

Alexander, J. (2004) 'The Shunned Houses of Takashi Shimizu', *Rue Morgue:Horror in Culture and Entertainment*, 40, July-August, 14-19.

Alexander, J. R. (2005) 'The Maturity of a Film genre in an Era of relaxing Standards of Obscenity: Takashi Ishii's *Freeze Me* as a Rape-Revenge Film', in *Senses of Cinema,* no. 36 (Jul-Sept 2005). On-Line. Available HTTP: www.sensesofcinema.com (11 March 2006).

Allison, A. (2000) *Permitted and Prohibited Desires: Mothers, Comics, and Censorship in Japan.* Berkeley and Los Angeles, CA: University of California Press.

Allsop, S. L. (2003) '*Battle Royale*: Challenging Global Stereotypes withinthe Constructs of a Contemporary Japanese Slasher Film', *The Film Journal*, volume 7, November. On-Line. Available HTTP: www.thefilmjournal.com/ (5 May 2005).

Aoyagi, H. (2000) 'Pop Idols and the Asian Identity', in Craig, T. J. (ed.) *Japan Pop!: Inside the World of Japanese Popular Culture.* New York & London: M. E. Sharp, 309-26.

Astruc, A. (1968) 'Birth of a New Avant-Garde: *La camera-stylo*' in Graham, P. (ed.) The *New Wave: Critical Landmarks.* Garden City, New York: Doubleday, 17-23.

Barenblatt, D. (2005) *A Plague upon Humanity: The Hidden History of Japan's Biological Warfare Program.* New York: Harper Paperbacks.

Barrett, G. (1989) *Archetypes in Japanese Film: The Sociopolitical and Religious Significance of the Principal Heroes and Heroines.* Selinsgrove: Susquehanna University Press.

Bataille, G. [1929-30] (1994), *Visions of Excess: Selected Writings, 1927-1939.* Minneapolis, Minnesota: University of Minnesota Press.

_____. (1957) *Erotism: Death and Sensuality.* London: Routledge

Batchelor, J. (2000) *Ainu of Japan: The Religion, Superstitions and General History of the Hair.* Mansfield Centre: Martino Publishing.

Baudrillard, J. (1988) *Selected Writings.* Stanford, CA: Stanford University Press.

_____. (1990) *The Transparency of Evil: Essays on Extreme Phenomena.* London and New York: Verso.

Behar, H. 'Jean-Luc Godard Press Conference at the 1995 Montreal Film Festival', *Film Scouts Interviews.* On-Line. Available HTTP: www.filmscouts.com. (9 March 2006).

Borges, J. L. (1964) *Labyrinths: Selected Stories and Other Writings.* San Fransisco, CA: New Directions Paperback.

Bornoff, N. (2002) 'Sex and Consumerism: The Japanese State of the Arts',Lloyd, F. (ed.) *Consuming Bodies: Sex and Contemporary Japanese Art.* London: Reaktion Books, 41-68.

Bradshaw, P. (2003) '*Dark Water* (Review)', in *The Guardian*, 6 June. On-Line. Available HTTP: film.guardian.co.uk/NewsStory. (9 March 2006).

Briggs, J. (1992) *Fractals – The Patterns of Chaos: Discovering a New Aesthetic of Art, Science, and Nature.* New York: Touchstone Press.

Broderick, M. (1996) *Hibakusha Cinema: Hiroshima, Nagasaki and the Nuclear Image in Japanese Film.* Kegan Paul Press.

Brottman, M. (1997) *Offensive Films: Towards An Anthropology of Cinema Vomitif.* Greenwood Publishing Group.

Bukatman, S. (1990) *Terminal Identity: The Virtual Subject in Post-Modern Science Fiction.* Durham and London: Duke University Press.

Caputi, J. (1992) 'Advertising Femicide: Lethal Violence against Women in Pornography and Gorenography', in Radford, J. and Russell, D. E. H. (eds.) *Femicide: The Politics of Killing Women.* New York: Twayne Publishers, 203-17.

Carter, A. (2001) *The Sadeian Woman: And the Ideology of Pornography.* New York and London: Peguin.

Cave, P. (2004) 'Bukatsudō: The Educational Role of Japanese School Clubs',*The Journal of Japanese Studies*, vol. 30, no. 2, 383-415.

Chow, R. (2000) 'Film and Cultural Identity', *Film Studies: Critical Approaches.* Oxford: Oxford University Press, 167-73.

Christopher, R. C. (1984) *The Japanese Mind.* New York: Fawcett Columbine.

'The Christopher Berthoud Case', *Beyond the Boundaries.* On-Line. Available HTTP: freespace.virgin.net/Alasdair.y/CASE.HTM. (9 March 2006).

Clover, C. J. (1992) *Men, Women and Chainsaws: Gender in the Modern Horror Film.* Princeton: Princeton University Press.

Cohen, J. J. (1996) 'Monster Culture (Seven Theses)', in Cohen, J. J. (ed.) *Monster Theory: Reading Culture.* Minneapolis: University Of Minnesota Press, 3-25.

Coniam, M. (2001) 'The Trouble with de Sade', in Black, A. (ed.) *Necronomicon: Book Four.* Hereford: Noir Publishing.

Conrich, I. (2005) 'Metal-Morphosis: Post-Industrial Crisis and the Tormented Body in the *Tetsuo* Films', in McRoy, J. (ed.) *Japanese Horror Cinema.* Edinburgh: Edinburgh University Press, 95-106.

Corliss, R. (2004) 'Horror: Made in Japan', *Time Magazine*, 2 Aug, 76.

Cousins, M. (2004) *The Story of Film*. New York: Thunder's Mouth Press.

Craig, T. (2000) 'Introduction', in T. Craig (ed.) *Japan Pop!: Inside the World of Japanese Popular Culture*. New York: M. E. Sharp, 3-26.

Crawford, T. (2003) 'The Urban Techno-Alienation of Sion Sono's *Suicide Club*', in S. J. Schneider (ed.) *Fear Without Frontiers: Horror Cinema Across the Globe*. Guildford: Fab Press, 305-11.

Creed, B. (1993) *The Monstrous- Feminine: Film, Feminism, Psychoanalysis*. London and New York: Routledge.

_____. (1995) 'Horror and the Carnivalesque: The Body Monstrous' in Devereaux, L and Hillman, R. (eds.) *Fields of Vision: Essays in Film Studies, Visual Anthropology and Photography*. Berkeley: University of California Press, 127-59.

Davies, R. J. and Ikeno, O. (2002) *The Japanese Mind: Understanding Contemporary Japanese Culture*. Vermont: Tuttle Publishing.

Davis, D. W. (1995) *Picturing Japaneseness*. New York: Columbia University Press.

_____. (2001) 'Reigniting Japanese Tradition within *Hana-Bi*', *Cinema Journal 40*, Number 4, Summer, 55-80.

Deleuze, G. and Guattari, F. (1987) *A Thousand Plateaus: Capitalism and Schizophrenia*. Minneapolis, Minnesota: University of Minnesota Press.

Deleuze, G. (1991) *Masochism: Coldness and Cruelty*. Boston: Zone Books.

_____. (2001) *Francis Bacon: The Logic of Sensation*. Minneapolis: University of Minnesota Press.

Dery, M. (1997) *Escape Velocity: Cyberculture at the End of the Century.* New York: Grove Press.

Desser, D. (1988) *Eros Plus Massacre: An Introduction to the Japanese New Wave Cinema.* Bloomington: Indiana University Press.

Desser, D. (1999) 'Gate of Flesh(tones): Color in the Japanese Cinema', in Ehrlich, L. C. and Desser, D. (eds.) *Cinematic Landscapes: Observations on the Visual Arts and Cinema of China and Japan.* Austin: University of Texas Press, 299-322.

Dika, V. (1987) 'The Stalker Film, 1978-81', in Waller, G. A. (ed.) *American Horrors: Essays on the Modern Horror Film.* Urbana and Chicago: University of Illinois Press, 86-101.

_____. (1990) *Games of Terror:* Halloween, Friday the 13th, *and the Films of the Stalker Cycle.* NJ: Fairleigh Dickinson University Press.

Dixon, W. W. (2000) *The Second Century of Cinema.* Albany, NY: State University of New York Press.

Dollimore, J. (2001) *Death, Desire and Loss in Western Culture.* London and New York: Routledge.

Felix-Didier, P. (2000) '*Cine y sexo en Japón*' *Film: On Line*, 15 April. On-Line. Available HTTP: www.filmonline.com. (9 March 2006).

Fernbach, A. (2002) *Fantasies of Fetishism: From Decadence to the Posthuman.* NJ: Rutgers University Press.

Gill, T. (1999) 'Transformational Magic: Some Japanese Super-heroes and Monsters', in D. P. Martinez, D. P. (ed.) *The Worlds of Japanese Popular Culture: Gender, Shifting Boundaries and Global Cultures.* Cambridge: Cambridge University Press, 33-55.

Grindon, L. (2001) 'In the Realm of the Censors: Cultural Boundaries and the Poetics of the Forbidden', in Washburn D. and Cavanaugh, C. (eds.) *Word and Image in Japanese Cinema.* Cambridge: Cambridge University Press, 293–317.

Grossman, A. (2002) 'The Japanese Pink Film: *Tandem, The Bedroom, The Dream of Garuda* on DVD', *Bright Lights Film Journal*, vol 36. On-Line. Available HTTP: www.brightlightsfilm.com. (9 March 2006)

Gruenberger, H. (2002) '*Naked Blood/Splatter*', *Metamovie*, 5 July. On-Line. Available HTTP: http://www.metamovie.de/. (9 March 2006).

Hand, R. J. (2005) 'Aesthetics of Cruelty: Traditional Japanese Theatre and the Horror Film', in McRoy, J. (ed.) *Japanese Horror Cinema*. Edinburgh: Edinburgh University Press, 18-28.

Hantke, S. (2005) *Horror Film: Creating and Marketing Fear*. Mississippi: University of Mississippi Press.

_____. (2005) 'Japanese Horror under Western Eyes: Social Class and Global Culture in Miike Takashi's *Audition*', in McRoy, J. (ed.) *Japanese Horror Cinema*. Edinburgh: Edinburgh University Press, 54-65.

Harootunian, H. D. (1989) 'Visible Discourses / Invisible Ideologies', in Miyoshi, M. and Harootunian, H. D. (eds.) *Postmodernism and Japan*. Durham and London: Duke University Press, 63-92.

Hawkins, J. (2000) *Cutting Edge: Art-Horror and the Horrific Avant-Garde.*, Minneapolis, MN: University of Minnesota Press.

Hasegawa, Y. (2002) 'Post-Identity *Kawaii*: Commerce, Gender and Contemporary Japanese Art', in Lloyd, F. (ed.) *Consuming Bodies: Sex and Contemporary Japanese Art*. London: Reaktion Books, 127-41.

Hendrix, G. (2006) '*Sigsaw* Review: Stop the Madness', *Kaiju Shakedown*.On-Line. Available: www.kaijushakedown.com. (9 March 2006).

Hendry, J. (2002) *Understanding Japanese Society, Second Edition*. London & New York: Routledge.

Hills, M. (2002) *Fan Cultures*. London and New York: Routledge.

_____. (2005) 'Ringing the Changes: Cult Distinctions and Cultural Difference in US Fans' Readings of Japanese Horror Cinema', in McRoy, J. (ed.) *Japanese Horror Cinema*. Edinburgh: Edinburgh University Press, 161-74.

Hull, E. A. and Siegel, M. (1989) 'Science Fiction', in Powers, R. G. and Kato, H. (eds.) *Handbook of JapanesePopular Culture*. New York and London: Greenwood Press, 243-75.

Hunter, J. (1998) *Eros in Hell: Sex, Blood and Madness in Japanese Cinema*. London: Creation Books International.

Hurley, K. (1995) 'Reading like an Alien: PostHuman Identity in Ridley Scott's *Alien* and David Cronenberg's *Rabid*', in Halberstam, J. and Livingston, I. (eds.) *Posthuman Bodies*. Bloomington and Indianapolis: Indiana University Press, 203-24.

Igarashi, Y. (2000) *Bodies of Memory*. New Jersey: Princeton University Press.

Indiana, G. (2000) *Salo or The 120 Days of Sodom*. London: British Film Institute.

_____. (2000) '*Salo or the 120 Days of Sodom* (Extract)', *British Film Institute*. On-Line. Available HTTP: www.bfi.org.uk/. (9 March 2006).

Internet Movie Database. On-Line. Available HTTM: www.imdb.com. (9 March 2006).

Ito Junji (2001) *Flesh-Colored Horror*. ComicsOne.

_____. (2001) *Tomie* vols. 1-2. ComicsOne.

_____. (2002-3) *Uzumaki* vols. 1-3. ComicsOne.

Ivy, M. (1995) *Discourses of the Vanishing: Modernity, Phantasm, Japan*. Chicago: University of Chicago Press.

Iwao, S. (1993) *The Japanese Woman: Traditional Image and Changing Reality*. Cambridge, MA: Harvard University Press.

Japan Shock DVD (2001) *All Night Long*. Japan Shock DVD Entertainment.

Kakiuchi, M. (2004) 'Made in Japan: From Video to Genocide', *Viceland*, 8 (9). On-Line. Available HTTP: www.viceland.com. (9 March 2006)

Kellner, D. (1995) *Media Culture: Cultural Studies, Identity and the Politics between the Modern and the Postmodern*. London and New York: Routledge.

Kellner, D. and Ryan, M. (1990) 'Technophobia', in Kuhn, A. (ed.) *Alien Zone: Cultural Theory and Contemporary Science Fiction Cinema*. London and New York: Verso.

Kakiuchi, M. 'Made in Japan: From Video to Genocide', *Viceland*, vol. 8, no. 9. On-Line. Available HTTP: viceland.com (9 March 2006).

Kawai, H. (1986) 'Violence in the home: Conflict between Two Principles:Maternal and Paternal', in Lebra, T. S. and Lebra, W. P. (eds.) *Japanese Culture and Behavior*. Honolulu, Hawai'i: University of Hawaii Press.

Kermode, M. (2003) 'Dread and Dripping: Japanese Horror Guru Hideo Nakata Combines Roeg and Polanski in a Masterpiece of Forboding', *The Guardian*, 8 June 2003. On-Line. Available HTTP: observer.guardian.co.uk (9 March 2006).

Kerr, A. (2001) *Dogs and Demons: Tales from the Dark Side of Japan*. New York: Hill and Wang.

Kinsella, S. (2000) *Adult Manga: Culture and Power in Contemporary Japanese Society*. Honolulu, Hawai'i: University of Hawai'i Press.

Kogawa, T. (2005) 'New Trends in Japanese Popular Culture', *Polymorphous Space*. On-Line. Available HTTP: anarchy.translocal.jp (8 March 2006).

Koreski, M. (2002) '*All About Lily Chou-Chou* (Review)', *Film Comment* 38, 4, Sept.-Oct, 77.

La Bare, J. (2000) 'The Future: "Wrapped…in that mysterious Japanese way"', *Science Fiction Studies*, 80, vol. 27, Part 1, March, 22-48.

Krafel, P. (1999) *Seeing Nature: Deliberate Encounters with the Visible World*. White River Junction, VT: Chelsea Green Publishing Company.

Lapper, C. (2005) '*Salò* and Censorship: A History', *British Film Institute*. On-Line. Available HTTP: www.bfi.org.uk. (9 March 2006).

Lu, A. (2002) 'Horror: Japanese-Style', in *Film Comment*, Jan/Feb, 38.

Livingston, I. (1997) *Arrow of Chaos: Romanticism and Postmodernity*. Minneapolis, MN: University of Minnesota Press.

Lyotard, F. (1984) *The Postmodern Condition: A Report on Knowledge*. Minneapolis, MN: University of Minnesota Press.

Macias, P. (2001) *TokyoScope: The Japanese Cult Film Companion*. VIZ Media LLC.

_____. (2003) 'The Scariest Horror Ever? *Juon*, Director Takashi Interview'*,Japattack*. On-Line. Available HTTP: japattack.com. (9 March 2006).

Makino, C. (2005) 'In Japan, Women's Constitutional Rights in Peril', in *WeNews*, 1 May. On-Line. Available HTTP: www.womensenews.org (9 March 2006).

Mandelbrot, B. B. (1982) *The Fractal Geography of Nature*. New York: W. H. Freeman.

Martinez, D. P. (1998) 'Gender, Shifting Boundaries and Global Cultures', in Martinez, D. P. (ed.) *The Worlds of Japanese Popular Culture: Gender, Shifting Boundaries and Global Culture*. Cambridge: Cambridge University Press.

Matsui, M. (2002) 'The Place of Marginal Positionality: Legacies of Japanese Anti-Modernity', in Lloyd, F. (ed.) *Consuming Bodies: Sex and Contemporary Japanese Art*. London: Reaktion Books, 142-65.

McRoy, J. (2004) 'The Technology of 'Nonfiction Filmmaking' in *Devil's Experiment* and *Flowers of Flesh and Blood*', in Hantke, S. *Horror Film: Creating and Marketing Fear*. Mississippi: University of Mississippi Press, 135-52.

_____. (2005) *Japanese Horror Cinema*. Edinburgh: Edinburgh University Press.

Menninghaus, W. (2003) *Disgust: The Theory and History of a Strong Emotion*.Albany, NY: State University of New York Press.

Mes, T. (2001) '*Pulse* (Review)', *Midnight Eye: The Latest and Best in Japanese Cinema*, 12 June. On-Line. Available HTTP: www.midnighteye.com (9 March 2006).

_____. (2001) '*All Night Long I* (Review)', *Midnight Eye: The Latest and Best in Japanese Cinema*, 1 August. On-Line. Available HTTP: www.midnighteye.com. (9 March 2006).

_____. (2001) '*All Night Long 3* (Review)', *Midnight Eye: The Latest and Best in Japanese Cinema*, 15 August. On-Line. Available HTTP: http://www.midnighteye.com (9 March 2006).

_____. (2003) 'Kiyoshi Kurosawa (Interview)', *Midnight Eye: The Latest and Best in Japanese Cinema*, 20 August. On-Line. Available HTTP: www.midnighteye.com (9 March 2006)

_____. (2003) *Agitator: The Cinema of Takashi Miike*. London: FAB Press.

Midori, M. 'The Place of Marginal Positionality: Legacies of Japanese Anti-Modernity', in Lloyd, F. (ed.) *Consuming Bodies: Sex and Contemporary JapaneseArt*. London: Reaktion Books, 142-65.

Mitchell, E. (2002) 'Film Festival Review: Alienated Teenagers Find Sanctuary in a Pop Star', *The New York Times*, 12 July. On-Line. Available HTTP: www.nytimes.com. (9 March 2006)

Modleski, T. (1986) 'The Terror of Pleasure: The Contemporary Horror Film and Postmodern Theory', in Modleski, T. (ed.) *Studies in Entertainment: Critical Approaches to Mass Culture*. Bloomington and Indianapolis: Indiana University Press, 155-66.

Najita, T. (1989) 'On Culture and Technology in Postmodern Japan', in Miyoshi, M. and Harootunian, H. D. (eds.) *Postmodernism and Japan*. Durham, N.C.: Duke University Press, 3-20.

Napier, S. J. (1996) 'Panic Sites: The Japanese Imagination of Disaster from *Godzilla* to *Akira*', in Treat, J. W. (ed.) *Contemporary Japan and Popular Culture*. Honolulu, Hawai'i: University of Hawai'i Press, 235-64.

Napier, S. (2000) *Anime: From* Akira *to* Princess Mononoke. New York: Palgrave.

Nolletti Jr., A. and Desser, D. (1992) *Reframing Japanese Cinema: Authorship, Genre, History*. Indianapolis: Indiana University Press.

O'Hehir, A. (2002) 'All About Lily Chou-Chou: This Electrified Tale of Teen Alienation Could Launch the Japanese New Wave Out of the Film Geek Ghetto', *Salon*, 24 July. On-Line. Available HTTP: www.salon.com. (9 March 2006)

Ohnuki-Tierney, E. (1987) *Illness and Culture in Contemporary Japan: An Anthropological View*. Cambridge: Cambridge University Press.

Orbaugh, S. (2002) 'Sex and the Single Cyborg: Japanese Popular Culture Experiments in Subjectivity', *Science Fiction Studies*, 88, Vol. 29, Part 3, November, 436-52.

Pasolini, P. P. (2005) 'A Mad Dream', *British Film Institute*, On-Line. Available HTTP: http://www.bfi.org.uk (9 March 2006).

Peng, I. (1996) 'Single-Mother Families in Japan: A Conspicuous Silence', *National Institute for Research Advancements*. On-Line. Available HTTP: www.nira.go.jp/ (9 March 2006).

Powers, R. G. and Kato, H. (1989) *Handbook of Japanese Popular Culture*.New York: Greenwood Press.

Radford, J. and Russell, D. E. H. (1992) *Femicide: The Politics of Killing Women*. New York: Twayne Publishers.

Rella, F. (1994) *The Myth of the Other: Lacan, Foucault, Deleuze, Bataille*. Maisonneuve Press.

Richie, D. (1999) 'The Influence of Traditional Aesthetics on Japanese Film', in Ehrlich, L. C. and Desser, D. (eds.) *Cinematic Landscapes: Observations on the Visual Arts and Cinema of China and Japan.* Austin, TX: University of Texas Press, 155-64.

_____. (2003) *The Image Factory: Fads & Fashions in Japan*. London: Reaktion Books.

Rimer, T. (1999) 'Film and the Visual Arts in Japan: An Introduction', in Ehrlich, L. C. and Desser, D. (eds.) *Cinematic Landscapes: Observations on the Visual Arts and Cinema of China and Japan.* Austin, TX: University of Texas Press, 149-54.

Rose, M. A. (1992) *The Post-Modern and the Post-Industrial.*Cambridge: Cambridge: Cambridge University Press.

Salamon, S. (1986) ' "Male Chauvinism" as a Manifestation of Love in Marriage', in Lebra, T. S. and Lebra, W. P. (eds.) *Japanese Culture and Behavior: Selected Readings*. Honolulu, Hawai'i: University of Hawai'i Press, 130-42.

Sato T. (1999) 'Japanese Cinema and the Traditional Arts: Imagery, Technique, and Cultural Context' in Ehrlich, L. C. and Desser, D. (eds.) *Cinematic Landscapes: Observations on the Visual Arts and Cinema of China and Japan*. Austin, TX: University of Texas Press, 165-86.

Scarry, E. (1985) *The Body in Pain: The Making and Unmaking of the World*. New York and Oxford: Oxford University Press.

Schaller, M. (1997) *Altered States: The United States and Japan since the Occupation*. Oxford: Oxford University Press.

Schneider, S. J. and Williams, T. (2005) *Horror International*. Detroit, MI: Wayne State University Press.

Schneider, S. J. (2004) *Fear without Frontiers: Horror Cinema from around the Globe*. Guildford: Fab Press.

Sharp, J. (2002) 'Juon', in *Midnight Eye: The Latest and Best in Japanese Cinema*, 23 December. Available HTTP: www.midnighteye.com (9 March 2006)

Sharrett, C. (1993) 'The Horror Film in Neoconservative Culture', *Journal of Popular Film and Television*, vol. 21, no. 3, 100-110.

_____. (1999) "Afterword: Sacrificial Violence and Postmodern Ideology', in Sharrett, C. and Grant, B. K. (eds.) *Mythologies of Violence in Postmodern Media*. Detroit: Wayne State University Press, 413-34.

Shaviro, S. (1993) *The Cinematic Body*. Minneapolis and London: University of Minnesota Press.

_____. (2003) *Connected, or What It Means To Live in the Networked Society*. Minneapolis, MN: University of Minnesota Press.

Shilling, M. (2003) 'Shooting a Work in Progress', in *The Japan Times*, 15 January. On-Line. Available HTTP: www.japantimes.co.jp. (9 March 2006).

Shimada, Y. (2002) 'Afterword: Japanese Pop Culture and the Eradication of History', in Lloyd, F. (ed.) *Consuming Bodies: Sex and Contemporary Japanese Art*. London: Reaktion Books, 186-91.

Skipp, J. and Spector, C. (1989) 'On Going Too Far, or Flesh-Eating Fiction: New Hope for the Future', in Skipp J. and Spector, C. (eds.) *Book of the Dead*. New York: Bantam Books.

Skov, L. (1996) 'Fashion Trends, Japanisme and Postmodernism', in Treat, J. W. (ed.) *Contemporary Japan and Popular Culture.* Honolulu, Hawai'i: University of Hawai'i Press.

Sugimoto, Y. (2002) *An Introduction to Japanese Society.* Cambridge: Cambridge University Press.

Stephens, C. (2001) 'Another Green World: On the Blossoming of Kiyoshi Kurosawa', *Film Comment*, Sept.-Oct., 64-72.

_____. (2002) 'High and Low Japanese Cinema Now: A User's Guide', *Film Comment*, Jan-Feb, 35-6.

Stremmel, H. (2004) *Realism (Basic Art).* Cologne: Taschen.

Sujimoto Y. (2002) *An Introduction to Japanese Society.* Cambridge: Cambridge University Press.

Suzuki, K. (2003), *Ring*, New York: Vertical Inc.

Tanaka, Y. (1996) *Hidden Horrors: Japanese War Crimes in World War II.* Colorado: Westwood Press.

Tasker, P. (1987) *The Japanese: A Major Exploration of Modern Japan.* New York: Truman Talley Books/E. P. Dunton.

Tateishi, R. (2003) 'The Contemporary Japanese Horror Film Series: *Ring* and *Eko Eko Azarak*', in S. J. Schneider (ed.) *Fear Without Frontiers: Horror Cinema Across the Globe.* Guildford: Fab Press, 295-304.

Tatsumi, T. (2000) 'Generations and Controversies: An Overview of Japanese Science Fiction', *Science Fiction Studies* 80, 27:1 (March), 105-14.

Thacker, E. (2002) 'Biohorror/Biotech', in Hantke, S. (ed.) *Horror.* Vashon Island, WA: Paradoxa Press, 109-29.

Thomas, K. (2005) 'Marebito: The Stranger from Afar', *Las Angeles Times*, 9 December. On-Line. Available HTTP: www.calendarlive.com (9 March 2006).

Tombs, P. (2000) 'Oh, Noh … Japan Has the Horrors Again', *Guardian Unlimited*, 18 August 2000. On-Line. HTTP. www.film.guardian.co.uk (9 March 2006).

Tsukamoto, S. (2005) 'Interview with the Director', *Vital* (DVD). Tartan Asia Extreme.

Tudor, A. (2002) [1997] 'Why Horror?' in Jancovich, M. *Horror: The Film Reader*. London and New York: Routledge, 33-55.

Turim, M. (1992) 'The Erotic in Asian Cinema' in Gibson, P. C. and Gibson, R. (eds.) *Dirty Looks: Women, Pornography, Power*. London: British Film Institute: 90-100.

Turner, B. (1992) *Regulating Bodies: Essays in Medical Sociology*. London and New York: Routledge.

Tsurumi, M. (2000) 'Gender Roles and Girls Comics in Japan: The Girls and Guys of Yūkan Club', in Craig, T. J. (ed.) *Japan Pop!: Inside the World of Japanese Popular Culture*. New York & London: M. E. Sharp.

Udden, J. 'The Future of a Luminescent Cloud: Recent Developments in a Pan-Asian Style', *Synoptique 10*. On-Line. Available HTTP: www.synoptique.ca. (9 March 2006).

Ueno, C. (1994) 'Women and the Family in Transition in Postindustrial Japan', in Gelb, J. and Palley, M. L. (eds.) *Women of Japan and Korea: Continuity and Change*. Philadelphia: Temple University Press, 23-42.

Ulaby, N. (2005) 'Ghosts, Chills, and 'Dark Water' from Japan', *Morning Edition, National Public Radio*, On-Line. Available HTTP: www.npr.org (9 March 2006).

Vuckovic, J. (2004) 'Inside the Ghost House', *Rue Morgue Magazine*, 40, July-Aug., 17-9.

Wardrope, T. (2005) 'An Exquisite Nightmare: New Asian Horror Sprays the Screen', in 'Primers', *Green Cine Daily*. On-Line. Available HTTP: www.greencine.com. (9 March 2006).

Weisser, T. and Weisser, Y. M. (1997) *Japanese Cinema Encyclopedia: Horror,Fantasy, Science Fiction*. Miami, Florida: Vital Books.

_____. (1998) *Japanese Cinema: The Essential Handbook*. Miami, Florida: Vital Books.

White, E. C. (1991) 'Negentropy, Noise, and Emancipatory Thought', in Hayles, N. K. *Chaos and Order: Complex Dynamics in Literature and Science*. Chicago, IL: University of Chicago Press,

_____. (2005) 'Case Study: Nakata Hideo's Ringu and Ringu 2', in McRoy, J. (ed.) *Japanese Horror Cinema*. Edinburgh: Edinburgh University Press, 38-50.

white pongo (2000) 'Essential Viewing', *Internet Movie Database* (User Comments), 3 October. On-Line. Available HTTP: us.imdb.com/ Title ?0217679#comment. (9 March 2006).

Williams, L. R. (2000) 'The Inside-Out of Masculinity: David Cronenberg's Visceral Pleasures', in Aaron, M. (ed.) *The Body's Perilous Pleasures: Dangerous Desire and Contemporary Culture*. Edinburgh: Edinburgh University Press, 30-48.

Williams, T. (2005) 'Case Study: *Battle Royale*'s Apocalyptic Millennial Warning' in McRoy, J. (ed.) *Japanese Horror Cinema*. Edinburgh: Edinburgh University Press, 130-46.

Wolfe, A. (1988) 'Suicide and the Japanese Postmodern: A Postmodern Paradigm', *South Atlantic Quarterly* (Summer), 87(3), 571-89.

Wu, H. (2002) 'Tracking the Horrific', *Spectator: The University of Southern California Journal of Film and Television Criticism*, 22:2 (Fall), 1-11.

Xu, G. G. (2005) 'Remaking East Asia, Outsourcing Hollywood', *Senses of Cinema*, 34, Jan-Mar. On-Line. Available HTTP: www.sensesofcinema.com. (9 March 2006)

Zahlten, A. and Kimihiko K. (2004-5) 'Norio Tsuruta (Interview)', *Midnight Eye: The Latest and Best in Japanese Cinema*, 22 December. On-Line. Available HTTM: www.midnighteye.com (9 March 2006).

Žižek, S. (1992) *Looking Awry: An Introduction to Jacques Lacan through Popular Culture*. Boston, Massachusetts: The MIT Press.

_____. (2003) *Organs without Bodies: On Deleuze and Consequences*. London & New York: Routledge.

Index

DATE DUE

DEMCO 38-296

Printed in the United States
132564LV00006B/126/A